Shalom and the Ethics of Belief

Shalom and the Ethics of Belief

Nicholas Wolterstorff's Theory of Situated Rationality

NATHAN D. SHANNON

Foreword by Nicholas P. Wolterstorff

◆PICKWICK *Publications* • Eugene, Oregon

SHALOM AND THE ETHICS OF BELIEF
Nicholas Wolterstorff's Theory of Situated Rationality

Copyright © 2015 Nathan D. Shannon. All rights reserved. Except for brief quotations in critical publications or reviews, no part of this book may be reproduced in any manner without prior written permission from the publisher. Write: Permissions, Wipf and Stock Publishers, 199 W. 8th Ave., Suite 3, Eugene, OR 97401.

Pickwick Publications
An Imprint of Wipf and Stock Publishers
199 W. 8th Ave., Suite 3
Eugene, OR 97401

www.wipfandstock.com

ISBN 13: 978-1-4982-0224-4

Cataloging-in-Publication data:

Shannon, Nathan D.

Shalom and the ethics of belief : Nicholas Wolterstorff's theory of situated rationality / Nathan D. Shannon ; foreword by Nicholas P. Wolterstorff.

xii + 204 p. ; 23 cm. —Includes bibliographical references and index.

ISBN 13: 978-1-4982-0224-4

1. Wolterstorff, Nicholas. 2. Belief and doubt—Moral and ethical aspects. 3. Knowledge, Theory of (Religion). 4. Religion—Philosophy. I. Wolterstorff, Nicholas. II. Title.

BD215 .S456 2015

Manufactured in the U.S.A.   04/15/2015

Contents

Foreword by Nicholas P. Wolterstorff | vii
Acknowledgments | xi

1 Nicholas P. Wolterstorff, Christian Philosopher | 1
2 Situated Rationality and the Doxastic Self | 23
3 Situated Rationality and Practices of Inquiry | 56
4 The Comprehensive Ethic of Shalom | 86
5 Theory and Praxis: Shalom Theorizing and Scholarship | 122
6 A Shalom Doxastic Ethic and the Status of Christian Belief | 157

Bibliography | 193
Index | 201

Foreword

In the essay that follows, Nathan Shannon skillfully brings to light the connections between two aspects of my thought that I myself have never explicitly connected in my published writings, namely, the theory of situated rationality that I developed in my writings on epistemology, and the account of justice and shalom that I developed in my writings on topics in social ethics.

From the time I first began to think and write about epistemological matters, two topics especially have intrigued me. One was the picture of the belief-forming self that one finds in the work of Thomas Reid. We are all created, says Reid, with dispositions to form beliefs of certain kinds upon having experiences of certain sorts, and with dispositions to form new belief-forming dispositions upon having experiences of certain sorts. Examples of the latter sort of belief-forming dispositions are the multiplicity of dispositions that we all have to form inductive beliefs. Adults living in the midwestern part of the United States all have the disposition, upon seeing lightning, to believe that thunder will follow. Those who have this disposition acquired it; it was not innate. What was innate was the disposition to acquire this disposition.

In some of my writings I have described this aspect of Reid's thought as the *historicizing* of the belief-forming self. The belief-forming dispositions that one has, at any particular point in one's life after infancy, are in good measure the result of one's personal history.

The other topic that, from the beginning, intrigued me within the field of epistemology was the connection between belief and obligation. I share the view of Reid and most other philosophers that beliefs are formed by dispositions, not by volition. We don't believe some proposition because we decided to believe it. Yet we commonly say such things as, "You should have known the answer," "You should have known better," "You shouldn't just believe what your eyes tell you in such a situation," "You should have believed what he told you." But if "You should have believed what he told you" cannot be understood as elliptical for "You should have *decided* to believe what he told you," how then is it to be understood?

To answer this question, I introduced the idea of *practices of inquiry*. Practices of inquiry are social practices aimed at finding something out. We all employ such practices. The practices of inquiry available to us vary to a considerable extent from person to person; their availability depends on the skills one has acquired, the state of technology in one's society, and so forth. Though we cannot decide to believe or not believe some proposition, what we can decide to do is employ some practice of inquiry, the hoped-for result of such employment being that we come to believe something.

Belief and obligation are connected through the intermediation of practices of inquiry. For each of us there are practices of inquiry that we *ought* to employ. At this point I introduce the concepts of *being entitled* to some belief and of *not being entitled*. In contemporary analytic epistemology the term "rationality" often functions as a multivalent word for a number of distinct merits in beliefs. Entitlement is one of those. Roughly speaking, one is not entitled to a certain belief just in case there is some practice of inquiry that one ought to have employed but did not and which is such that, had one employed it, one would not hold that belief. The merit of entitlement is attached to some belief just in case the demerit of non-entitlement is not. One is entitled to a belief that one has if it is permissible for one to have it.

And how do we determine which practices of inquiry a particular person is obligated to employ? Some philosophers have held that we are dealing here with a distinct species of obligation, purely intellectual obligation, and that it is possible to give a universalistic formulation of the obligation. That was the view, for example, of Roderick Chisholm, who wrote: "We may assume that every person is subject to a purely intellectual requirement—that of trying his best to bring it about that, for every proposition h that he considers, he accepts h if and only if h is true."

My own view is that there are no purely intellectual obligations; the practices of inquiry that one is obligated to employ are a function of one's obligations in general. And the obligations that one has vary from person to person depending on one's situation: one's maturity, one's role in society, the state of knowledge in one's society, and so forth. The theory of rationality (entitlement) that I develop is thus a theory of *situated rationality*.

Shannon lays out these ideas lucidly in chapters 2 and 3 of his essay. He then goes on to note that while my theory of rationality (entitlement) depends crucially on the concept of obligation, in my writings on epistemology I offer no account of obligation. I assume that there are obligations and that, to a considerable extent, these vary from person to person; and I let it go at that. What Shannon then rightly observes is that my writings on justice and shalom fill in the gap.

The Hebrew word *shalom* occurs often in the Hebrew Bible/Old Testament. In most English translations it is translated as "peace"; I strongly prefer translating it as flourishing. An indispensable component of flourishing, as it is understood in the Hebrew Bible/Old Testament, is that the members of society treat each other justly—treat each other as they are obligated to treat each other. Genuine flourishing goes beyond doing what we ought to do and beyond being treated justly; but those are its ground floor. I hold that a person's obligations are determined by what she, in her situation, is required to do by way of pursuing the shalom of her neighbors and herself. Thus it is that Shannon speaks of my *shalom doxastic ethics*. It's not a term that I myself used; but I gladly accept it.

The final two chapters of Shannon's essay are a judicious discussion of the ways in which my Christian convictions have shaped my philosophical thought on these matters. I will refrain from giving the reader a peek in advance at what he says.

Nicholas Wolterstorff
Noah Porter Professor Emeritus of Philosophical Theology, Yale University
Senior Research Fellow of the Institute for Advanced Studies in Culture,
University of Virginia

Acknowledgments

I was first introduced to the work of Nicholas Wolterstorff in Scott Oliphint's apologetics courses at Westminster Theological Seminary. It was clear to me then as it is now that Dr. Oliphint's admiration, great as it is, for the work of contemporary Dutch Reformed philosophers stands in the shadow of his devotion to the Christ of Scriptures and the authority of the Word of God. I am grateful for his example. Only so far as I preserve in my thinking and my work the unqualified authority of Scripture may I remain useful. But I am also grateful since from his example I gained a steadfast interest in the relationship of Christian (or any) philosophical thought to the teaching of Scripture, and without that I would not have undertaken or anyway certainly would not have completed this study.

The present text would still be an incomplete, unfocused, and poorly articulated bit of self-assured confusion were it not for the scrupulous guidance of Gijsbert van den Brink, my doctoral supervisor at the VU Amsterdam. His careful reading and re-reading (and re-reading again) of every page led the way toward the refinement of my own self-critical awareness and rigor, and a much improved final product. Few among us are so well equipped as he to handle both the patois of analytic epistemology and the richness of historic Dutch Reformed theology, and my unwieldy manner of working to boot.

My co-supervisors Rene van Woudenberg and W. L. van der Merwe also offered invaluable feedback and insight, without which the project would have emerged severely deficient. Rene in particular subjected the entire text to his high standard of clarity in both concept and expression, and not a few times helped steer the project wide of ruin.

I would also like to thank Nicholas Wolterstorff for providing the foreword, for serving on my thesis committee, for encouraging conversations—electronic and conventional—and of course for the raw material for these, my modest secondary reflections. I have learned a great deal from careful study of his writings, and I have been challenged and edified by his example as a philosopher, a scholar, and a Christian.

My good friends Jonathan Brack, Paul Maxwell, and Deryck Barson have encouraged me toward completion of this project, directly at times, but most importantly by keeping my theological and philosophical oil burning day and night. How good and pleasant.

My family most of all has been committed in untold ways to my studies. The conclusion of this particular academic task is but a small indication of the direction our life together has taken and of commitments we have made as a family to particular forms of service to the Lord. To dedicate this text to my lovely wife or to our precious little ones seems to me, in comparison, a petty thing.

1

Nicholas P. Wolterstorff, Christian Philosopher

The central concern of the present study is Nicholas Wolterstorff's theory of situated rationality. In Wolterstorff's view, the traditional focus on the justification of true beliefs displays Cartesian heritage in that its conceptions of the subject and the subject's relation to its beliefs are treated as abstract and impersonal. Wolterstorff instead considers the subject within its full, individualized, social and moral context and argues that the chief epistemic merit—entitlement rather than justification—accrues to doxastic conduct that is morally defensible in a subject's particular situation.

Beliefs are not justified abstractly. Rather, subjects are entitled to their beliefs (or their believings are entitled) in so far as they manage their doxastic affairs so as to meet the ethico-doxastic norms of their concrete situations as far as can be reasonably expected of them. Epistemic merit, therefore, is normative, and has to do principally with the subject's proper doxastic conduct. This much is Cartesian. But for Wolterstorff the doxastic practices available to the subject and the relevant ethico-doxastic norms are situationally (rather than subjectively) constituted. Epistemic merit is normative but then also practical and situational.

In Wolterstorff's view, furthermore, the availability of doxastic practices includes a situationally given, ethically significant assumption regarding the truth-conduciveness of such practices. Actual truth-conduciveness is not the principal factor in the ethico-doxastic significance for the subject of available doxastic practices; situationality is. So, as Wolterstorff claims, there are no specifically doxastic norms. Doxastic ethics are a refraction of the responsibilities and obligations bearing on a subject in terms of various relationships (to one's self, to God, to others). Belief entitlement thus raises a rather expansive question of moral value and ethics, without an answer to which situated rationality drifts unsecured. The obvious candidate in Wolterstorff's work for completing his theory of the ethics of belief is his notion of shalom. And so my thesis: Wolterstorff's theory of situated rationality is a *shalom doxastic ethic*.

Our entry point is decidedly epistemological, but my thesis will require us to bring into view the relevant biblical, theological, ethical, and historical philosophical material. This being a daunting task, it will help to know something of Wolterstorff's background and development. So we begin with a bit of intellectual biography.

1.1 NICHOLAS P. WOLTERSTORFF, CHRISTIAN PHILOSOPHER

In 2002, Nicholas P. Wolterstorff added "emeritus" to his title as Noah Porter Professor of Philosophical Theology at Yale University. The list of titles Wolterstorff has held throughout his career is long and prestigious. It includes Fulbright and National Endowment for the Humanities fellowships, a senior fellowship at the American Academy of the Arts and Sciences, and, most recently, a senior fellowship at the Institute for Advanced Studies in Culture at the University of Virginia. He has held endowed lectureships, among many others, at Oxford, the Free University of Amsterdam, Princeton, Yale, and St. Andrews, and teaching appointments at dozens of American universities. Wolterstorff has been awarded at least four honorary doctorates and has served as the president of the Society of Christian Philosophers and the American Philosophical Association's Central Division. His publications include some two dozen books, over one hundred and fifty peer-reviewed articles, and countless short pieces on a wide range of current issues. In recent years, several volumes of Wolterstorff's collected essays have been released, including one on epistemology, another on philosophical theology, another on justice and human dignity, and a fourth on liberal democracy, while the pace of production of new material remains steady.[1]

It is difficult to pinpoint Wolterstorff's most influential, most significant, or most acclaimed publications or lectures. At least one reason for this

---

1. The four collected volumes are Wolterstorff's *Inquiring about God*; *Practices of Belief*; *Hearing the Call*; and *Understanding Liberal Democracy*. Also recent are *Justice: Rights and Wrongs*; *Justice in Love*; *Mighty and the Almighty*; and *Journey toward Justice*.

is that he has made significant contributions in several different fields. The person interested in the arts would regard highly Wolterstorff's *Art in Action*, a text just as fresh and insightful but more accessible than his *Works and Worlds of Art*.[2] The philosophical theologian might argue that Wolterstorff's writings on the doctrines of eternity and aseity, on theological predication, and on divine speech, cannot, in any fair assessment of Wolterstorff's work, be overlooked.[3] The philosopher or historian of philosophy would certainly find Wolterstorff's work on Locke, including his *John Locke and the Ethics of Belief* and numerous articles, his work on Reid—again, a book, *Thomas Reid and the Story of Epistemology*, along with numerous shorter pieces— and indeed his incisive, critical writing on foundationalism, all deserving of mention.[4] Wolterstorff has also been prolific on the topic of education, writing extensively on a Christian and specifically Calvinist view of public and higher education.[5] He has written on political philosophy, engaging Robert Audi and Richard Rorty on the role of religion in public discourse,[6] and his recent publication *Justice: Rights and Wrongs* offers a carefully researched account of the history of the concepts that constitute what Wolterstorff calls our "moral subculture," including natural human rights and human dignity. And this is only a partial list.

Most crucial for the topic of this study is a connection I shall draw between two bodies of Wolterstorff's work: one on rationality and another on the biblical notion of shalom. Exposition of Wolterstorff's thought on these topics takes up much of the present work because together they constitute

---

2. Wolterstorff, *Art in Action*; ibid., *Works and Worlds of Art*. Wolterstorff has also published a number of articles in the *Journal of Aesthetics and Art Criticism* and in *Idealistic Studies*, and also lectured on art and aesthetics for, among others, the International Arts Movement (IAM) in New York and the C. S. Lewis Institute.

3. On eternity, see Wolterstorff, "God Everlasting." On aseity, see Wolterstorff's contributions to Ganssle and Helm, *God and Time*, and his comments on divine simplicity in Wolterstorff, "Is It Possible?," 37–42. Wolterstorff gave the Wilde Lectures at Oxford in 1993. Those lectures were later published as *Divine Discourse*.

4. Wolterstorff, *John Locke*; *Thomas Reid and the Story*. Still important for understanding Wolterstorff's critique of classical modern foundationalism is his essay, "Can Belief in God Be Rational If It Has No Foundations?" The piece was originally published in Plantinga and Wolterstorff, *Faith and Rationality* (1983) and was republished in Wolterstorff, *Practices of Belief*. There are a few, but no significant, changes in the 2010 republication. Subsequent references to this essay are to the republication in *Practices of Belief* unless otherwise noted.

5. See especially Wolterstorff, *Educating for Life*; and *Educating for Shalom*.

6. Audi and Wolterstorff, *Religion in the Public Square*. Wolterstorff wrote an uncharacteristically polemical piece targeting Rorty's views on this topic, "Engagement with Rorty," which was published alongside Rorty's "Religion in the Public Square" in the *Journal of Religious Ethics*.

the proper framework for my thesis. The connection between them is, briefly, as follows.

For Wolterstorff, rationality has to do with the ethical significance of believing, and believing should be understood not as a stale, removed, purely intellectual disposition, but as a behavior embedded in a web of practices that are socially and culturally significant. Rationality addresses the moral significance of believing when believing is woven into the moral fabric of social living. And shalom, as we will see, is a grand, perhaps even eschatological, ethical vision, drawn from Christian sources, that conditions the full scope of human moral situationality and accountability.

This connection is essential to my thesis, but an additional benefit of clarifying the organic relation between Wolterstorff's work in specifically these two areas is a glimpse into the structural unity of Wolterstorff's thinking and writing as a whole. Over the course of my time producing the present study, I have come to understand Wolterstorff as a systematic and remarkably self-consistent thinker.[7] I have also noted that many of his readers, who might benefit from one area of his work or another, show little appreciation for the substructure which unifies his diverse and varied work. A brief intellectual biographical sketch will help us begin to appreciate this, and begin even at this early stage to clarify my claim that there is an intimate connection between Wolterstorff's theory of rationality and his notion of shalom.

Wolterstorff was born to Dutch immigrants during the Great Depression, in "a tiny farming village in the prairies of southwest Minnesota, Bigelow."[8] "We did not take means of sustenance for granted," he recounts, ". . . my family was poor."[9] If they may have lacked materially, it seems the Wolterstorffs and their community were rich in tradition. Wolterstorff recounts in delightful detail the intense, resolute, even austere piety and the unshaken reverence for the Scriptures which permeated his childhood church and home.[10] And he recalls with wonder and nostalgia the

---

7. Wolterstorff has dropped some clues to the contrary: "I have written a good deal about art over the course of my career, not because philosophy of art was a chapter in some system that I was developing but because art intruded itself, begging for attention. And I have written a good deal about liturgy, because liturgy intruded itself." (Wolterstorff, "How My Mind Has Changed," in ibid., *Hearing the Call*, 437). However, I trust that this study proves without a doubt that Wolterstorff is a systematic and, indeed, a global thinker, and that his vast and varied output reflects a limited number of core concerns.

8. Wolterstorff, "Grace That Shaped," in *Hearing the Call*, 1. This essay was originally published in Clark, *Philosophers Who Believe*, 259–75.

9. Ibid.

10. "The piety in which I was reared was a piety centered on the Bible, Old Testament

tough-minded and tough-spirited atmosphere of Bigelow and Edgerton, Minnesota.

It is equally remarkable that his early intellectual role models were almost to a person farmers and laborers as it is that their faith and tradition, looking back, thrived immune to, because either unaware of or uninterested in, the theological crises of modernity—critical threats to the trustworthiness of Scripture, scientific challenges to the theistic worldview, and so on. Years later, Wolterstorff would continue to reflect on the strangeness of simply claiming for oneself the right to 'just talk about God.'[11] Without a doubt, the Dutch Reformed tradition has been deeply formative in Wolterstorff's thinking: "If you ask who I am, I reply: I am one who was bequeathed the Reformed tradition of Christianity."[12]

Wolterstorff went on to undergraduate studies at Calvin College where he studied the intellectual legacy of both the Dutch Reformed tradition and of the wider Western world. At Calvin, Wolterstorff encountered a thriving Dutch neo-Calvinism.[13] He also formed a few personal relationships there,

---

and New Testament together. Centered not on experience, and not on the liturgy, but on the Bible; fsor those themselves were seen as shaped by the Bible" (ibid., 5).

11. This is a theme that runs deep in Wolterstorff's theory of rationality, as we will see, and he reflects on it in many of his critical writings on classical foundationalism. For example, see Wolterstorff, "Is It Possible?," 35–55.

12. Wolterstorff, "Grace That Shaped," 268.

13. The term "neo-Calvinism" may be used to refer to two distinguishable but related emphases. The two emphases include the theological and the cultural, both aspects of a movement that emerged from within the Dutch Reformed churches in the nineteenth and early twentieth centuries. Vos provides a concise analysis in a review of the first volume of Herman Bavinck's *Gereformeerde Dogmatiek* (Vos, *Redemptive History*, 475–84; originally published in *The Presbyterian Review* 7 [1896] 356–63). Vos explains Bavinck's view that although a "Calvinistic type of theology never died out entirely, not even in the darkest period of the history of his country," it "lacked for a long time the scientific impulse" of that "purely theological interest" distinctive of historic Calvinism, particularly of the post-Reformation Reformed scholastics (Vos, *Redemptive History*, 475). It was particularly the work of Abraham Kuyper, whose *Encyclopedia of Sacred Theology* Vos calls "the first mature fruit of this movement," which evoked renewed theological rigor within Reformed circles (ibid.). Bavinck's first volume stands "next to this comprehensive work," and gives "the center and heart of theological science," Vos says, its "adequate treatment" (ibid., 475–76). Vos also distinguishes two aspects of this revival of Calvinist theology in the Netherlands: "In the first place it has displayed a high degree of historic sense," a feature of Bavinck's *Dogmatiek* for which Vos expresses appreciation (ibid., 475). "In the second place . . . [t]here has been a conscious effort to develop further the Calvinistic principles, and to shape the Reformed dogma to a form suitable and congenial to the consciousness of the present age" (ibid.). Thus the two aspects mentioned, recognized by Vos already in 1896, one of theological and doctrinal rigor, the other an interest in Calvinism for the modern age. Kuyper and Bavinck both display—even embody—that dual interest, and as we will see, Wolterstorff does as well. This duality and the question of the consistency between doctrinal and cultural

such as a lasting friendship with Alvin Plantinga, that would become, over the years, considerable influences in the direction of his thought and career.

When reflecting on the intellectual forebears of Calvin College, Wolterstorff mentions Abraham Kuyper and Herman Dooyeweerd, in that order. What little Wolterstorff has written on Dooyeweerd has not been terribly appreciative; it might be fair to say that Wolterstorff will follow Dooyeweerd only as far as Dooyeweerd has followed Kuyper, but no further.[14]

Kuyper bequeathed to the North American Dutch Reformed world a sense of Christian Reformed identity which emphasized coordinately the integrity and totalism of Christian truth and life and the idea of the antithetical clash of religious ("regenerate" and "unregenerate") presuppositions. A soteriological antithesis between the elect and non-elect, and the attendant antithesis between the cultural activity of the regenerate and the unregenerate—categories exhaustive of the human species—were determinative for Kuyper.[15]

---

interests are hallmarks of neo-Calvinism. For a brief, if critical, study of the history of the cultural and socio-political emphases of neo-Calvinism, see Dennison, "Dutch Neo-Calvinism."

14. Wolterstorff's unpublished short piece, "Herman Dooyeweerd: An Appreciation," is in fact not very appreciative at all. It was originally written sometime in the 1960s and delivered at a Calvin College Faculty Forum.

15. The Kuyperian antithesis is fundamentally a soteriological one between sinners who have been "regenerated" by the Spirit of Christ and sinners who remain "unregenerate," and its cultural implications feature prominently in Kuyper's view of science: "This regeneration breaks humanity in two, and repeals the unity of human consciousness" (Kuyper, *Encyclopedia of Sacred Theology*, 152). See also Kuyper, *Lectures on Calvinism*, particularly chapter 4, "Calvinism and Science." There, Kuyper says that "[f]ree investigation leads to collisions. One draws the lines on the map of life differently from his neighbor. The result is the origin of schools and tendencies. Optimists and pessimists. A school of Kant, and a school of Hegel . . . Everywhere contention, conflict, struggle, sometimes vehement and keen, not seldom mixed with personal asperity. And yet, although the energy of the difference of principle lies at the root of all these disputes, these subordinate conflicts are entirely put in the shade by the *principal conflict*, which in *all* countries perplexes the mind most vehemently, the powerful conflict between those who cling to the confession of the Triune God and His Word, and those who seek the solution of the world-problem in Deism, Pantheism, and Naturalism" (ibid., 130–31). Kuyper does not see this as a conflict between faith and science, but between competing faiths: "Notice that I do not speak of a conflict between faith and science. Such a conflict does not exist. Every science in a certain degree starts *from faith*" (ibid., 131). Elsewhere, Kuyper says that "faith in this connection is taken formally, and hence considered quite apart from all content. By 'faith,' here, then, we do not mean the 'faith in Christ Jesus' in its saving efficacy for the sinner, nor yet the 'faith in God' which is fundamental to all religion, but that formal function of the life of our soul which is fundamental to every fact in our human consciousness" (ibid., *Encyclopedia of Sacred Theology*, 125). See ibid., §43–51. Helpful secondary resources include Klapwijk, "Antithesis and Common Grace"; van Woudenberg, "Abraham Kuyper"; Mouw, *Challenges of Cultural Discipleship*.

By contrast, modern thought, Wolterstorff often explains, is captivated by the idea of an ultimate, platonic unity of humanity, accessible only by transcending (or perhaps by wishing away) the frailties and weaknesses of individuality and historical situatedness and arriving at the human being itself. Modern thought is, consequently, devoted to constructing, through the impersonal powers of abstract reason, an ideal, pristine body of independent and self-verifying scientific knowledge. In practical terms, this modern, secular view meant that the Western academy was to pursue the sciences *simpliciter*, or even science *simpliciter*, and Western intellectuals were to be *just intellectuals*, leaving their religion, personalities, personal histories, and cultural baggage at the door.[16]

Kuyper found this vision not only untenable but dangerous. Dangerous because, as a kind of religious view itself, it threatened to relegate Christian thought to both theoretical and practical irrelevance, and consequently, with speed and resolve, to the dusty annals of history.[17] It was also dangerous because of the political realities to which, Kuyper foresaw, it was conducive: various forms of political totalitarianism.[18] Standing his ground against the accelerating secularization of a post-Christian Europe, Kuyper embraced the antithesis between Christian and secular culture as a kind of eschatological battle line between, as he saw it, Trinitarian Christian theism and various forms of pantheism and atheism.[19] Furthermore, he found the modern theory of science untenable because, as Wolterstorff himself would later argue, there simply is no such thing as the ideal or platonic human being itself—the claim itself is rather eerily religious—and therefore no such thing as science *per se*, in platonic abstraction from individual, religiously committed scientists. Kuyper argued, at the end of the day, that

---

16. Wolterstorff writes, "[I]n my days as a graduate student at Harvard there were no such things as feminist studies, African-American studies, or any such perspectival studies. Had anyone at the time proposed any such study, they would have been greeted with blank incomprehension . . . the response would have been that any such study would be a biased study, and hence had no place in the academy" ("Postscript: A Life in Philosophy," in Wolterstorff, *Practices of Belief*, 415).

17. Kuyper says, for example, that "[t]o believe that an absolute science in the above-given sense can ever decide the question between truth and falsehood is nothing but a criminal self-deception. He who affirms this, always takes science as it proceeds from his own subjective premises and as it appears to him, and therefore *eo ipso* stigmatizes every scientific development which goes out from other premises as pseudo-science, serviceable to the lie" (Kuyper, *Encyclopedia of Sacred Theology*, 118).

18. Kuyper, *Lectures on Calvinism*, 85. He names two: "[p]opular-sovereignty, as it has been anti-theistically proclaimed in Paris in 1789; and that of *State-sovereignty*, as it has of late been developed by the historicopantheistic school of Germany. Both these theories are at heart identical" (ibid.).

19. See Kuyper, "Pantheism's Destruction of Boundaries."

a religious-like faith rendered 'life-systems'[20] and modes of doing science irreconcilable at a basic level, shattering the modern hope for a superhuman *scientia*.[21]

Thus, a basic plurality of worldviews and religious presuppositions is a staple of the Kuyperian legacy. Without a doubt, this principle is operative in Wolterstorff's work as well, as this study seeks to demonstrate.[22]

When reflecting on his student days at Calvin, Wolterstorff invariably mentions two personal relationships: a lasting friendship struck with Alvin Plantinga and the influence of his professor of philosophy, William Harry Jellema. While at Calvin Wolterstorff was instilled with a sense of duty to capture and fortify a Christian perspective, specifically on issues philosophical, and to forge a self-consciously Christian presence in the world. He recounts having been persistently encouraged to view the intellectual history of the West from a Christian point of view, as a critical, Christian observer, but also to actively pursue the growth and fortification of the kingdom of God in the world. "'There are two cities,' said one of our teachers, Henry Jellema, with gripping charisma . . . 'the *civitas Dei* and the *civitas mundi*. Your calling is to build the *civitas Dei*.'"[23] Later collaborations with Plantinga would put Wolterstorff at center stage in the Christian intellectual world, in

---

20. The awkward term "life-system" is synonymous with "worldview." It represents the leading concept in Kuyper's *Lectures on Calvinism* (the first lecture is entitled, "Calvinism as a Life-system"), and it is a central theme in Dutch neo-Calvinism. See Wolters, "On the Idea of Worldview and its Relation to Philosophy."

21. Ultimately, says Kuyper, "the conflict is not between faith and science, but between the assertion that the cosmos, as it exists today, is either in a normal or an abnormal condition. If it is normal, then it moves by means of an eternal evolution from its potencies to its ideal. But if the cosmos in its present condition is abnormal, then a disturbance has taken place in the past, and only a regenerating power can warrant it the final attainment of its goal. This, and no other is the principal antithesis, which separates the thinking minds in the domain of Science into two opposite battle-arrays" (Kuyper, *Lectures on Calvinism*, 131–32). In the unpublished essay "Herman Dooyeweerd: An Appreciation," Wolterstorff explains Dooyeweerd's pointed critique of the Kantian ideal of a uniform, non-religious body of scientific knowledge, also indicating Dooyeweerd's agreement with Kuyper on the role of religious presuppositions in science. Wolterstorff writes, "By contrast, one of Dooyeweerd's fundamental theses is that we must live in the expectation that over and over, in the academic disciplines, disagreements will arise of so fundamental a nature that there is and can be no agreed-on method for settlement. That at least is what we must expect in a religiously pluralistic society and tradition. For Dooyeweerd's contention is that we must expect divergence in *religious* commitment to lead to such disputes. Thus, Dooyeweerd took the radical position of holding that there are no *scientiae* on the traditional concept" (Wolterstorff, "Herman Dooyeweerd: An Appreciation," 3).

22. Particularly in chapter 6.

23. Wolterstorff, "Grace That Shaped," 268.

the world of Reformed thought, and indeed in the Anglo-American philosophical scene, Jellema's charge being realized through the production of, by most accounts, the most influential Christian philosophy of the twentieth century.

Wolterstorff went on to study philosophy at Harvard, where he graduated with his Ph.D. in 1956. As Wolterstorff remembers,

> There were, as I recall, twenty-one of us who were admitted as first year grad students in philosophy that year . . . A requirement of the program was that one take written prelims at the end of the first year, four in two days. The results were posted about a week after the exams were concluded. Four of us were allowed to continue to the Ph.D. . . . The rest were sent packing, a few with master's degrees, most without.[24]

Wolterstorff finished his course work in two years and wrote his dissertation, "Whitehead's Theory of Individuation," in a single year. "I have not looked at the dissertation since turning it in," he said in 2007.[25]

We should also mention Wolterstorff's contribution to what has come to be called Reformed Epistemology. In retrospect, Plantinga's *God and Other Minds*, published in 1967, represents a charter moment for Reformed Epistemology, though the term did not appear until 1983.[26] In that text, Plantinga argues that no more defense is needed for the rationality of belief in the existence of God than for the rationality of belief in the existence of other minds, or rather, that a defense is no more possible for the one than for the other, and that, therefore, the demand imposed on theists to provide such a defense, the default charge of irrationality, and the insistence that religious beliefs may be rational only by providing such a defense, is groundless and self-defeating. We are forced to choose between classical foundationalism and the rational permissibility not only of religious beliefs but of a great swath of basic beliefs such as belief in the existence of other minds and belief that the world is more than a few moments old. Reformed Epistemology says, 'so much the worse for classical foundationalism.'

Plantinga adopted, if incipiently, what Wolterstorff later called an "innocent until proved guilty"[27] approach to the rationality of theistic belief, a

---

24. "Postscript," 409–10.

25. Ibid., 411–12.

26. In the introduction to *Faith and Rationality*, Wolterstorff writes, "a third theme which weaves in and out of these essays is what might be called, admittedly not very felicitously, 'Calvinist epistemology,' or 'Reformed epistemology'" (Plantinga and Wolterstorff, *Faith and Rationality*, 7).

27. Wolterstorff says, for example, "The deliverances of our credulity disposition

theme largely consistent with Plantinga's later approach to warrant.[28] The fullest statements of Reformed Epistemology, of both its critique of classical foundationalist rationality—what Wolterstorff in places calls the "regnant" rationality of our time—and indications of viable alternative theories of rationality, appeared in the acclaimed *Faith and Rationality*, published in 1983.

Plantinga later proposed a theory of properly basic belief in two texts on warrant, *Warrant: The Current Debate* and *Warrant and Proper Function*. He then argued that Christian belief may qualify as one of these properly basic beliefs in his *Warranted Christian Belief*. Plantinga's notion of properly basic belief is a more fully developed "innocent until proved guilty" approach to rationality than anything that had come from the Reformed epistemologists up to that point, and it is heavily Reidian in its common sense response to skepticism and its approach to rationality. While Plantinga's work is characterized by penetrating critiques of classical foundationalism, Wolterstorff's work developed more broadly through his search for a historical account of the pervasive influence of it, despite its painfully obvious internal problems. Plantinga's work tended to maintain the a-historical tenor of analytic philosophy, while Wolterstorff's work developed more historically. Wolterstorff's own proposals also followed Reid, who he found to have been not only unjustly neglected by historians of philosophy, but also to be a most effective critic of classical foundationalism and modern skepticism. Wolterstorff's appreciation of Reid goes beyond Plantinga's, not only historically but also in terms of his development of an account of the doxastic self.

As we will see in some detail, Wolterstorff rejects modern epistemological anthropology as an unilluminating and unhelpful abstraction. He replaces it with a heavily Reidian, mobile, historically conditioned, and socially accountable doxastic subject, one upon whose every moment, every

---

are innocent until proved guilty, not guilty until proved innocent" (Wolterstorff, "Can Belief in God Be Rational," in *Practices of Belief*, 247).

28. The same basic position enjoys theological precedent, according to Wolterstorff. See "Herman Bavinck." Of the "innocent until proven guilty" principle of belief entitlement, Wolterstorff writes, "This, so I have argued, is the right approach" (ibid., 143). Bavinck's realism has been widely debated, particularly in terms of its theological merits and consistency with Bavinck's take on relevant theological doctrines. A section of Bavinck's *Prolegomena* entitled "Realism," and the entirety of the seventh chapter, "Scientific Foundations," has received a great deal of critical attention. It caught the attention of Vos, who gave it special mention in his review (mentioned above). Van Til, though much indebted to Bavinck otherwise, brought additional critical attention to this material. See Van Til, *Introduction to Systematic Theology*, 93–98. See also Oliphint, "Bavinck's Realism."

thought and action, weigh the ethical components of his personal, social, and historical situation. This doxastic anthropology leads Wolterstorff to his theory of *situated rationality*.[29] As we will see, the theory is explicitly Reidian, but it also retains elements of Kuyper's thought, and it stands in an intimate and organic relation to Wolterstorff's notion of shalom, his own version of Kuyperian neo-Calvinism.

Already in this brief introduction we have seen many of the traditions, personalities, and themes that have influenced and informed Wolterstorff's thinking in relevant ways—Kuyper and neo-Calvinism as well as Reformed Epistemology's critique of foundationalism and its constructive use of Thomas Reid. This provides us with the necessary background against which I will begin to develop a defense of my thesis, that Wolterstorff's theory of rationality is essentially a shalom doxastic ethic. We turn now to an exposition my claim and its relevance.

1.2 THE TOPIC AND ITS RELEVANCE

The claim that situated rationality is a shalom doxastic ethic suggests a profound relationship between Wolterstorff's theory of rationality and his own Christian belief. So it is worth noting at the outset that Wolterstorff's work on epistemology and rationality is not explicitly Christian. What I mean is that a defense exclusively of Christian belief or a presentation of a distinctly Christian point of view are rarely, if ever, his express intention. His writing on these topics is decidedly philosophical; it is intended for the philosophical reader, sensitive to the history of philosophy, and forged in philosophical categories.[30] Wolterstorff's epistemologically focused readers are unlikely to

---

29. The term "situated rationality" does not figure prominently in Wolterstorff's work, but it appears consistently over time. In his seminal essay, "Can Belief in God Be Rational If It Has No Foundations?," he says pointedly, "Rationality is always *situated rationality*" (Wolterstorff, Can Belief in God Be Rational," in *Practices of Belief*, 239), by which he means, "[o]ur noetic obligations arise from the whole diversity of obligations that we have in our concrete situations" (ibid., 231). In "Entitlement to Believe and Practices of Inquiry," written some twenty years later, he writes, "Obligations to employ practices of inquiry are *personally situated* obligations" (111). See also 238–39, 262–63; Wolterstorff, *Divine Discourse*, 272–73. Sloane uses the phrase in *On Being a Christian* (his third chapter is titled "Wolterstorff's Situated Rationality"), as does Coyle in "Nicholas Wolterstorff's Reformed Epistemology." Wolterstorff says of Reid's theory of rationality, "Reid very clearly gives what may be called a theory of *situated rationality*" (Wolterstorff, "Thomas Reid on Rationality," 65).

30. As he says of Reformed Epistemology, "Its discussion partners have been philosophers, not theologians; it employs the conceptuality of philosophy" (Wolterstorff, "Herman Bavinck," 146).

get the impression that he understands his work as related in any significant way to a Christian worldview, to the kingdom of God, to the Christian faith, biblical ethics or a biblical view of history. Even his writing on religious epistemology, one notices, bears none of the marks of a positive articulation of a distinctively Christian view, and may just as well have come from the pen of a follower of another religion, or even an epistemologist without religious commitment. Some might count this along the foremost merits of Wolterstorff's work, even from an apologetic point of view. I include myself here. But the fact is, Wolterstorff's work appears to be somewhat of an anomaly in this sense: while the success of his work toward upsetting the presumptive bias against religious or specifically Christian believing in much of twentieth century philosophy, if not in Anglo-American academia more broadly, is uncontested, he has not, to my knowledge, produced a single argument for the existence of God, much less the truth of Christianity, nor does he anywhere in publication, again, to my knowledge, directly engage an atheist or a critic of one kind or another on the question of the ationality of specifically Christian belief, that is, on the unique (epistemic) merits of the faith he calls his own.[31]

31. Wolterstorff's introduction to *Faith and Rationality* offers some insight here. He describes the first three of the four themes of the volume as follows: First, he says, "Perhaps the most basic theme is that of the collapse of *classical foundationalism*" (*Faith and Rationality*, 1). "A second theme which weaves in and out of these essays is that of the evidentialist challenge to religious belief, a challenge first issued decisively in the European Enlightenment . . . the fundamental contentions of the Enlightenment still prove persuasive to many" (5). Third, notice, "Characteristic of the Continental Calvinistic tradition has been a revulsion against arguments in favor of theism or Christianity . . . that this tradition has characteristically viewed in a dim light the project of offering evidence for theism and for Christianity is clear" (7–8). In other words, historically speaking, stopping short of offering evidence for Christian belief is a distinctly Reformed habit. Wolterstorff continues, "[M]ost often the position taken was that such arguments are unnecessary for putting a person in the position where he is within his rights in being a Christian" (8). In sum, "The third theme that weaves in and out of these essays, then, is that of the antievidentialist impulses of the Reformed tradition. Of course, by taking up an antievidentialist position in their response to the Enlightenment, these essays *perforce* ally themselves with that impulse in the Reformed tradition" (7–8). In other words, this antievidentialist commitment, as Wolterstorff sees it, is a large part of the Reformed pedigree of Reformed Epistemology. Wolterstorff's claim that Calvinism of the European continent is characterized by a "revulsion" to positive arguments for Christian theism is, however, not entirely accurate. Even if there is some ambiguity here between apologetics and natural theology, there are notable advocates of both within the Reformed tradition. On the Reformed tradition and natural theology, see the recent study by Sudduth, *The Reformed Objection to Natural Theology*. Even though the Reformed objection to natural theology has a noble history, the philosophico-theological influence of Thomas Aquinas, particularly with reference to the doctrine of simplicity, is pervasive in the history of Reformed thought. See, for example, Bavinck, *God and Creation*, 118–77. Regarding apologetics, even Kuyper was not decidedly against it, as

The fact that no such arguments have come from Wolterstorff's pen is due to the particular nature of his apologetic methodology, if we may call it that, or to his view of epistemic merit and doxastic ethics, which include, as we have already seen to some extent, important aspects of the work Thomas Reid and of the thought of Dutch theologians Abraham Kuyper and Herman Bavinck, and even the public and social concerns of John Locke. Wolterstorff is committed to a common sense, "innocent until proven guilty" principle of belief entitlement. A given belief (believing) is innocent—rational, justified, permissible, or entitled, for Wolterstorff—until and unless the believer is permissibly aware of a compelling reason that the belief in question represents some kind of epistemic malpractice or dereliction of epistemic duty. Simple enough. As I seek to demonstrate here, however, this formulation has a rich theological pedigree.[32]

Just as in Wolterstorff's own work on epistemology and rationality, where the theoretical influence of Christian commitments is not immediately apparent, much of the initial, formative work of Reformed Epistemology is decidedly neither an argument for the irrationality of unbelief nor a positive argument for the unique or particular epistemic credentials of Christian belief *per se* nor a defense of any distinctly Christian theological claims. Reformed Epistemology has consistently affirmed a different goal, that of rebuffing the regnant assumption that religious belief as a class is *prima facie* non- or irrational, or that for a religious belief to be rational it

---

one recent study argues: "Kuyper's role for apologetics was not to abolish it, but to give it a role of little importance" (Anderson, *Reason and Worldviews*, 49). Warfield wrote that Kuyper had demoted apologetics to "a subdivision of a subdivision," and that, on Kuyper's method, Christianity remained "the great assumption" (Warfield, "Introduction to Beattie's *Apologetics*," in *Selected Shorter Writings*, 95). If Kuyper was not a great advocate of apologetics, certainly he did not express revulsion to it. See also Edgar and Oliphint, *Christian Apologetics*, 331–35, on Kuyper, and 453–56 on apologist Van Til, who considered himself a Kuyperian in many respects.

32. See Wolterstorff, "Herman Bavinck," 143. The basic thesis of this article is that Reformed Epistemology came about by capitalizing on an important shift in philosophy (the emergence of metaepistemology) as an opportunity to give voice to the philosophical implications of themes in Reformed theology going at least as far back as Dutch neo-Calvinism. That yield is precisely this "innocent until proven guilty" approach to belief entitlement. It is also telling that, from an early age, Wolterstorff understood his faith as bequeathed, received, and held on non-foundationalist bases: "My induction into the tradition, through words and silences, ritual and architecture, implanted in me an interpretation of reality—a fundamental hermeneutic. Nobody offered 'evidences' for the truth of the Christian gospel; nobody offered 'proofs' for the inspiration of the Scriptures; nobody suggested that Christianity was the best explanation of one thing or another. Evidentialists were nowhere in sight! The gospel was report, not explanation. And nobody reflected on how we as 'modern men' can and should believe all this" ("Grace That Shaped," 263).

must be supported by inference from self-evident beliefs or beliefs immediately evident to the senses. The methodology of Reformed Epistemology is, consistently, to defend an "innocent until proved guilty" rationality of believing, just believing—Christian believing receives no special attention. This is not to say that Christian belief does not benefit from this work; it does, but neither directly nor uniquely. Reformed Epistemology frees Christian belief—and religious belief generally, along with a broader class of basic beliefs—from the constraints of classical foundationalism indirectly.

Much of *Faith and Rationality* confirms this. The arguments there are directed against the purported irrationality of Christian belief only as a species of religious belief as a species of belief-in-general, defending the rationality of generic religious belief or of belief-in-general by undercutting the demands of classical foundationalism and the evidentialist requirement, by demonstrating decisive internal inconsistencies in foundationalism itself. Consequently, *Faith and Rationality*, and much of the relevant writing of Reformed epistemologists since, treats religious belief as a doxastic category without particular theological content or significance. The object of religious doxastic intentionality remains unspecified; or, the referent of the term 'God' in religious propositions is inconsequential, and anyway never defined. The anti-foundationalist and anti-evidentialist arguments presented in *Faith and Rationality* make no claim at all about the unique nature of religious beliefs, much less Christian belief in particular.[33]

Wolterstorff makes this clear when he writes, "[c]entral to Christianity, Judaism, and Islam, is the conviction that we as human beings are called to believe in God . . . Presumably it is rational for a person to believe *in* God only if it is rational for him to believe various propositions *about* God—in particular, that there is such a being as God."[34] Here, however, a problem emerges: is it really the case that Jewish, Christian, and Islamic faiths are largely interchangeable as far as the cognitive aspect of faith is concerned? Does not the Christian mean something significantly different by "belief

---

33. Exemplifying this approach is Wolterstorff's essay "Can Belief in God Be Rational" and also his "Epistemology of Religion." The latter was originally published in *The Blackwell Guide to Epistemology* and was republished in *Practices of Belief*, 144–72. I offer some critical reflections on the theological implications of this methodology in Shannon, "Believe and Confess."

34. Wolterstorff, "Can Belief in God be Rational," in *Practices of Belief*, 217. Note also the following statement, which appears in the piece on Bavinck: "This leaves open the possibility that [foundationalism] nonetheless holds for beliefs about God, but defending that possibility requires that one find a relevant difference among perceptual beliefs, memorial beliefs, and the like, on the one hand, and beliefs about God, on the other hand . . . Here I have to call it off and declare that no one has yet succeeded in pinpointing a relevant difference" (Wolterstorff, "Herman Bavinck," 137).

in God" than the Muslim does? And what might this imply in terms of Wolterstorff's approach to the epistemic status of Christian belief? Even setting aside the question of the referent of the term "God," does not the cognitive side of faith itself enjoy theological attention within each of these traditions? So there is a sense in which Wolterstorff's work on these topics, and the work of Reformed Epistemology in general, obviously stands to be of service to the church, but also a sense in which it proves to be somewhat of a conundrum, particularly for the Christian theologian and the apologist interested in defending the unique merits of Christian faith.

So the theologian might be somewhat irked to find that theistic believing, as Wolterstorff tends to treat it, is not itself essentially theological. What I mean is that it is clear that Wolterstorff approaches the topic of the rationality of religious belief from a philosophical point of view, as though there was, first, believing, generically speaking, within which, second, we find religious believing, distinguished from other species of belief by the uniqueness of its (unspecified) grounds (revelation or religious experience of the divine, a supernatural something or someone), and then, third, by finer, (unarticulated) distinctions separating Jewish, Christian, and Muslim believings. And so these finer distinctions bear little or no weight in terms of the epistemic features of religious believings. What we find then is no substantive role for religious beliefs themselves, much less for their content—for the specific Christian-ness of Christian belief—in the formulation of a theory of rationality.

Religious beliefs are just as uninvolved in the process of drawing up norms for believing as they are treated unexceptionally by those norms once clarified. Religious belief is subject to the same standards of rationality as any other belief in Wolterstorff's theory of rationality no less than in the modern theories he rejects. Viewing religious belief from the philosophical side of things leaves us with the impression that there is a pre- or non-theological way to think about religious believing, so that we can say "certain attributes of God" (beginning with existence) or "religious propositions" are the objects of religious belief without concerning ourselves with the actual referents of such beliefs (i.e., "which god?" or "what does 'god' mean?"), with whether the true God is relevantly similar to the abstract attribute in question, or with the redemptive categories relevant to one's confession or rejection of religious claims. The implication of all this appears to be that our discussions of religious believing will be generally uninterested in theological specifics. But one might expect that an approach which grows out of a theological atmosphere, such as Wolterstorff's Kuyperian background, instead of a modern philosophical one, might come at things the other way around, finding the generic "religious believing" somewhat confusing, theoretically unfruitful, if not flatly objectionable.

The Christian theologian or apologist may not be as eager to speak of religious belief in this generic way. His starting point will be a Christian theological one: belief in the triune God of Scripture and in Christ as lord and savior, perhaps commitment to "the faith that was once for all delivered to the saints," or to the apostolic "pattern of sound words."[35] The theoretical difference is this: belief is theologically defined, it is a theologically constituted category, and it is ethically significant ultimately for theological reasons: the Bible enjoins us to believe. Belief in this case is an aspect, the cognitive aspect, of Christian faith; but here it is inseparable from the content of that faith. So the theologian may not be so easily discouraged from using even trinitarian categories to define Christian faith and the relevant doxastic attitudes. If, as in a classical Reformed perspective, one's soteriology begins in the eternal counsel of peace and the triune economies of both the *historia* and the *ordo* of salvation, belief will always and everywhere be a function of the sinner's status as either in Adam or in Christ, a context in which saving faith is a gift of God by the indwelling of the Holy Spirit. And other religions will understand belief through distinct categories of their own. So from a theological point of view, the parity among religious believings that is implied when we speak about religious belief as a generic epistemological category is somewhat of an oddity.

Wolterstorff's theory of situated rationality offers a fresh perspective on belief entitlement and rationality, one which, in my view, is distinctly Christian but also philosophically informed.[36] And any attempt at achieving this balance invites a number of questions, especially from the Christian point of view: is it rational to hold Christian beliefs? And if it is, is it irrational *not* to hold Christian beliefs, or to reject Christian theism? In what sense it is rational to be a believing Jew or Muslim, or to be an agnostic, a skeptic, or an atheist—again, from a Christian point of view, or from Wolterstorff's own Christian vantage point? More broadly, what is the relationship between Wolterstorff's theologically informed theory of rationality, the theology which informs it, and the rational status of Christian belief according to it? And so, the research question of this study is: *how are we to understand*

---

35. 2 Tim 1:13; Jude 1:3.

36. So, for example, in my view, for Wolterstorff the parity between various religious believings is implied by a logically prior commitment to the unique merits of the Christian faith. In other words, in Wolterstorff's view, Christian belief itself commends a view of rationality in which various religious beliefs enjoy, *prima facie*, equal footing. Religious diversity is a Christian (epistemic) value.

the relationship between Wolterstorff's theory of rationality and his theological commitments?

My response comprises two main components. The first is situationality. Wolterstorff insists that rationality is always and everywhere a function of a person's situation. The second is shalom. Wolterstorff appears to understand all moral significance to be reducible to the biblical notion of shalom. So he rejects the abstract, de-personalized epistemology of modern tradition and replaces it with a situated, personally conditioned reconfiguration of doxastic and practical responsibility, and that responsibility is permeated through and through with moral accountability ultimately given in the Christian vision of shalom. As will be clear later on, situated rationality is not merely consistent with shalom, it is the theory of rationality commended by shalom. The connection is necessary. But is Christian belief rational? There is no generic answer; it 'all depends.' It all depends upon a person's situation. The implication is this: Wolterstorff's theory of rationality is a shalom doxastic ethic within which Christian belief itself is situationally entitled.

1.3 APPROACHING THE QUESTION

In order to understand situated rationality as a shalom doxastic ethic, one might examine those publications in which Wolterstorff directly addresses the question of the epistemological credentials and the rational merits of religious believings. And a number of Wolterstorff's best-known works speak directly to this way of approaching the question.[37]

The principal disadvantage of this procedure is that, as a direct approach to the *what* question, it promises nothing in terms of *why*.[38] We may learn from numerous publications directly and efficiently how Wolterstorff goes about defending the rationality of religious belief, so directly and efficiently that phrasing a research program this way impugns the need for an extended secondary study. But more importantly, this approach fails to engage the issue with the requisite breadth, since interaction with the primary (philosophical) literature alone offers no opportunity to ask those outstanding questions about theological motivation, and no opportunity to address the concerns of the Christian theologian or apologist, who benefit I think a great deal from the apologetic achievements of Reformed Epistemology.

So if our goal is to clarify the relationship between situated rationality and shalom, certainly Wolterstorff's epistemological work is indispensable,

---

37. For example, Wolterstorff, *Reason within the Bounds*.
38. And anyway, such a study has been done: Sloane, *On Being a Christian*.

but on its own it is insufficient. In order to defend my claim that Wolterstorff's theory of rationality is borne by theological ideas, by shalom in particular, I must clarify the connections between the relevant bodies of his work, between Wolterstorff's work on epistemology and rationality and his work on shalom and related ethical topics (education, scholarship and theorizing, justice, human dignity, etc.). As noted, this connection is essential to the descriptive proposal I offer here. So my approach to the relationship between shalom and situated rationality is as follows. I begin with Wolterstorff's epistemological work and then argue for a point of fundamental dependence of his contributions in this area upon his notion of shalom. I then explore the particular ways in which a shalom ethic informs theorizing and the ethics of belief. Finally, I examine the theological distinctives which are in my view constitutive of Wolterstorff's approach to situationality and doxastic ethics.

Epistemology and the ethics of belief have been the focus of a great deal of Wolterstorff's writing, teaching, and public lecturing throughout his career. He has written extensively on related topics toward historical, analytical, and more creative goals, and he has made significant contributions of all three kinds. And while his thought on these issues continues to develop, with some of his latest creative work appearing in print only very recently, a sustained, theologically informed analysis of this material still waits for an author.[39] It is my hope that the present study will begin to answer that need.

1.4 OUTLINE AND PROCEDURE

After a short introduction, I take a moment to define Wolterstorff's notions of rationality, justification, and entitlement (§2.1). The core of chapter 2 begins with an analysis of Wolterstorff's critique of the abstractness characteristic of the Western epistemological tradition (§2.2). In Wolterstorff's estimation, modern and contemporary epistemologists have tended to work with a notion of the epistemological or doxastic subject that is noticeably de-historicized, and which has very little to do with the living, moving, and socially engaged sorts of thinkers and believers we actually are. Wolterstorff rejects this starting point and adopts a Reidian view of the doxastic self and of belief-forming dispositions. We treat his doxastic anthropology next

---

39. The only book-length studies of Wolterstorff's work I know of are Sloane's *On Being a Christian* and Coyle's "Nicholas Wolterstorff's Reformed Epistemology," mentioned above. Both attempt to synthesize Wolterstorff's work to some degree, but neither attempts to incorporate theological categories of Wolterstorff's own Dutch Reformed tradition as a unifying or integrating substructure, as I do here.

(§2.3). We are able to view some of the features of Reid's thought which are appealing to Wolterstorff in further detail through an analysis of what Wolterstorff refers to as Reid's "credulity disposition" and Reid's psychological account of belief in testimony, as Wolterstorff has understood them (§2.4). Reid's theories of belief and knowledge depend in large part on a doxastic optimism which is really quite peculiar in the modern context.[40] Since Wolterstorff benefits from Reid's doxastic optimism so much, and because it proves to be theologically significant, I devote some time to Wolterstorff's adoption of Reidian doxastic optimism (§2.5). This attention to Reidian optimism reveals some points of continuity and some of discontinuity between Wolterstorff and Plantinga in terms of doxastic anthropology (§2.6).

Wolterstorff views rationality in terms of a normative notion of doxastic permissibility which he calls "entitlement." Because it is normative, rationality thus understood requires some notion of intentional action in the order of the formation of beliefs, since one cannot be held accountable for something over which one has no control. Wolterstorff rejects strong doxastic voluntarism, the idea that we can, by sheer force of will, determine to believe or to not believe something, even, perhaps, against the evidence; but he affirms that there are many ways in which we may "govern" our belief-forming faculties. So, a person can only be accountable for beliefs (or believings) over which he is able to exercise some control—"eluctable" beliefs, Wolterstorff calls these; and we have within our power many means of responsible doxastic action.[41] Thus resting rationality, in terms of entitlement, on intentional action locates believing and belief-governing practices within a broader web of actions and a more general moral context. Rationality is always both practical and moral. I turn to these issues in the third chapter.

Wolterstorff's understanding of rational permissibility and accountability in terms of situationality is the first topic covered in chapter 3 (§3.1). Next I examine situationality itself in terms of the availability of beliefs and doxastically significant actions, actions Wolterstorff calls "practices of inquiry" and "ways of finding out," and relevant social, historical, and

---

40. One recent study, De Bary, *Thomas Reid and Scepticism*, argues for a reliabilist understanding of Reid's response to skepticism, an approach to Reid that is, at least broadly, not unlike the one Wolterstorff takes. I understand Wolterstorff as holding that Reidian doxastic optimism is a close philosophical relative of Herman Bavinck's positions on belief in God and the foundation of theology, again, as Wolterstorff has interpreted Bavinck. He says, for example, that there are "some astoundingly Reidian-sounding passages in Bavinck's *Reformed Dogmatics*" (Wolterstorff, "Herman Bavinck," 146).

41. Wolsterstorff, "Can Belief in God Be Rational," in *Practices of Belief*, 246.

personal delineations (§3.2). The closing section of chapter 3 introduces the question of moral value (§3.3).

Jointly, chapters 2 and 3 comprise an analysis of situated rationality, of rationality as practical, situational, and deontological. Focusing in chapter 2 on the doxastic subject and in chapter 3 on the subject's (doxastic and moral) situation will provide us with an account of Wolterstorff's theory of rationality in terms of entitlement sufficient for articulating the relevance of shalom.[42]

I proceed in chapter 4 with an analysis of shalom, an ethical vision in many ways of Kuyperian, neo-Calvinist pedigree. My intention in the fourth chapter is to demonstrate that shalom is of the background for situated rationality, most notably its moral foundation. After a brief introduction, I seek a definition of shalom (§4.1). I then introduce its biblical and theological roots, as Wolterstorff has articulated them (§4.2), and next discuss Wolterstorff's interaction with contemporary representatives of neo-Calvinism (§4.3–5). I also bring a wider range of issues into the discussion—worship, liturgy, biblical anthropology, biblical theology and eschatology—in order to fill out shalom as Wolterstorff's governing ethical vision. I give special attention to Wolterstorff's thought on shalom and liturgy (§4.5), a theme which draws together the theological and ethical concerns of the chapter.

Chapter 5 presents a more detailed analysis of the practical implications of shalom, specifically, how Wolterstorff envisions a shalom-guided Christian presence in the academy. Wolterstorff has put much of what he has to say on this issue in terms of the theory versus praxis question relative specifically to academic work. I introduce Wolterstorff's thought on that question (§5.2) and then, in order to demonstrate the practical potential of the ethic of shalom, I retrace Wolterstorff's shalom-based treatment of it (§5.3). Wolterstorff has analyzed the potential role of shalom in scholarly activities in terms of various levels of theorizing and scholarly self-consciousness. After introducing these categories (§5.3), I turn very briefly to point out the odd fact that shalom, on the one hand, is a biblical concept, but, on the other, provides a pluralistic doxastic ethical context. Wolterstorff embraces this fact and defends what he calls "dialogic pluralism." We then revisit neo-Calvinism, since, in light of an enhanced view of shalom, we are able to view in greater detail Wolterstorff's interaction with this tradition (§5.4). Chapter 5 concludes as we bring into view a point Wolterstorff makes with particular clarity in *Reason within the Bounds of Religion*: that theorizing is not by any means a strictly academic endeavor, but is in fact a basically human activity. In other words, however Wolterstorff has shown

---

42. Sloane offers a more detailed analysis. See *On Being a Christian*, 79–110, 165–79.

shalom to bear on the scholarly life, it bears *mutatis mutandis* on the daily life of every person, and it thus relates directly to a general theory of rationality (§5.5).

The analysis of shalom in the fourth and fifth chapters serves our overall interest by demonstrating the fact that Wolterstorff sees shalom as an expansive ethical vision: all people, if Christians most self-consciously, are always and everywhere accountable to shalom. Shalom is our duty. A Christian scholar is a shalom-scholar, and the value of his work and accomplishments are weighed against shalom, and the direction and focus of his scholarship should serve shalom. This means, alternatively, that believing, indeed all doxastic activity, is always and everywhere shalom-believing and shalom-doxastic-activity, doxastic activity, that is, forged through humanity's existential accountability to the creating and redeeming God. Rationality itself then stands wholly under the governance of shalom, and the ethical vision conspicuously absent at the close of chapter 3, the moral grounding of situated rationality, is now before us.

If chapters 2 and 3 comprise an analysis of situated rationality, and chapters 4 and 5 of shalom, it would appear that we have done things the wrong way around. We began with what turned out to be the effect—situated rationality—and traced it back to the cause: shalom and Christian belief. But we have discovered, in sum, that Wolterstorff's theory of situated rationality is implicit, in his view, in his understanding of the Bible's teaching on redemptive history, on creation, fall, and redemption. And yet, as we will note at several points, situated rationality is itself a happily pluralistic doxastic framework.

I begin chapter 6 with a survey of the evidence from each of the preceding chapters for a connection between shalom and rationality (§6.1). The goal here is to bring into view a coherent narrative unifying chapters 1 through 5 that demonstrates my thesis. I then focus narrowly on the question of the epistemic status of Christian belief, since it appears both as Wolterstorff's actually entitled belief in the shalom of the Christian God and as situationally rational. The relationship between the theoretical function of shalom in Wolterstorff's approach to the ethics of belief and the status of Christian belief downstream, under the theory of situated rationality, is pivotal for my interpretation of situated rationality. In order to clarify and defend the connection between them, I propose a few interpretive concepts, including 'redemptive-historical epistemic humility' and a 'Wolterstorffian' theology of situationality (§6.2). I consider two potential objections to the interpretation I propose (§6.3), and in the final section of chapter 6, I articulate a line of theological inquiry directed toward Wolterstorff's notion of situationality (§6.4). A few summary remarks bring the sixth and final chapter to a close.

Throughout this study, I attempt to track Wolterstorff's interaction with two closely related traditions. As we have seen, Wolterstorff understands himself as having inherited the tradition of historic Dutch Calvinism, and he is consistently appreciative of its theology, intellectual rigor, expansiveness of vision, and even its distinctive doctrinal emphases. But Wolterstorff is also an established authority on the Western philosophical tradition, and his engagement with it is an important part of this study.

I have attempted to trace the implications of a single question, the question of the relationship between belief entitlement and theological commitment, through the deep structures of Wolterstorff's vast oeuvres, and the substructure of Wolterstorff's work is rich both theologically and philosophically. Because Wolterstorff's thought, in my assessment of it, is proven to be systematic at its core, and related organically at every point to the same basic themes, in theory we could begin our inquiry anywhere. I have elected to begin where any Calvinist might happily begin, with iconoclasm: the smashing of an idol of the secular tradition.

2

Situated Rationality and the Doxastic Self

Chapters 2 and 3 are related in the following two ways. Together they rehearse the development of the theory of situated rationality, beginning in chapter 2 with Wolterstorff's charge that something is amiss in traditional epistemology and moving incrementally, through to the conclusion of chapter 3, to the theory fully developed. We might also think of the second and third chapters as an exposition of the theory of situated rationality that begins in chapter 2 with the psychology of the doxastic subject and expands in chapter 3 to bring into view the subject's socially constituted ethico-doxastic situation.[1] This image of an incrementally expanding scope of analysis might also be thought to encompass chapter 4 as well, where we move beyond social and historical situations to the super-situational ethical vision of shalom.

I begin chapter 2 with preliminary matters: defining rationality, justification, and belief entitlement, according to Wolterstorff. Then, my analysis

---

1. One drawback of this procedure is the potential to fail to appreciate the fact that situated rationality is essentially a theory of practical rationality, which has implications for doxastic or epistemic rationality in terms of doxastic or belief-governing practices. Where the tradition of the ethics of belief seeks to articulate norms for believing, Wolterstorff argues that there are no specifically doxastic norms, but there are norms for believing when doxastic activity is understood as located within a broader context of practical deontology. The danger of the approach I am outlining here is that the impact of this distinctive feature of Wolterstorff's thought on the ethics of belief is somewhat overlooked. The extended treatment in chapter 3 of socially constituted doxastic practices should, however, steer us clear of this potential pitfall.

of situated rationality begins at the flashpoint of Wolterstorff's break from epistemological tradition: his critique of the abstract, platonic epistemological subject of the modern, Cartesian tradition (§2.2). We then encounter Wolterstorff's mobile, socially engaged, and ethically responsible epistemological subject (§2.3). Introduced in this section are features of the doxastic self that receive careful attention from Wolterstorff, "belief-forming dispositions." Next is a detailed study of one particular such disposition, the "credulity principle," and belief in testimony (§2.4). Wolterstorff adopts the basic idea of belief-forming dispositions in general and of the credulity principle in particular from the work of the Scottish common sense philosopher Thomas Reid. We will notice that Wolterstorff also adopts from Reid an optimism that I shall call "Reidian doxastic optimism" (§2.5). Doxastic anthropology of a Reidian stripe also figures heavily in Alvin Plantinga's work on the epistemic desideratum he calls "warrant." A comparison between Plantinga and Wolterstorff on the doxastic self will clarify unique features of Wolterstorff's doxastic anthropology, and thus conclude the first stage of our analysis of situated rationality (§2.6).

In the third chapter I expand the sphere of analysis, moving next to the ethical significance of the subject's place in his "sphere of moral responsibility," and then to the role of social, cultural, and historical situatedness in the availability and status of doxastic actions. We will see how, in dialogue with the tradition but also through fresh and incisive critique, Wolterstorff charts a significant and innovative path beyond the standard approaches to rationality. This is especially clear in Wolterstorff's critique of the solitary, immobile reactor of traditional epistemology, and in his locating the doxastic subject within his particular socio-historical context. Before we address these issues, some definitions are in order.

2.1 RATIONALITY, JUSTIFICATION, AND ENTITLEMENT: PRELIMINARY DEFINITIONS

Even a cursory survey of the relevant literature confirms Wolterstorff's observation that "'rational' is a word protean in its meanings."[2] The broadest use of the term refers to an evaluative notion of practicality, of mean-ends suitability. Says one standard text, "rational" is "a normative concept that philosophers have generally tried to characterize in such a way that, for any

---

2. "Thomas Reid on Rationality," 45. He says elsewhere, "[H]ere our situation is surely that our English word 'rational' is unusually protean, having a large number of different, albeit connected, senses" ("Can Belief in God be Rational," in *Practices of Belief*, 225).

action, belief, or desire, if it is rational we ought to choose it."[3] If we are thinking of instrumental rationality, some principle like the following might be operative:

> *Principle of Instrumental Rationality*: If you intend that a situation, X, occur and you believe, in agreement with your evidence, that another situation, Y, is the most effective means to X, then you rationally should aim to have Y occur.[4]

Purely instrumental rationality in not concerned with the (rational) status of goals; it is concerned only with the (instrumental) expediency of the means. In such cases, we are tasked only with the clarification and articulation of a given goal and the discovery of the right means, given circumstantial variables and other factors. A so-called substantialist approach to rationality, on the other hand, holds that ends too are rationally assessable and, therefore, that only certain ends are rational. In these Aristotelian and Kantian traditions, since ultimate goals are rationally assessable, rationality is not purely instrumental.

Another important distinction is that between rational permissibility and rational obligation. Not to choose from among those actions which are rationally obligatory or required would be irrational and blameworthy. Alternatively, some actions are rationally permissible but not obligatory. To either perform or avoid these is neither necessarily rational nor necessarily irrational.[5] But all this is somewhat beside the point, and too generic, since we are interested specifically in epistemic or doxastic rationality at this point. We find complications there as well.

"Until rather recently," Wolterstorff explains, "analytic epistemology in the twentieth century was conducted as if there were—apart from truth itself—just one truth-relevant merit in beliefs, that one typically called either 'justification' or 'rationality.'"[6] Though there is, Wolterstorff writes, "a large number of distinct truth-relevant merits in beliefs . . . neither 'justification' nor 'rationality' picks out any single such merit; both are highly ambiguous terms . . ."[7] In this sense too, then, the term is too vague for our purposes.

This vagueness creeps into Wolterstorff's use of the term as well. The reason is, in my estimation, that Wolterstorff *begins*, so to speak, in interaction with the tradition of taking "rational" to refer to this singular

---

3. Gert, "Rationality," 772.

4. Moser, Mulder, and Trout, *The Theory of Knowledge*, 130. Instrumental rationality is "goal-oriented, as opposed to goal-determining" (124).

5. Ibid., 125–6.

6. "Epistemology of Religion," in *Practices of Belief*, 145.

7. Ibid.

truth-relevant epistemic merit, calling it something like "intellectual justification," but then, as he moves toward his own theory, he re-defines the term to mean something more specific and concrete.[8] It may be helpful to think of Wolterstorff's use of the term "rational" in three different ways or three steps, representing three stages in the development of his theory of situated rationality.[9]

First, we find Wolterstorff adopting traditional usage: "I shall use it, as I have already suggested, in such a way that rational belief is understood as intellectually justified belief."[10] But he quickly moves toward breaking new ground in terms of specificity: ". . . that just moves the question over one step. What is an intellectually justified belief?"[11]

"My contention," he writes, "is that there is a large number of distinct truth-relevant merits in beliefs."[12] Wolterstorff specifies his notion of epistemic justification in deontological terms: "Justification in beliefs, as I understand it, is essentially connected to duties and responsibilities. Justification is a normative concept."[13] And he says:

> Intellectual justification, in my judgment, is tied up with attempting to get in touch with reality, by trying to avoid falsehood in one's beliefs and trying to expand one's hold of true beliefs. In each of us there are certain belief-forming mechanisms. Likewise in each of us there are certain abilities for controlling these belief-forming mechanisms so as to diminish the amount of falsehood in our beliefs and to attain truth. *Intellectual responsibility* pertains to how we *ought* to use those governing abilities for the purpose of avoiding falsehood and attaining truth. Each of us is *obliged* to use those governing capacities in certain ways, toward the goal of being in touch with reality on certain matters; those constitute our *intellectual responsibilities*.[14]

This is a second use of the notion of rationality: doxastic self-governance with reference to alethically defined intellectual responsibility.[15] Along these lines, Wolterstorff offers a detailed criterion for rational believing:

---

8. This transition is explicit in "Thomas Reid on Rationality," as we will see below.

9. This following three-step definition is my own way of attempting to define the terms in question according to Wolterstorff's use of them.

10. "Thomas Reid on Rationality," 45.

11. Ibid.

12. "Epistemology of Religion," in *Practices of Belief*, 145.

13. "Thomas Reid on Rationality," 45.

14. Ibid., 46; emphasis added.

15. "Alethic" means having to do with truth. Wolterstorff writes, "Locke

> A person S is rational in his ineluctable and innocently produced belief B*p* if and only if S does believe *p*, and either
>
> S neither has nor ought to have adequate reason to cease from believing *p*, and is not rationally obliged to believe that he *does* have adequate reason to cease;
>
> or,
>
> S does have adequate reason to cease from believing *p* but does not realize that he does, and is rationally justified in that.[16]

Most distinctive of Wolterstorff's theory of rationality is the location of doxastic conduct within a broader field of behavior and responsibility, within a field, that is, of ethically significant action and practical rationality. The third use of the notion of rationality then, unique to Wolterstorff, begins with recognition of the similarities between doxastic and practical responsibility:

> Just as there are duties and responsibilities pertaining to one's treatment of other human beings, so too there are duties and responsibilities pertaining to one's use of the intellect. It is not true that 'anything goes' in our actions regarding other persons; neither is it true that 'anything goes' in our believings. The justified belief, then, is the belief that is in accord with the norms for believing.[17]

And so, "[a]ccording to this understanding," he explains, "to be justified in one's believings amounts to doing as well is one's believings as can be rightly demanded of a person." On the one hand, "[j]ustification consists in doing one's duty by one's believings." But on the other, "[t]he justified in the domain of belief is like the permissible in the domain of morality; the morally permissible action is the action in accord with the norms for moral actions; the justified belief is the belief in accord with the norms for believing."[18] And, in fact, "Our noetic obligations arise from the whole diversity of obligations that we have in our concrete situations."[19] Elsewhere he says, "[t]

---

assumes—rightly in my judgment—that we have an obligation to govern our assent with the goal in mind of getting more amply in touch with reality" ("Can Belief in God Be Rational," in *Practices of Belief*, 228).

16. Ibid., 253.
17. "Thomas Reid on Rationality," 46.
18. Ibid., 46.
19. "Can Belief in God be Rational," in *Practices of Belief*, 231.

he clue to the applicability of deontic concepts to our believings lies in the notion of a *doxastic practice* . . ."[20]

Along the lines of this third notion of rationality in terms of broader, situated, practical responsibility, we find Wolterstorff's notion of entitlement. Rationality in terms of private doxastic conduct (the second notion) is broader (though more specific) than merely intellectual justification (the first); and entitlement (the third), a normative, deontological notion reflecting a broad, socially constituted ethic, is more expansive yet than rationality in terms of private, doxastic conduct.[21]

"A characteristic error of epistemologists," Wolterstorff writes, "has been to suppose that our noetic obligations are disconnected from our other obligations. The truth is that in good measure the particular shape that the obligation to attain truth and avoid falsehood assumes for each person is determined by her obligations in general."[22] Notice then that Wolterstorff's criterion for entitled belief is largely his criterion for rational believing, where doxastic conduct is put in terms of what he calls "doxastic practices":

> . . . a person S is *entitled* to his belief that *p* just in case S believes *p*, and there's no doxastic practice D pertaining to *p* such that S ought to have implemented D and S did not, or S ought to have implemented D better than S did.[23]

At times Wolterstorff will use the term "rationality" in the traditional way, as a catch-all epistemic merit roughly equivalent to epistemic or intellectual justification. We will also find Wolterstorff claiming, against this notion, that rationality is principally a deontological notion with reference to the general obligation of getting "more amply in touch with reality," or with properly governing one's belief-forming faculties toward true beliefs. This second notion stands as a corrective to epistemological tradition, and when it is enhanced beyond the limitations of private doxastic self-governance to include socially constituted "practices of belief," it becomes Wolterstorff's distinct notion of belief entitlement, the chief epistemic desideratum of Wolterstorff's theory of situated rationality.

---

20. *Divine Discourse*, 269. I explore this connection in chapter 3.

21. Sloane also sees entitlement is a development of rationality—basically the same "innocent-until-proven-guilty" notion, with the incorporation of practices of inquiry. He calls it "a later development of this model" (*On Being a Christian*, 95). Entitlement, he says, "is simply a clarification of his prior criterion of *rationally justified belief* which avoids the potentially misleading words *rational* and *justification*, without substantially altering its central tenets" (96).

22. "Can Belief in God Be Rational," in *Practices of Belief*, 231.

23. *Divine Discourse*, 272.

All this is can be confusing, certainly. It might help to think of chapters 2 and 3 as reflecting a three-step development: grappling with the traditional notion of rationality as intellectual justification broadly speaking appears in section §2.2. Recasting the notion of rationality in deontological terms with private doxastic self-governance in view appears in sections §2.3–4. In chapter 3, we find the notion of rationality taking the shape of situationality and incorporating socially constituted practices of inquiry, and we find entitlement at the center of it.

2.2 THE SOLITARY IMMOBILE REACTOR

Wolterstorff's theory of situated rationality is an attempt to chart the full range and moral significance of the activities and actions which constitute a person's doxastic life. His aim is to understand the rationality of believing as a refraction of a person's personal, social, professional, and even cultural obligations and responsibilities—in a word, as an aspect of moral situationality.[24] So Wolterstorff argues that doxastic norms are not separate from the rest of a person's life; indeed they are inseparable and inextricable from the full scope of a person's roles and responsibilities.[25] This is a significant departure from the way epistemologists have typically understood doxastic norms and subjectivity.

Following philosophy's otherwise "admirable penchant"[26] for universalizing, contemporary analytic philosophy, no less than historic modern philosophy, has with few exceptions employed an image of the epistemic subject and the doxastic life so abstract and de-personalized as to bear little relation to actual human life. "The picture that comes to mind," Wolterstorff explains,

> is that of a solitary person sitting in a chair passively receiving such sensory stimulation that comes his way, taking note of the beliefs that that stimulation evokes in him, recalling certain events from his past, observing what is going on in his mind,

---

24. Here I only have space to summarize the general motivation behind Wolterstorff's notion of "practices of inquiry" (see his "Entitlement to Believe and Practices of Inquiry," in *Practices of Belief*, 86–143).

25. Wolterstorff explains, "A characteristic error of epistemologists has been to suppose that our noetic obligations are disconnected from our other obligations. The truth is that in good measure the particular shape that the obligation to attain truth and avoid falsehood assumes for each person is determined by her obligations in general ... Our noetic obligations arise from the whole diversity of obligations that we have in our concrete situations" ("Can Belief in God Be Rational," in *Practices of Belief*, 231).

26. "Entitlement to Believe," in *Practices of Belief*, 104.

and drawing inferences . . . The body enters the picture only so far as sensory stimulation requires a body. And even that requirement is treated as a contingency . . . How different is the actuality, which presumably it is the task of epistemology to illuminate.[27]

Coordinately, rationality is often construed as a kind of independent moral law, wielding super-personal, super-situational normativity. This normativity is articulated in various ways, as, for example, a function of epistemic structure (foundational certainty, for example), or of factual or evidential accuracy (dependent upon the reliability of doxastic faculties), or right measures of probability according to evidence, or some such meta-epistemological scheme. In such cases, rationality is de-personalized and context-indifferent, paying the individual no heed, accounting for no personal or moral concerns—concerns which no actual person ever finds himself without. The result is a strange and artificial isolation of the doxastic life from all other morally and personally significant matters.

Wolterstorff rejects the implication that entitlement,[28] he calls it, or rational permissibility, can be a function of a universal or abstracted conception of rationality. Human beings are not in fact brains in vats (in any event, it is certainly more reasonable to suppose we are not), nor are the doxastic activities of real people carried out with the cool remove of laboratory tests. Our believing, thinking lives are rife with human action and intention and imbued with situational and existential obligation and constraint, in an embodied and socially significant manner reflective of human nature generally. Believing is always *human* believing, the believing of concrete, situated individuals.

Wolterstorff finds John Locke's insight into the situatedness of the doxastic process helpful. "Which deficiencies in one's system of beliefs is one obligated to remove or forestall, or try? I think John Locke was right when he said that the answer varies from person to person. For The Human Being as Such, there is no answer. It all depends."[29] Wolterstorff finds Locke aware of the fact that "Only in the light of the complete contour of obligation that holds uniquely for a given person at a given point in time in her life, and

---

27. Ibid., 86. For more on the ways in which a platonic, "idealized" epistemology has influenced Western philosophy, see Wolterstorff's "Epistemology of Religion."

28. Again, entitlement is Wolterstorff's epistemic merit of choice. It is a normative, deontological notion, roughly equivalent to rational permissibility. Referring to the "innocent until proved guilty" doxastic ethos of early Reformed Epistemology, Sloane says, correctly I think, that Wolterstorff's notion of entitlement is "a later development of this model" (*On Being a Christian*, 95).

29. "Entitlement to Believe," in *Practices of Belief*, 103.

in the light of that person's convictions about the accessibility, acceptability, and promise of various practices of inquiry for removing the deficiencies of belief, can this question be answered."[30]

But Locke's insights turn out to be his undoing. Locke's rich elucidation of doxastic situatedness and the individuality of epistemological processes and commitments, and his recognition of the constitutive role that situated limitations may play on the range of doxastic permissibility and obligation, prove devastating for Locke's own hope for a universally enforceable standard of belief entitlement, the singular goal of the fourth book of the *Essay*.[31] Nevertheless, against these terrible odds, it was to that hope—a universal, generic, ground of rationality—which Locke held till the end:

> I submit that what was deepest in Locke's thought was the idea of putting aside the unreliable contingencies of our immersion in some particular tradition so as to get to the reliable necessities of our shared human nature. Deeper in Locke than evidentialism concerning theistic belief was his passion to circumvent all contingent doxastic programming, to circumvent all tradition, and to employ nothing but our reliable hard-wiring when it comes to matters of maximal concernment. For our programming is full of obstructive and deleterious affect.[32]

30. Ibid. Notice that operative in Wolterstorff's thought at this point is an image of the human being as always forming beliefs. Rather than asking how one ought to form beliefs, he asks how one ought to go about pruning and managing one's believing. Removing or forestalling epistemic "deficiencies" is a kind of after the fact doxastic house-keeping. We remove or forestall beliefs or doxastic tendencies we find ourselves already with. "[W]e are looking at the person who already has an array of beliefs, so as to give him and others a criterion for picking out those that are rational for him to hold from those that are not. What we are after is not rules for the direction of the mind but a criterion for separating one's rational beliefs from one's non-rational beliefs" ("Can Belief in God be Rational," in *Practices of Belief*, 245–46). As this chapter seeks to demonstrate, this is due in large part to the fuller and more active doxastic anthropology Wolterstorff works with.

31. Following Wolterstorff's view, these situational limitations devastate Locke's project because his epistemic standard is an idealized and impersonal belief-forming subject. Wolterstorff recognizes the very same 'situational' complications as Locke; situated rationality represents Wolterstorff's theoretical appreciation for the situatedness of the epistemic subject.

32. "On Being Entitled to Beliefs About God," in *Practices of Belief*, 326. In terms of interpreting Locke, it is important to distinguish between the functional situatedness mentioned here, which to Locke's mind presented normal and acceptable doxastic limitations, and the situatedness and individuality of personal epistemic constitution and experience. The former, normal situatedness in a web of circumstantial limitations and ulterior obligations means only that a person's volitional doxastic concerns have to be prioritized. The latter are, for Locke, a host of nearly unavoidable but dangerously subversive epistemological misfortunes and misdoings. It is these that appear toward

Locke attempted a universal theory of entitlement, one functionally oblivious to the situatedness of the belief-forming subject and the doxastic industry generally, a theory of rational permissibility in tension with the natural and historical limitations of human subjectivity. And even with Locke's failure there for all to see, hope for such a theory has remained strong. The same drive toward universality and the same interest in the super-situational subject is exemplified in W. K. Clifford's famous evidentialist moralism, and, though different in the details, remains undiminished in the work of Roderick Chisholm.[33] Chisholm argues that an obligation to do one's best to maximize the ratio of true beliefs to false ones bears on all people at all times, "for every proposition *h* that he considers."[34]

Wolterstorff responds with three objections. First, Chisholm's obligation to truth is a "total abstraction from the social availability, the personal accessibility and acceptability, and the personally estimated promise, of ways of finding out."[35] In other words, Chisholm entirely overlooks rational (situational) permissibility, dissolving it into rational (universalizable) obligation. Wolterstorff claims that Chisholm needs to consider the limited availability of beliefs, and to then distinguish that availability from obligation, the one preceding the other. Second, Wolterstorff argues, it cannot really be the case that for every proposition that a person considers, the truth value must be assessed with scientific precision and diligence, as Chisholm appears to maintain. This is a practical impossibility, for one thing, and in many situations moral obligations force a prioritization of occupations of this kind such that only at the cost of a moral violation could one devote equal attention to all propositions or all competing hypotheses relative to a particular question. So the obligation as Chisholm defines it lacks nuance

---

the closing sections of his *An Essay concerning Human Understanding*, and that Locke views as truly nefarious. Wolterstorff says that there is "no better example of 'deconstruction' in the history of Western philosophy," so devastating are these concessions to Locke's goal of a universal theory of belief entitlement (Wolterstorff, *John Locke*, 97).

33. I refer to Clifford's essay, "The Ethics of Belief," in *The Ethics of Belief and other Essays*, originally published in *Contemporary Review* in 1877, in which he writes, "[I]t is wrong always, and everywhere, for anyone, to believe anything on insufficient evidence," and "It is wrong in all cases to believe on insufficient evidence; and where it is presumption to doubt and to investigate, there it is worse than presumption to believe" (77, 96). In "Does the Role of Concepts Make Experiential Access to Ready-Made Reality Impossible?," in *Practices of Belief*, chapter 2, Wolterstorff explains that the same Platonic image of the doxastic subject is dominant in Kant. For this point regarding Chisholm, see Wolterstorff, "Ought to Believe—Two Concepts," in *Practices of Belief*, 62–85, esp. 103–4.

34. Chisholm, *Theory of Knowledge*, 14, quoted by Wolterstorff, "Entitlement to Believe," 103.

35. Wolterstorff, "Entitlement to Believe," in *Practices of Belief*, 103.

and is too broad. Third, in a different sense, "the thesis is too limited"; we are often obligated to seek out new propositions.[36]

The "philosopher's penchant for reaching for necessarily true universalizations" is not in itself problematic. "It's an admirable penchant; I share it," Wolterstorff writes. He qualifies his appreciation, however, arguing that there is no way, as demonstrated by repeated failure to find a way, to understand doxastic entitlement "by looking up in the Platonic heaven at The Human Being Itself."[37]

Instead, entitlement is found only "by looking down to the particular human being herself so as to discern her unique location in the space of moral obligation."[38] It is this morally rich space, and a person's location within it as an intentional and responsible agent, which infuses the doxastic life with ethical significance. On the one hand, beliefs to which a person is entitled, which are permissible for a person, are those which are offered to him situationally. Similarly those beliefs which it is incumbent upon a person to have (or to form responsibly) also must be found or available within a situational-personal context. Entitlement, in other words, is a function of which beliefs are available and accessible to me, here and now, but also of what is, subjectively, within my doxastic grasp. Guilt is not accrued when a belief is either subjectively or objectively unavailable, since responsibility and accountability are functions of availability. Conversely, beliefs wielding particular deontological weight are, of all those beliefs to which I am entitled, those toward which my location in the space of moral obligation demands I direct my attention most urgently.[39] If I am a baseball umpire, I had better know all the rules of the game; but if I am only a fair-weather spectator, that obligation is not a serious one. If I am behind the wheel of a car, I am rightly expected to have full control of my faculties and to have clear understanding of my responsibilities, of the traffic laws, of how to operate a car, and so on. The epistemology of the "solitary, immobile reactor,"

---

36. Ibid., 104.
37. Ibid.
38. Ibid.
39. I speak too loosely here of "belief," when what should be understood is propositions regarding which beliefs may be formed or held, propositions as the objections of doxastic intentionality. In the relevant literature, the reader often has to contend with ambiguous uses of the term "belief," which sometimes refers to the act of believing, or is even inclusive of a range of doxastic actions (withholding assent, believing, relinquishing belief, perhaps believing with varying degrees of confidence), and sometimes even refers specifically to propositions.

Wolterstorff explains, must be replaced by an epistemology of the "socially engaged, mobile agent."[40]

2.3 THE DOXASTIC SELF AND BELIEF-FORMING DISPOSITIONS

Wolterstorff's doxastic anthropology follows in many ways the thought of Thomas Reid. In both his critique of the "solitary, immobile reactor" of Lockean epistemology and his constructive rethinking of the doxastic subject, Wolterstorff was preceded by Reid and in large part works from the foundation laid by him. But Wolterstorff does not simply pit Locke against Reid and side with one against the other; there is at least one concern all three have in common. Locke and Reid share an interest in a self-consciously religious approach to doxastic anthropology and the right conducts of the mind;[41] and religious self-consciousness is basic to Wolterstorff's approach as well. Hume too figures in Wolterstorff's understanding of the doxastic self, particularly in terms of the development of inductive belief-forming dispositions. Thus we can see Wolterstorff's view of the doxastic self come together through interaction with Locke, Reid, and Hume.[42]

Wolterstorff views the doxastic subject as a changing and developing, thinking and believing, socially engaged person whose doxastic faculties operate and develop (as is their nature to do), within the changing contexts of individual history and experience. His understanding of the doxastic subject balances the general and the particular by viewing natural doxastic anthropology as designed for particularized social and historical doxastic conditions and development.

We have an innate doxastic design, which Wolterstorff calls "doxastic hard-wiring." And we are hard wired both to modify and refine natural belief-forming dispositions and to develop new ones as we learn from experience. The development of doxastic faculties that occurs according to

---

40. "Entitlement to Believe," in *Practices of Belief*, 86. See also 90–91.

41. I want to be careful not to exaggerate the role of theological language in Reid; his is not a theological epistemology, to be sure. Wolterstorff notes, for example, "Reid never cites any theistic propositions as principles of common sense. And he never explains this omission" ("Thomas Reid on Rationality," 60).

42. Wolterstorff writes, "By intent there will be no originality in what I have to say, since one of the points I want to make is the historical point that a recognition of the historicized character of the belief-forming self was a prominent feature of the thought of Hume and Reid—and in a rather curious way, a component of Locke's as well" ("Historicizing the Belief-Forming Self," in *Practices of Belief*, 120).

the original hard-wiring Wolterstorff calls "doxastic programming."[43] In this sense Wolterstorff moves beyond the bare design plan defended by Plantinga (who also works from a Reidian framework), arguing that the doxastic faculties operative at any given moment involve more than a mere original design; they involve a developed complex of belief-forming faculties honed and refined through personal experience.[44] Wolterstorff's is a thoroughly Reidian approach, and we have come a long way from Locke.

Locke conceded, if begrudgingly, that a generic doxastic anthropology should be recognized as to some degree idealistic and fraught with difficulty (as any idealism is), and anyway, very unlike any actual human being.[45] Very often, the circumstances of both personal and epochal history are influential in the constitutions of doxastic selves, molding and conditioning, indeed corrupting, Locke would say, the ideal and original doxastic self in unpredictable and unmanageable ways. Locke names four particularly pervasive corrupting influences.[46] The first occurs when "propositions that are not in themselves certain and evident, but doubtful and false," are accepted as true early in life and continue to exercise undue and even religious-like authority in a person's thinking.[47] The second occurs when peoples' "understandings are cast into a mold, and fashioned just to the size of a received hypothesis."[48] The third occurs when personal inclinations and passions undermine right reason, and the fourth when the authority of ecclesial or public opinion usurps the role of evidence.[49] Clearly Locke sees little chance that belief formation will proceed as planned and as it ought to, uninfluenced by experience and uncorrupted by personal inclination or selfish mo-

---

43. On doxastic hard-wiring and programming, see "Historicizing the Belief-Forming Self," in *Practices of Belief*, 135-43.

44. Wolterstorff writes, "We human beings are all hard-wired for belief; we all have an innate dispositional constitution that, when activated by one event or another, yields belief. That's the beginning of the matter," he says, "and it is this beginning of the matter that Plantinga emphasizes" ("Historicizing the Belief-Forming Self," in *Practices of Belief*, 136). So he argues, "To fully account for the beliefs that actually get formed in a person on a given occasion one has to know not only the belief-forming faculties of that person but how that person has been programmed" (ibid.). Therefore "Plantinga's account [needs to be] amplified by adding the concept of *doxastic programming*" (ibid., 143). For Plantinga on the design plan, see his *Warrant and Proper Function*, esp. chapters 3-5. More on the differences between Wolterstorff and Plantinga on the doxastic self in section §2.6.

45. See especially Locke, *Essay*, II.xxxiii; IV.xx.

46. Locke, *Essay*, IV.xx.7-17.

47. Ibid., IV.xx.8.

48. Ibid., IV.xx.11.

49. Ibid., IV.xx.12-17. For Wolterstorff's discussion, see *John Locke*, 92-97.

tive, even though much of the *Essay* displays both his tenacious hope that it might and his somewhat embarrassing conviction that it should.[50]

Locke is on his own in this regard. Hume on the other hand is convinced that belief formation cannot proceed free of historical conditioning.[51] In his view, the historical and individualized acquisition and refinement of belief-forming dispositions—the malleability of the doxastic self—is natural, normal, and necessary for daily life. And Reid views acquired dispositions even more favorably as the unfolding of the design of the divine creator and as refined through experience and, thus, as truth-conducive.[52] But Locke looks upon acquired doxastic dispositions and acquired principles with extreme suspicion, even disdain. Acquired dispositions and principles are subversive and, as for the most part would seem to be Locke's foremost concern, socially parlous, a threat to the peaceful cohesion of a civilized society.[53] Believing the uncorrupted balance of the conduct of the mind to be so crucial for political and social stability, Locke would likely have viewed Reid's optimism as naïve or even reckless.

This important difference particularly between Locke and Reid in terms of the personal and historical complications in the belief-forming process is reflected in their distinct employments of theological language. Such language is prominent in both Locke's and Reid's writing, and there is little reason to doubt that some or even much of this rhetoric is sincere, if not theologically significant. The difference between them may be viewed in terms of their respective views of original design. Both appear to believe

---

50. Wolterstorff does not reject Locke's concern outright. On the contrary, he expresses sympathy with it. He welcomes Locke's belief that "in addition to whatever flaws there may be in one's hard-wiring and operating system, the programming of each of us includes a good many defective components, those defects in programming yielding defects in output" (Wolterstorff, "Historicizing the Belief-Forming Self," in *Practices of Belief*, 134, 137)

51. See ibid., esp. 129–31. Wolterstorff says, "In short, what's to be learned from Hume is that one component of the historicized belief-forming self consists of all those belief-forming dispositions that we acquire by undergoing experiences of a sort apt for the formation of those particular dispositions—inductive dispositions being prime examples of such, though perhaps there are others as well" (ibid., 129).

52. See ibid., 131–32.

53. Locke, Wolterstorff writes, "did his philosophizing, and perceived himself as doing his philosophizing, in a situation of cultural crisis, a crisis induced by the widespread consensus that the European moral and religious tradition was fractured and that new 'foundations' for knowledge and belief had to be discovered" (ibid., *John Locke*, 3). He adds, "The England of Locke's day was a special case . . . Here the religious antagonisms erupted into civil war." So, "In the background of Locke's epistemology was the general European crisis . . . in the foreground was the specific, intensely antagonistic, form which that crisis was taking in English culture and society in Locke's day" (ibid., 7). See also Locke, *Essay*, II.xxxiii; IV.xx.

that whatever is creationally original and in accord with divine intention and design is as such good and trustworthy, and whenever and however the belief-forming faculties deviate from the maker's design, they are corrupted, spurious, and untrustworthy. Reid believes that the origin design included prescriptions for development; Locke thinks that belief-forming faculties have no other function but to weigh the strength of evidence and that modifications or external influences of any kind serve only to stifle the clear voice of pure factuality, empirical perception, and the testimony of evidence.

Both agree on the pervasiveness of life experiences effectual for belief-forming faculties. But Locke's hope that such influences are avoidable, at least in some cases, at least pertaining to some beliefs, remains steadfast, because he believes that their influence is unnatural and deleterious. According to Reid (and Hume), that hope is groundless, and beside the point. Locke hopes to avoid the influences of acquired doxastic practices; Reid welcomes them. Both adorn their concerns with pious language.

Locke's is the more pessimistic view, since he finds the subject's susceptibility to historical conditioning wholly disruptive of reasoning faculties in their purest, God-intended form. He appears to associate susceptibility to historicity with impiety and lack of self-control. Reid, by contrast, views the historical conditionality of the doxastic subject as a good and natural complexity anticipated in the creational design. It is fair to say then that both Reid and Locke have roughly the same phenomena in view, but contrary doctrines of their theological significance.

Nonetheless, as noted, Locke's abstracted, ahistorical doxastic subject serves us very little in understanding belief formation and the holding of beliefs by real people. Wolterstorff finds Locke's generic doxastic anthropology contrived and untenable. Alternatively, he recognizes in Reid's work an analysis of the belief-forming self which is truer to fact and corrective of many of Locke's oversights. So he adopts Reid's view of a dynamic, responsive, and socially engaged subject.

Wolterstorff borrows from Hume as well. Hume believed that inductive beliefs were formed by acquired habits or custom.[54] Phenomena *P* are taken to indicate or represent fact *F*, and only habit or custom supports the inference. But Hume goes further, Wolterstorff explains, than simply attributing the formation of inductive beliefs to pre-cognitive or uncritical habit: "A regularity in my prior experience . . . has produced in me a new belief-forming disposition . . ."[55] A new *disposition* is formed or acquired

---

54. Wolterstorff discusses Hume's view of induction in "Historicizing the Belief-Forming Self," in *Practices of Belief*.
55. Ibid., 129.

through repeated experience. So according to Hume, a belief-forming disposition takes shape in response to repeated experience, a disposition to form immediate beliefs in response to types of experiences.

Wolterstorff finds Reid and Hume in agreement on this point.[56] He takes Hume to affirm, or at the very least to imply, the Reidian idea that innate to the doxastic subject are dispositions to form belief-forming dispositions, dispositions, that is, for the development of new belief-forming faculties: "if I am to form this disposition I must have a *disposition* to form this disposition and others like it; and that disposition to form particular inductive dispositions has to be innate in me."[57] On this point, the possession of natural dispositions governing and prescribing the refinement of dispositions and the acquisition of new ones, Reid and Hume are one.[58] According

---

56. There is some ambiguity here. First, Reid certainly held that there are dispositions to form new belief-forming dispositions; this "is not a point Hume emphasizes," but it is a natural implication of what he says about the formation of inductive beliefs ("Historicizing the Belief-Forming Self," in *Practices of Belief*, 129). Secondly, Wolterstorff does not doubt that Hume believes that there is a malleable inductive belief-forming disposition to form beliefs *immediately, not* by inference. Within the course of his article "Historicizing the Belief-Forming Self," Wolterstorff says both that this is also Reid's view and that it was not Reid's view, that Reid believed rather that the disposition to form inductive beliefs was a disposition to form such beliefs *by inference*, not immediately. At one point Wolterstorff says that his original view was the latter (that Reid believed inductive beliefs are formed by inference), but that he later came to view Reid as holding the former (that inductive beliefs are formed immediately, as Hume held) (ibid., 130n9). In that case, "his [Reid's] analysis, is the same as Hume's" (ibid., 130). Later in the same article, Wolterstorff clearly endorses the view that he says he held originally but later rejected, that Reid holds that inductive beliefs are formed by inference: "Reid differed from Hume in that, whereas Hume thought that inductive beliefs were formed immediately, Reid thought they were the product of inference. What's innate in us, on Hume's view, is the disposition to form inductive belief dispositions upon perceiving regularities; what's innate in us, on Reid's analysis, is the disposition, upon perceiving those same regularities, to form generalized conditionals about the course of nature—along with the disposition to infer instantiations of these generalizations when confronted with instances of the antecedents of the generalized conditionals" (ibid., 139). In the end, on this issue Wolterstorff sides with Hume, and with Reid as long as Reid agrees with Hume: "Our faculties of perception, of rational intuition, and perhaps of credulity, are designed to produce beliefs *immediately*" (ibid.).

57. Ibid.

58. Except for the fact that Reid believed the formation of an inductive disposition was part of the creator's design. God, he writes, "implanted in human minds an original principle by which we believe and expect the continuance of the course of nature, and the continuance of those connections which we have observed in time past. It is by this general principle of our nature, that when two things have been found connected in time past, the appearance of the one produces the belief of the other" (Reid, *Inquiry*, VI.xxiv; 197).

to both, says Wolterstorff, "My belief-forming self is, in this respect, a product of my personal history."[59]

History and experience contribute to the formation of belief dispositions, and the formation of new dispositions in response to experience must be grounded innately, in the form of a natural disposition to form new dispositions. Natural dispositions interact with external phenomena and both modify old dispositions and form new ones. Wolterstorff summarizes approvingly: "it is the explicitly held view of Reid and Reidians that our belief-forming selves are (in good measure) the creatures of history—not just of the broad sweeping currents of social history, but of our personal histories." And, "What the Reidian emphatically adds, however, and emphasizes, is that this personal formation occurs in accord with our nature," so that "Reidian *doxastic anthropology* . . . represents a blending of the natural and the historical."[60]

As noted, Wolterstorff has called the organic process of the acquisition and formation of new belief-forming dispositions in response to history and experience, "programming," or "doxastic programming." And doxastic programming occurs according to our doxastic "hard-wiring." At any point, the full picture of a person's doxastic constitution should take into account both that person's doxastic programming as it has developed in response to personal history, and the hard-wiring which has directed that development. Working largely from a Reidian template but benefiting from Locke and Hume as well, Wolterstorff replaces the static, idealized reactor of traditional epistemology with an individualized and historically conditioned doxastic subject.

2.4 REID'S CREDULITY PRINCIPLE AND BELIEVING TESTIMONY

As we have seen, belief-forming dispositions, the innate dispositions of doxastic hard-wiring and the particular dispositions of doxastic programming,

---

59. "Historicizing the Belief-Forming Self," in *Practices of Belief*, 131.

60. Ibid., 120. See 136–43. "Doxastic hard-wiring" is roughly equivalent to what Plantinga calls "design plan." The addition of historically developing doxastic programming demonstrates what we will see in more detail below, that Wolterstorff finds mere design plan insufficient for filling out an accurate picture of the ethically charged doxastic life. He writes, "To fully account for the beliefs that actually get formed in a person on a given occasion one has to know not only the belief-forming faculties of that person but how that person has been programmed." And so, "My own suggestion is that . . . Plantinga's account be amplified by adding the concept of *doxastic programming* to those other concepts with which he works." (ibid., 136, 143).

are central to Wolterstorff's doxastic anthropology. In this section, we focus on one doxastic disposition in particular, what Reid called the "credulity disposition."[61]

It is of course important for a young person to possess a strong and securely pre-critical inclination to believe what other people tell him. If a child were consistently incredulous and regularly disregarded the counsel of other people, if he were committed to a cautious skepticism, his safety and even his survival would hang in the balance. It would only be a matter of time until the child elected to test a claim or disregard a warning issued by an experienced elder and his methodological doubt would cost him dearly. Multiplied many times, trust in testimony provides the cohesion necessary for tradition and cumulative culture. The credulity disposition, is the means by which a person is inducted into and participates in a tradition and a distinctive culture. In this sense it is a basic anthropological reality. It is fair to say then that the credulity disposition, an innate credulity toward testimony, is really quite pervasive and indeed essential to normal human life. Characteristically, Reid ignites his exposition with doxology: "The wise and beneficent Author of nature ... intended that we should be social creatures," that we should be relationally dependent, and trusting.[62]

Reid understood the credulity disposition as unqualified and unconditioned in children.[63] As we might expect, he argues that "our innate credulity disposition gets modified in the course of experience," and because that experience is always personal experience, it may be the case that the credulity disposition "varies considerably from one adult to another depending on their experience of truth-telling and falsehood-telling."[64] Individuals who have endured repeated betrayal are often burdened with a profound and intractable reluctance to trust others. The credulity disposition of such a person has been shaped by experience. Wolterstorff explains that, "as a consequence of our experience, our innate credulity disposition gets modified in such a way that eventually we believe what certain sorts of people

61. Following Reid, Wolterstorff refers to it both as a "principle" and a "disposition." He refers to "the *credulity* disposition, as Reid rather fetchingly called it" ("Can Belief in God Be Rational," in *Practices of Belief*, 232), and he notes that "Reid's own suggestion ... is that indigenous to our human constitution is a *principle of credulity*, as he calls it" ("Epistemology of Religion," in *Practices of Belief*, 159). I think this can be explained, but anyway, I stick with "disposition" in order to avoid confusion.

62. Reid, *Inquiry*, VI.xxiv: 193, quoted by Wolterstorff, "Historicizing the Belief-Forming Self," in *Practices of Belief*, 132.

63. Wolterstorff says that "[i]t is a moot point whether the credulity disposition is present in us at birth. But very little maturation is required for it to put in its appearance" ("Can Belief in God Be Rational," in *Practices of Belief*, 234).

64. "Historicizing the Belief-Forming Self," in *Practices of Belief*, 132.

say on certain sorts of topics in certain sorts of situations more firmly than we would have originally, whereas we believe less firmly or not at all what those same people tell us on different sorts of situations, or what other sorts of people tell us."[65]

In the normal course of experience, a child who begins with unconditioned trust in his parents might learn that after he has eaten some number of cookies, consistently more than three or four, his mother often tells him that the supply of sweet snacks is depleted. He may learn as well, however, that precisely these circumstances very often include his mother making such claims despite their being false. By contrast, the child's father may very frankly declare that "yes, there are more cookies; but no, you may not have any more." The child learns that, despite a natural tendency and desire to trust his mother, the harsh reality is that in a particular set of circumstances, mommy is a stone-cold liar. Repeated experiences of this kind nuance the credulity disposition.[66] There are many other such examples; so many, in fact, that it is difficult to imagine normal, adult interaction taking place without nuanced and highly sophisticated credulity dispositions. People do not simply announce raw and untailored truth claims, in the way that calculators display numbers or road signs display distances and street names. Rather, normally functioning human beings communicate in dynamic, socially sensitive, sophisticated ways, which require highly refined credulity dispositions.

We learn to distinguish "types of testimony that regularly prove true and types of testimony that regularly prove false."[67] As these experiences are confirmed over the course of time, the doxastic self adapts by taking account of those experiences. Doxastic hard-wiring is in place so that adaptability is constitutive of what the doxastic self is, so that doxastic programming is real, personal, and natural. "What we learn from our fellows is not just stored in memory to be brought out as the occasion demands; it becomes a component of our programming."[68] Locke seemed to think that in some cases, if a person had both the resolve and analytic capacity, it would be possible to circumvent those influences, to re-wire or short-circuit, as it were, the doxastic self, in order to purge the reasoning faculties of acquired, inherited, or uncritical beliefs or belief-forming dispositions. Not only is this impossible,

---

65. Ibid.

66. This is my own illustration. See Wolterstorff's discussion in "Epistemology of Religion," in *Practices of Belief*, 159–60.

67. "Historicizing the Belief-Forming Self," in *Practices of Belief*, 133.

68. Ibid., 136–37.

in Wolterstorff's view, it is undesirable, since it would mean unmaking the individual and effacing doxastically formative personal history.

The credulity disposition, as Wolterstorff sees it, is a largely trustworthy disposition, and is for the most part, by its own nature and through experience, reliably in touch with reality. The trustworthiness that characterizes Wolterstorff's Reidian take on belief in testimony is a distinctive feature even more broadly of Wolterstorff's approach to rationality. We shall call it Wolterstorff's Reidian doxastic optimism.

2.5 WOLTERSTORFF'S REIDIAN DOXASTIC OPTIMISM

In this section, we note two themes closely associated with Wolterstorff's Reidian doxastic optimism.[69] One is this. Wolterstorff inherits both Reid's doxastic optimism and the role that Reid's optimism plays in his polemic against what Reid called "the way of ideas."[70] This polemically lucrative employment of Reidian doxastic optimism has become a trademark of Reformed epistemology. It is easily recognizable in Plantinga's work as well. The second theme related to Wolterstorff's incorporation of a Reidian doxastic optimism is this. We find that Wolterstorff also follows Reid in depending on an ultimately theological account of the truth-conducivity and trustworthiness of doxastic faculties.

First, the polemical import of Reid's doxastic optimism. As we have seen, Wolterstorff takes the doxastic programming which he has adopted

---

69. I say optimism, while Wolterstorff characterizes Reidian Common Sense in terms of trust: "One can think of Reid's doctrine of Common Sense as taking this theme of *taking on trust*, or *taking for granted*, and running with it!" (*Thomas Reid*, 218). See 260–61, where Wolterstorff calls "trust" "the most fundamental component of Reidian epistemology."

70. This odd phrase refers broadly to the mental representationalism of early-modern British empiricism. It is "as familiar as anything in modern philosophy," Wolterstorff says (ibid., 23). Wolterstorff explains the phrase this way: "[T]he seventeenth and eighteenth century proponents of the Way of Ideas unambiguously held that items of reality are presented to each of us for our acquaintance ... Assuming the tenability of the ontological distinction between mental entities and all others, the Way of Ideas held that, at any moment, that with which one has acquaintance consists at most of oneself, of one's present mental acts and objects, and of those of one's present mental states that one is then actively aware of—along with various facts, contingent and necessary, consisting of the interrelationships of these." Wolterstorff takes Reid to use the phrase to refer largely to Locke and Hume: "Locke seems to have functioned for him as the paradigmatic figure, while Hume takes the brunt of his polemical ire" (24). See esp. chapter 1, "Reid's Questions," and chapter 2, "The Way of Ideas: Structure and Motivation," in ibid., 1–44. For a detailed study of Reid's use of the term, see Greco, "Reid's Critique of Berkeley and Hume: What's the Big Idea?"

from Reid as highly trustworthy, as reliably truth-conducive. Wolterstorff says, "contrary to what our sociologists of knowledge tell us, our programming, though it sometimes constitutes a barrier between us and reality, is often if not usually a means of access."[71] But is this optimism warranted?

Experience, even repeated experience, does not always accurately or truthfully represent reality to us. The possibility stands plainly before us that doxastic programming will mean the incorporation of faulty processes or even of false beliefs or assumptions. Wolterstorff recognizes this: "Beliefs are not the outcome simply of reality's impact on our hard-wired dispositions for belief-formation but the outcome of reality's impact on our hard-wiring *plus our programming, with all its glitches.*"[72] If glitches are part of our programming, how can we account for this confidence that we have reliable contact with reality? On what grounds can we choose, or does Wolterstorff choose, between Lockean suspicion and Reidian optimism?

Wolterstorff's view of the doxastic self implies that a number of "belief components in our programming" reliably improve our access to reality, since they are refined by interaction with the outside world and continually corrected by means of that contact. Only malfunction or some corrupting influence can engender habitual inference which contradicts the testimony of repeated experience. Since doxastic programming happens in response to experiences of reality, we can expect that in due time, fallacious inferential habits will be corrected without unnatural intervention, and that in general we will form true beliefs.

Far more recognizable than Locke's solitary, immobile reactor, is the dynamic, socially and contextually sensitive human subject, an epistemological agent whose faculties balance a degree of optimism in terms of objective truth and a measure of subjectivity in terms of doxastic development. It is hard to imagine a serious account of the 'self' and of trust in our own thinking without the recognition that history—in personal, familial, communal, and wider socio-cultural dimensions—is in a significant way constitutive of our doxastic lives and practices. Hard to imagine, indeed—and that is precisely the point. For Reid, the burden of proof lies not with the doxastic optimist, but wholly with the skeptic.

This point deserves more careful attention. The skeptic Reid has in mind targets specifically the positive doxastic intentionality, directed toward an existential proposition, that emerges from a perceptual experience. In such instances, a perceptual experience evokes in the subject a belief in the

---

71. "Historicizing the Belief-Forming Self," in *Practices of Belief*, 138.
72. Ibid., 137.

extra-mental existence of the object of perception.[73] The skeptic challenges the epistemic credentials or the certainty of this belief and the validity of that inference from mental representation to the extra-mental existence of the object of perception, supposedly corresponding to the mental. And so, according to the skeptic, any philosopher justly so-called ought to maintain a healthy attitude of suspicion and withhold assent to existential beliefs inferred from perception until a critical account of the reliability of such beliefs can be established. That is, skepticism regarding perceptual beliefs is the only reasonable position. Wolterstorff says that "Reid's skeptic . . . is a classically modern foundationalist with respect to entitlement . . ."[74] And to some extent, Reid is sympathetic to the skeptics' charge. The skeptic rightly points out that we are "so constituted as to fall short of that ideal," the ideal, Wolterstorff explains, of having only beliefs that are rationally grounded.[75]

Reid finds fault with the skeptical requirement that this ideal should be satisfied, however, on several fronts. First, great philosophers have failed to satisfy it: Malebranche, Descartes, and Locke, among others.[76] Wolterstorff asks, echoing Reid, whether these three philosophers, having failed to provide the necessary arguments to vindicate the epistemic trustworthiness of perception and memory, were thereby obligated to renounce perceptual beliefs and beliefs formed on the basis of memory. Clearly not, for even if it were possible to do so, by no account would it be reasonable to do so: "if a person—a philosopher, say—really began to refrain from believing what the skeptic says philosophers ought to refrain from believing, we wouldn't regard this as a noble achievement . . . we'd try to get treatment for him."[77] This is a rather pointed *reductio*: no one in his right mind could or ought to take the skeptic's demands seriously, not even the skeptic. On a practical level, the skeptic's recommendations reach to the heights of foolishness.

A second problem internal to the foundationalist challenge is arbitrariness. The skeptic notes, rightly, that perception and memory are not always reliable guides to truth. In fact, there is no way of ensuring that all the

---

73. Wolterstorff's example: "In perceiving the sun, that sun evokes in me a sensation that is a sign of itself; and that sensation evokes in me an apprehension of the sun and the immediate belief, about it, that it exists as something in my environment" (*Thomas Reid*, 185).

74. Ibid., 191.

75. Ibid., 193. He continues: "It is this particular 'falling short' that is the burr under the saddle of Western philosophy which the philosopher is restlessly trying to remove."

76. Reid writes, "For these three great men, with the best good will, have not been able, from all the treasures of philosophy, to draw one argument, that is fit to convince a man that can reason, of the existence of any one thing without [outside] him" (*Inquiry*, I.iii: 18, quoted by Wolterstorff, *Thomas Reid*, 193).

77. *Thomas Reid*, 196.

doxastic deliverances of perception and memory are not fictitious and the faculties themselves untrustworthy. Reid, explains Wolterstorff, concedes as much. But the skeptic insists therefore that perception and memory be examined in the court of reason. Only a nod from reason can vindicate our doxastic dependence on them. But this is no better, responds Reid. "[W]hat difference is there," asks Wolterstorff, "between perception and memory on the one hand, and consciousness and reason on the other, that would authorize this radical difference in treatment for this purpose?"[78] By whom or what has reason been proven? Says Reid:

> The skeptic asks me, Why do you believe the existence of the external object which you perceive? This belief, sir, is none of my manufacture; it came from the mint of nature; it bears her image and superscription; and, if it is not right, the fault is not mine: I even took it upon trust, and without suspicion. Reason, says the skeptic, is the only judge of truth, and you ought to throw off every opinion and every belief that is not grounded on reason. Why, sir, should I believe the faculty of reason more than that of perception; they came both out of the same shop, and were made by the same artist; and if he puts one piece of false ware into my hands [as the skeptic claims], what should hinder him from putting another?[79]

And so, not only, says Wolterstorff, was it "sheer illusion on Descartes' part to suppose that incorrigibility was to be found in his introspective beliefs," deference to reason over perception is indefensible.[80] Wolterstorff concludes, "[t]he arbitrariness of the discrimination undermines the injunction."[81]

But the skeptic's presumption is yet more egregious. As Wolterstorff explains, false doxastic deliverances of perception are very often found out by perception itself. A clearer perceptual experience produces a belief contrary to that produced by a prior, less clear one, and when the two conflicting beliefs meet, naturally one prefers the deliverance of the clearer experience and renounces its competitor. But "clearer" is also perceptual. Perception is

---

78. Ibid., 198.

79. Reid, *Inquiry*, VI.xx: 168–69, quoted by Wolterstorff in *Thomas Reid*, 199. This excerpt from Reid's *Inquiry* bares openly not only several key talking points of Wolterstorff and Plantinga *vis-à-vis* classical modern foundationalism, but also the fundamental posture of Reformed epistemology relative to the anti-theism characteristic of modern epistemology. The same passage is quoted in Plantinga, *Warranted Christian Belief*, 221.

80. *Thomas Reid*, 201.

81. Ibid.

its own most diligent auditor, while it remains true that perception is liable to error. The skeptic trumpets this difficulty, and Reid responds by pointing to the same difficulty, *mutatis mutandi*, with regard to reason. Thus Descartes's bias and egregious oversight, and Hume's, too.

The capstone of Wolterstorff's Reidian position *vis-à-vis* classical modern foundationalism is the realization that in the critiquing and evaluating of our belief-forming faculties of any kind—whether perceptual self-review, critique of perception by reason, reason's self-evaluation, or perception checking the deliverances of reason—the reliability of our doxastic faculties is and in fact must be taken for granted. There is no avoiding dependence upon the very faculties which are under examination. Explains Wolterstorff,

> . . . coming to believe that something one believed is false presupposes trusting one's faculties; and coming to believe, more generally, that one of one's belief-forming faculties is not reliable in such-and-such conditions presupposes trusting one's faculties. We have no choice but to treat our belief-forming faculties as innocent until proved guilty.[82]

As far as this argument goes, this unavoidable taking-for-granted leaves us all on level ground—but for the fact that the skeptic is left with the simple, unsecured taking-for-granted of the reliability of his belief-forming faculties. Reid and his beneficiaries, including Wolterstorff and Plantinga, may here claim a significant advantage. Reid speaks vaguely, though typically for his time, of 'the wise Author of nature' or even just of 'nature,' but the point is this: "the person who believes in a good, wise, and powerful God does, thereby, have a belief from which he can appropriately infer the overall reliability of his basic native faculties," and the person who does not so believe must abuse this doxastic trustworthiness which he has on loan from his religious neighbor.[83] In other words, we have no explanation for the truth-directness and trustworthiness of our cognitive faculties, which we take for granted even in critiquing them, but that God ordained them trustworthy. The implication, if one may put loosely, is that the skeptic is taking a substantial leap of faith in taking for granted the trustworthiness of the very cognitive faculties (reason) which he claims discredit perceptual beliefs (or theism, for that matter), where the necessity of that 'taking for granted' is the only excuse on offer for his presumption. And since reason is no more reliable and no less dependent on circular self-review than perception is, the skeptic is unwarranted, if not pointedly self-incriminating, in his

---

82. Ibid., 211.
83. Ibid., 212.

presumptive scrutiny of the doxastic deliverances of sense perception and memory by the rule of reason.[84]

The second theme related to Wolterstorff's Reidian doxastic optimism, then, is its theological underpinnings. An important distinction between Locke and Reid relative to their respective assessments of the doxastic ideal is reflected in their employments of theological language. For Locke, it is our God-given duty as creatures of God, and the essence and fulfillment of this-worldly piety, to conduct our believings in accord with this de-personalized vision.[85] Alternatively, Reid accepted the belief-forming person as he finds himself in the world as to a large degree reflective of, and even revelatory of, who and how God intended him to be.[86]

Reidian doxastic optimism is an integral part of Reid's constructive epistemology, but he also employs it as a polemical strategy. As we have seen, Reid's polemical strategy against the "way of ideas" comes down to his refusal to accept the burden of proof for basic and normal beliefs. Reid exerts tremendous effort dispensing impressive rhetorical artillery to push the philosophical skeptic back into a defensive posture: he who doubts what everyone else happily and safely assumes and what everyone else is thus by (near) consensus fully within his rights in believing, and he who doubts the very faculties required to articulate his skepticism, bears the burden of explanation. The audacity of doubting the existence of an external world, Reid argues, default incredulity of testimony, and highbrow distrust of the belief-forming constitution of human beings ought to be recognized for what it is: impiety and philosophy unwound. Reid has little patience for the presumptions of the philosopher, tucked away in his study, pretending to undermine the most basic and pervasive features of the cognitive life of normal people and the doxastic constituents of community and culture. Thus Reid's work on common sense is in part a retrenchment, a stern reminder that the philosopher too lives a normal human life, having experiences which he must

---

84. Notice that we find ourselves on the cusp of Plantinga's argument that naturalism contains its own defeater. See his *Where the Conflict Really Lies*, esp. Part IV entitled "Deep Conflict."

85. See Wolterstorff, "John Locke's Epistemological Piety," where he goes so far as to say that "Christianity . . . provides the fundamental pattern and dynamic of Locke's philosophy" (572).

86. "Thomas Reid on Rationality," 56–63. Wolterstorff observes, "Over and over Reid says it is God who has endowed us without native belief-dispositions," and so, "when all is said and done, the person who believes in a good God does, thereby, have a belief from which he can appropriately infer the reliability of his native noetic faculties" (57). In another place, Wolterstorff writes, "Reid observed that the person who believes that it is God who has endowed us with our faculties can and will on that account regard them, whatever their deficiencies, as fundamentally reliable" (*Thomas Reid*, 211).

and always does take for granted, living and moving and having his being in a world which he must and always does assume to be real, even while insisting that belief in such things is beyond the bounds of doxastic right and rationality. Turning the tables against the skeptic, Reid insists that the philosopher himself invites suspicion and distrust when he refuses to afford those regular believings any theoretical value, and when his impressive epistemological theory handily dismisses our most intuitive and common sense commitments.[87]

Wolterstorff's theory of situated rationality utilizes the same view of the doxastic subject and natural belief forming capacities, and the same optimism, that we find in Reid. Wolterstorff's optimism, like Reid's, views the human person and all his faculties as created by God. If man is created by God, an inductive study of the way the human creature functions may be expected to discover the design and intention of a good and trustworthy creator. Reid and Wolterstorff share this basic starting point.

Furthermore, Wolterstorff and Plantinga both confront modern, foundationalist skepticism toward theistic belief and ask, as Plantinga might put it, why think a thing like that? Both foundationalism and modern philosophies of science hold high the value of certainty, but they hold it unreasonably high, inhumanly and artificially high, so high as to be no worldly good.[88] So in Reidian fashion, Wolterstorff and Plantinga have both responded by asking, on what grounds can it be justifiable to call into doubt and to regard with suspicion the host of beliefs all people consistently hold in non-foundationalist fashion, even without 'sufficient evidence'?[89] On the contrary, philosophy should be judged by this common sense, not common

---

87. I paraphrase, but this is the tenor of Reid's response to "the skeptic," as Wolterstorff describes it. See chapter 8 of *Thomas Reid*, "Reid's Way with the Skeptic," esp. 197–214; and chapter 9, "Common Sense." In his essay "Thomas Reid on Rationality," Wolterstorff's analyzes Reid's response to the skeptic in the following way: "The Reidian skeptic, remember, is the person who holds that we are to admit nothing amongst our beliefs but what has been established by reasoning. In other words, Reid's skeptic is the person who holds that we are justified in believing something only if we hold it on the basis of other beliefs which constitute adequate evidence for it" ("Thomas Reid on Rationality," 53). Wolterstorff summarizes Reid's response to this claim in two points. "The first point Reid makes in response to the skeptic is the *ad hominem* observation that such skeptics . . . violate this very principle in their philosophizing. But accept, without having established its reliability, the testimony of consciousness" (ibid.). "A second argument which Reid launches against the position of the skeptic is that his position is completely arbitrary. The skeptic apparently holds that we are justified in accepting the deliverances of inference without having adequate evidence that inference is a reliable belief-producing mechanism" (55–6).

88. Logical positivism is everyone's favorite case in point.

89. This is much the spirit of Plantinga's *God and Other Minds*.

sense by the fancies and speculations of philosophers. But if (Christian) theism is true, on the other hand, we have every reason to trust the human doxastic design plan. The question is not, may we believe these things?—as though we may for a moment pretend not to—but rather, finding that we take these beliefs (e.g. belief in a world external to the mind) as basic and universal, and cannot indeed believe otherwise, how is it that our beliefs are formed and held? This is the question that a Reidian doxastic anthropology seeks to answer.

In Wolterstorff's rethinking of the doxastic subject, the marble-sculpted ideal of modernism is set aside, and doxastic normativity is cut down to size, or particularized, and doxastic virtue is transferred from the realm of the idealized doxastic nobody to the situated and personalized individuality of real persons in social interaction.

2.6 WOLTERSTORFF AND PLANTINGA ON THE DOXASTIC SELF

For Plantinga, warrant accrues to a belief when it is formed by belief-forming faculties functioning properly in the appropriate context—functioning, that is, according to a "design plan." Plantinga's "design plan" is roughly Wolterstorff's "hard wiring," and both concepts benefit from Reid's theologically grounded doxastic optimism. But where Wolterstorff considers doxastic hard-wiring to be only a basic starting point from which the doxastic self develops into a complex individual, Plantinga works only in terms of the function of the design plan. His doxastic self does not see the complex development that Wolterstorff's does. But Wolterstorff suggests that the most significant difference between their views has to do with belief-governance and ethico-doxastic accountability. He is concerned that Plantinga's stunted doxastic anthropology leaves no room for relevant intentional action, and thus precludes our speaking of doxastic accountability.

In his *Thomas Reid and the Story of Epistemology*, Wolterstorff writes, "A good deal of Reid's disagreement with the Way of Ideas theorists [especially Locke, but Hume as well] was over the identification of our hard wiring."[90] A distinguishing feature of Reid's account is that "Reid regarded our hard wiring as much more elaborate than the Way of Ideas theorists were willing to concede."[91] Wolterstorff hints here at some timidity, or sheer shortsightedness, on the part of Locke and Hume, relative to the full scope of belief-forming faculties, in contrast to Reid's emphasis on a richer and

90. *Thomas Reid*, 116.
91. Ibid.

more complex picture of the doxastic self. That reluctance, says Wolterstorff, may have been a philosopher's well-groomed mystery anxiety—a condition from which Reid appears not to have suffered so acutely.

But while Reid contended that there was much more to the original belief-forming self than Locke and others were willing to grant, "he thought much less could be explained than they thought."[92] The Reidian picture is then more optimistic, but also both a more complicated and ultimately a more mysterious image of the doxastic self. Perhaps Reid would have attributed his resolve in the face of philosophical mystery with reference once again to theology. But why the anxiety from Locke's point of view?

Locke and others held steadfast to a Newtonian hope regarding two things: the analytic powers of the human mind, and the intelligibility of the natural world and the human person. This bold vision of the new science lured philosophers with promises of explanatory riches and dreams of a wholly scrutable world. While Locke, for one, regularly if perfunctorily attributed the complexities of the human constitution to their Maker, he nonetheless banished mystery from his investigative hypotheses and philosophic vocabulary.

Reid demurred, arguing that the original doxastic faculties of the human creature are vastly more complex than Locke and Hume would concede. Given this immense complexity, the claim that much at all of the depths of epistemic anthropology will be within theoretical reach is at least naïve, probably impious, certainly incorrect. We must yield, Reid appears to say, to divine mystery as inference to the best (and more pious) explanation. "A good deal of Reid's disagreement with the Way of Ideas was over the identification of the original principles of the mind—the identification of our hard wiring," Wolterstorff explains. And Reid held that "Of the workings of our original principles we can give no explanation—other than to declare that things work that way because that's how our Creator makes them work."[93]

It appears once again that theological confessions bears more weight in Reid's account of belief formation than it does for Locke. Reid's doxastic optimism, which Plantinga and Wolterstorff share, rests upon trust in the creator. Locke attributes to the human constitution the ability to know with certainty so very little that the epistemic life is largely relegated to belief and probability, and he reminds his reader repeatedly that it is, therefore, to God that the duty of right and prudent doxastic conduct(the uncorrupted weighing of evidence) is owed. Reid on the other hand appears to draw on

92. Ibid.
93. Ibid.

theistic premises in order to explain the ever present shadow of mystery, in order both to call it mystery and to allow mystery to remain. His theistic emphasis provides not only for a more optimistic view of the acquisition of beliefs through the use of those original faculties, but also for trustworthy (truth-conducive) doxastic conditioning, refinement, and development. Reid is thus able to conceive of the doxastic self as meant (by God) or designed (by God) to acquire beliefs in a variety of ways. So it is not a mal- but a rightly dubbed "proper" function of the doxastic self to, say, believe the testimony of other people and to see the credulity disposition refined over time through experience, and to understand immediately, or at least with relative ease, from the sign the thing signified, and so on.

Plantinga and Wolterstorff agree up to this point. They agree that there are ways in which people are 'designed' to form beliefs, that we are in possession of natural doxastic faculties designed by God for truth-conducivity, and that these faculties are in large part not corruptions or epistemic perils or shortcomings, as Locke and Hume held, but *proper* to the human constitution—again, as created by God. But Plantinga and Wolterstorff disagree in what else we may say about the doxastic subject. Plantinga has worked mainly in terms of only this basic and original arrangement, treating it alone as complete doxastic anthropology. Wolterstorff on the other hand tracks with Reid in taking the basic and original arrangement to be merely seminal and developmentally basic. The original arrangement, Wolterstorff might say, has its whole life ahead of it.

To see what Wolterstorff has in mind, let us return momentarily to Reid's "principle of induction," discussed in section §2.3 above. As Wolterstorff explains this principle, it is operative in the acquisition of perceptual beliefs in much the same way in which we have seen it operative in the refinement of belief-formation based on testimony. The processes of accumulating both perceptual experience and experiences in linguistic communication are inductive. So while such beliefs lack deductively certain justification, they can be accounted for, and, furthermore, relied upon, due to the inductive principle and its divine givenness.[94] Wolterstorff explains,

> The way sensations and perceptions acquire these additional powers is as follows: There is in all of us the disposition to acquire customs or habits. This is one of the original principles of our constitution (Reid calls it the 'inductive' principle.) It's repetition of one sort and another that accounts for the activation

---

94. Wolterstorff writes, "The deepest similarity between, on the one hand, language acquisition and our acceptance of testimony, and, on the other hand, acquired perception, is that in both cases the inductive principle is at work" (ibid., 183).

of this disposition, and thus, for the acquisition of a particular habit or custom. In the case before us, it's the repeated observation of a constant, or nearly constant, conjunction in nature that accounts for the formation of the relevant custom or habit. . . . It's only on account of our acquisition of the requisite customs that most of the informational potential of our sensations can be interpreted—in the perceptual way, not in the inferential and theoretical way.[95]

Reid believed that a disposition for the development or acquisition of further faculties or dispositions is included among the "hard wiring" or original faculties of belief formation. The original constitution or design plan, the 'hard-wiring,' is only the, say, operating system, such that at any moment, epistemic function is really a great deal more than that original material, while what is in fact operative has developed in accordance with the primary operating design.

Plantinga's doxastic self is something like a child born healthy, with cognitive abilities in good working order, but who never grows, never learns to converse, never acquires the sophistication for tactful social interaction, never reaps the benefit of doubting and never learns from his doxastic mistakes. Plantinga works only with the design, neglecting, we might say, the concrete individual.[96] By contrast, Reid writes:

> To a man newly made to see, the visible appearance of objects would be the same as to us; but he would see nothing at all of their real dimensions, as we do. He could form no conjecture, by means of his sight only, how many inches or feet they were in length, breadth, or thickness. He could perceive little or nothing of their real figure; nor could he discern that this was a cube, that a sphere; that this was a cone, and that a cylinder . . .[97]

---

95. Ibid., 117–18, 120.

96. Phrasing it this way risks overstating the matter. There is no principled difference between Plantinga and Wolterstorff in terms of doxastic anthropology; Wolterstorff's amplifications in terms of individual persons and personal histories could easily be incorporated into Plantinga's work.

97. Reid, *Inquiry*, VI.iii: 84–85. At least in theory, perceptions are distinguishable between those provided for by the primary or original faculties and those acquired through experience: "Our perceptions are of two kinds: some are natural and original, others acquired, and the fruit of experience" (ibid., VI.xx). Wolterstorff explains that "What happens in the course of experience, then, is that sensations acquire powers of suggestion well behind [beyond?] those that they have by virtue of our hard wiring. That is to say, they acquire the disposition to evoke many other apprehensions and beliefs than those that they evoke by virtue of one's hard wiring" (*Thomas Reid*, 117).

The difference between a blind man "newly made to see" and a normally functioning adult who has behind him years of epistemic and perceptual development, is analogous to the difference between a normally functioning adult and an infant. Both possess similar original designs, but only the adult has the benefit of formative experience.

Plantinga's emphasis on proper function is a welcome move away from a doxastic ideal like Locke's, granted what Wolterstorff thinks is its inadequacy in terms of dynamic historicity and its consequently narrow conception of the doxastic self. And related to this concern is the principal weakness Wolterstorff spots in Plantinga's theory of proper function: that it is insufficient for doxastic governance, and thus for belief obligation and doxastic normativity.[98]

While it is true, Wolterstorff and Plantinga agree, that neither in terms of original doxastic programming nor subsequent doxastic development, are beliefs within direct or even remote volitional range—they are not subject to willful manipulation—it is not the case, Wolterstorff contends, that there is no intentional action involved with the formation of beliefs: "for the most part if not entirely, believings are the outcome of the dispositional rather than the volitional side of our nature . . . But . . . it doesn't follow," he says, "that intention has no role whatsoever in the formation of beliefs."[99] Even though proper function affords a glimpse of rationality or belief permissibility, since it includes no role for the will with respect to the formation of beliefs, proper function is ultimately insufficient for entitlement and obligation. *Can* is necessary for *ought*; if there is no volition involved in the formation of beliefs, there can be no accountability. I am no more responsible for my doxastic affairs than I am for my circulatory system. Another way of putting this is to say that at the same time that proper function, in its emphasis on a de-historicized design plan, neglects the historically organic and socially engaged doxastic *person*, it also neglects historical and social contexts, which represent a kind of doxastic playing field within which the doxastic subject is ever so actively and intentionally aware of doxastic habits, customs, and responsibilities, of what Wolterstorff calls practices of belief and inquiry. There is still, we might say, a slight modern influence

---

98. Wolterstorff traces this deficiency to Reid: "We must . . . speak about the locus of epistemic obligation. Here we go beyond Reid; for Reid speaks almost exclusively about epistemic practices, hardly at all about epistemic obligation." So in this regard the Reidian model is inadequate for epistemic obligation and doxastic deontology. The reason is that for Reid, "Beliefs are not the outcome of decisions but of dispositions" ("Evidence, Entitled Belief, and the Gospels," 452).

99. "Ought to Believe—Two Concepts," in *Practices of Belief*, 67.

in Plantinga's doxastic anthropology, evident in its removed and idealized character.

Wolterstorff, following Reid more closely, insists that while what a person perceives evokes in him, irresistibly and even immediately, a number of beliefs about his environment, that person also retains the ability to avert his gaze or to inspect more carefully, and to determine a course of action with the express intention of influencing his doxastic state. Some of these doxastically significant actions will be generically human, such as looking away or pausing to look more closely; others will be historically or situationally specific. If I want an estimate of the population of Beijing, I can google it, or consult an expert.

Our believings and belief-forming dispositions are governed, Wolterstorff explains, but not directly controlled. "A ruler's governance of his subjects does not consist in calling them into existence."[100] Doxastic governance does not consist in exercising direct control, but in laying out parameters and in directing our belief-forming mechanisms, trusting that they will function as they are meant to. The important point is that in very many ways we are able to do so, and whatever scope of possibility that ability provides is the scope of epistemic accountability. Only if I could have known is it possible that I should have, and may be blameworthy if I did not.

Wolterstorff's critique of proper function comes down to this, that it cannot account for an ethic of belief because it stops short of the role of volition in the formation of beliefs.[101] We are culpable for our believings if and only if we are able to govern them, and only to the extent that we are able to do so. We are accountable only for knowledge which is available to us, which we should have had, or could have had, by means situationally and personally available.

Wolterstorff describes that availability as a function not only of generalized doxastic faculties and personal subjective situationality, but also of broader socio-historical factors. Relative to other people and to society, and in terms of what means of inquiry are available and acceptable to a given person in a given situation, a complex web of ethically significant

---

100. "Can Belief in God Be Rational," in *Practices of Belief*, 231.

101. Distinguishing his own view from Plantinga's, Wolterstorff writes, "Most of one's belief-forming dispositions are not to be found in our human design plan—or not to be found there in the form in which they actually exist in one. The belief-forming dispositions that each of us actually possesses at any particular time have been produced in us across the course of our lives. Though their production has occurred *in accord with* our design plan, they are not themselves *to be found within* our design plan. Furthermore, it is not one's designed belief-forming self that is relevant to the determination of warrant, but the belief-forming self produced in accord with the design" ("Historicizing the Belief-Forming Self," in *Practices of Belief*, 118–19).

relationships weighs on our doxastic practices and responsibilities. Wolterstorff understands situational availability, intention, and responsibility as introducing rational normativity into the doxastic life in the form of socially constituted "practices of inquiry." But that is a discussion for another day.

In sum, we have seen Wolterstorff lay bare the inadequacies of the traditional view of the doxastic subject as solitary, immobile, and passive—a stoic and staid, idealized nobody, without personal relations, social roles, or the ability to learn and develop. We have also examined Wolterstorff's appreciation for Reid's notions of belief-forming dispositions and a more dynamic and life-like doxastic subject, his response to the skeptic of the Way of Ideas, and a theologically grounded doxastic optimism. Finally, we noted the fact that Wolterstorff distinguishes his Reidian doxastic anthropology from Plantinga's in the interest of maintaining an organic unity of the historically located, individual believer and a fuller appreciation for the moral significance of the doxastic life.

We now have a detailed understanding of Wolterstorff's doxastic anthropology. In the next chapter we examine situationality, the doxastic subject's morally charged sphere of intentional action. We will see that Wolterstorff understands situational availability, intention, and responsibility as introducing rational normativity into the doxastic life in the form of socially constituted "practices of inquiry."

3

Situated Rationality and Practices of Inquiry

As noted, Wolterstorff's chief epistemological concern is rationality in terms of belief entitlement. His position, as discussed in section §2.1, is that rationality is (1) situational, (2) practical, and (3) deontological. Chapters 2 and 3 unpack these features of "situated rationality" by focusing first on the doxastic self in chapter 2, and then, in the present chapter, on practices of inquiry.

Wolterstorff's doxastic anthropology, as I have called it, is a response to the platonic abstractions of philosophical tradition: the "solitary, immobile reactor." In response, Wolterstorff proposes a Reidian account of a historically situated and socially responsible believing subject. In the second chapter, we focused on the noetic structure of the historicized subject in terms of belief-forming dispositions and historical conditioning. The value of this material for an analysis of situated rationality is that it individualizes and historicizes the doxastic subject and the doxastic life. Wolterstorff's doxastic anthropology essentially lays to rest the abstract propensities of traditional epistemology, and in effect forces the epistemologist to recast epistemic norms in terms of individualized and historicized subjectivity. In this way, Wolterstorff's doxastic anthropology has set us on the path toward a *situated* rationality.

If obligation implies ability, or ought implies can, the next step in an analysis of Wolterstorff's theory of rationality ought to be a defense of the role of the will in belief formation. This is the goal of the present chapter. According to Wolterstorff, doxastic self-governance is a function of those doxastic practices which are available in a subject's situation (reading a book, consulting an expert, doing an online search, etc.). A particular socio-historical situation and a person's belonging to or in it are in large part constituted by such practices, since such practices represent a set of socio-historically distinctive epistemological and metaphysical commitments.[1] Doxastic practices, then, advance our understanding of situated rationality by (1) concretely representing a subject's (doxastic) situation, (2) translating epistemic rationality into practical rationality, and (3) locating the subject's doxastic practices within a socially constituted, moral (deontological) situationality.

In the present chapter, I expand the scope of analysis in order to examine the doxastic situation in which a subject always finds himself, and the socially and ethically charged actions which constitute a subject's unique ethico-doxastic situation. The main subject in chapter 3, therefore, is situated rationality and what Wolterstorff calls "practices of inquiry." Wolterstorff's article "Entitlement to Believe and Practices of Inquiry" will be a principal source for this step in our study,[2] along with relevant passages from *Divine Discourse*, the seminal essay, "Can Belief in God Be Rational If It Has No Foundations?" and other articles.[3]

---

1. See "Entitlement to Believe and Practices of Inquiry," in *Practices of Belief*, 95–98. Wolterstorff refers in that section to Alasdair MacIntyre, *After Virtue*. Wolterstorff says, "Social availability comes and goes across time and space with the coming and going of the frameworks of conviction that give rationale to those ways of finding things out and make them interpretable," and "[p]ractices of inquiry acquire their point and plausibility, and their results become interpretable, within a context of ontological and epistemological conviction" ("Entitlement to Believe," 94, 97–8).

2. "Entitlement to Believe" and another essay, "On Being Entitled to Beliefs about God" (*Practices of Belief*, 313–33), are taken from Wolterstorff's 1995 Gifford Lectures. Of these two pieces, Terence Cuneo, the editor of the collected essays, writes, "When combined with Alvin Plantinga's work on warrant and William Alston's work on justification and perception of God, they provide the most complete picture of so-called Reformed epistemology to date" (*Practices of Belief*, vii–viii). Wolterstorff's aim in "Entitlement to Believe and Practices of Inquiry" is to clarify the notion of belief entitlement through an inductive study of how relevant terms are used and how people tend to view, even if somewhat uncritically, the ethical side of cognitive conduct. In the essay, he explores his contention that there are actions which are both morally significant and essentially doxastic or epistemological. Here he means to refute the claim that epistemology does not deal in moral (deontological) value; indeed it does. These morally significant doxastic actions are "ways of finding out" and "practices of inquiry." Such actions are historically, socially, and personally given, defined, and restricted. Section §3.2 explores these ideas in detail.

3. Respectively, *Divine Discourse*, esp. chapter 15; and "Can Belief in God Be Rational," in *Practices of Belief*, 217–64. Other studies of Wolterstorff's theory of situated rationality include Sloane, *On Being a Christian*; and Coyle, "Nicholas Wolterstorff's Reformed Epistemology."

I focus first on the situational availability of beliefs and the significance of intention and volition for doxastic responsibility (§3.2). I then focus on socially constituted doxastic practices, what I shall call, following Wolterstorff, "practices of inquiry" (§3.2). These practices are, we might say, the instruments of socially and morally significant doxastic behavior. Wolterstorff's claim that epistemic rationality should be understood as woven into the fabric of a practical, situational deontology should be clear at that point.

In the final section of this chapter (§3.3), I introduce the question of moral value: namely, what is the theory of moral value informing situational deontology? By the end of the chapter, we will have discussed in detail the situational presence of doxastic obligation in terms of a person's broader moral situation. The burden of the final section of the present chapter is to demonstrate that thus far no account has been given for moral value, while moral value is incontestably essential to Wolterstorff's analysis of rationality as it appears both here and in chapter 2. So the question of accounting for that moral value remains outstanding as our analysis of practices of inquiry draws to a close. At the conclusion of chapter 3, we move toward answering the question of moral value by introducing Wolterstorff's notion of shalom. In the fourth chapter, we find that, for Wolterstorff, moral value emerges from Christian scripture in the redemptive and semi-eschatological theme of shalom.

3.1 THE DOXASTIC ETHICAL SITUATION: AVAILABILITY AND INTENTION

The goal of this section is to explore two necessary conditions for doxastic deontology and to see how these conditions advance our understanding of the notion of situationality that is central to Wolterstorff's theory of rationality. The two conditions are: intentional doxastic action and the situational availability of beliefs. Intentional action is necessary because a subject can be held accountable for his believings only insofar as he has control over those believings.[4] The situational availability of beliefs is a necessary condition for doxastic deontology in the sense that a subject may be held accountable only for beliefs situationally available to him.

Following a discussion of these themes, we shall examine their significance relative to our analysis of Wolterstorff's notion doxastic situationality.

---

4. Wolterstorff suspects Reid of assuming the same principle: "I suspect it is Reid's conviction... that one is never obliged to do what one *cannot* do. Accordingly, in showing that some of our immediate beliefs are ineluctable he has shown that we are *justified* in holding them" ("Thomas Reid on Rationality," 55).

The situational availability of beliefs and the role of intentional doxastic action provide a link between the doxastic anthropology outlined in chapter 2 and the subject of this chapter, practices of inquiry. First, intention and availability as these relate to doxastic obligation.

Wolterstorff understands rational obligation, and more broadly, moral obligation, to be a function of intentional action.[5] He understands intention as necessary for responsibility and accountability. Intention connects an agent to an action or an utterance or belief, in an ethically significant way, so that only where one intentionally carries out an action or intends to carry it out, may one be held morally accountable for that action.[6] "It's to intentions and only to intentions that the required, the prohibited, and the permitted attach . . . What's required, prohibited, or permitted of me is the forming of intentions to do things, along with intentional undertakings and doings."[7]

We can see the value of this connection for Wolterstorff in his critique John Locke's doxastic deontology. Following Wolterstorff's analysis, there appear to be two sources of the moral value of believings which compete for prominence in Locke's *Essay*. One is religious: we owe the duty of right believing to our creator.[8] The other is social: irresponsible believing is a threat

---

5. "We must first speak about the locus of epistemic obligation. Here we go beyond Reid; for Reid speaks almost exclusively about epistemic practices, hardly at all about epistemic obligation" ("Evidence, Entitled Belief, and the Gospels," 452). And we move beyond Alston as well, whose position is "that though the concept of obligation . . . has some application to beliefs, its applicability is so marginal as to make it pointless for the epistemologist to pay it any attention" ("Ought to Believe—Two Concepts," in *Practices of Belief*, 69). The reason for this is that according to both Reid and Alston, "Belief is almost entirely—if not indeed entirely—the outcome of the dispositional side of our nature, not of the volitional side . . . But if this is right, how can obligations attach to our believings? Believings are not all that different from startle-reflexes" (ibid., 66).

6. "[S]omewhere obligation enters the picture. Where? At those points where we, by decision, can affect the workings of our doxastic practices—can *govern* their workings . . . By acts of will we can direct attention of our epistemic faculties, by acts of will we can impair or improve our epistemic faculties, and by acts of will we can attempt to keep in or near the forefront of consciousness something we already believe" ("Evidence, Entitled Belief, and the Gospels," 452).

7. "Ought to Believe—Two Concepts," in *Practices of Belief*, 67. In the same article he says, "Blaming a person for a belief he has is appropriate only when he's accountable for having that belief; malformation is not sufficient for that. 'It's through no fault of his own,' we say. What he's accountable for is the intentions he forms and tries to act upon, and for the intentions that he could have formed and could have tried to act upon" (ibid., 82).

8. See Wolterstorff, "John Locke's Epistemological Piety." Wolterstorff expresses sympathy with this concern: "But this whole array of believings, that God said or is saying so-and-so, cries out for appraisal. Some are so bizarre as to lack whatever merit one can think of. Many have proved utterly appalling in their consequences: human blood has been shed, oppression imposed, suffering experienced, as the consequence of one and another person believing that God had spoken to him" (*Divine Discourse*, 267).

to social well-being and political stability, so it is the duty of every citizen to govern his believings rightly—duty owed, in this case, to the state or the body politic, to one's fellow human beings.[9] So Locke portrays the value of doxastic conduct as flowing from either or both of these interpersonal contexts: God-human or human-human.

Part of Wolterstorff's critique of Locke's theory of belief is that, while laying so much emphasis on moral doxastic accountability in these two ways, Locke expresses serious doubts as to whether a necessary component of moral accountability is there to begin with, namely, a sufficient volitional aspect of belief formation.[10] In Wolterstorff's view, Locke's socio-religious doxastic deontology is quite heavy-handed; while at the same time, he (Locke) denies that most people, or perhaps anyone at all, have any direct control over their believings.[11] Locke offers a famously forceful doxastic obligation; but he denies doxastic ability.

So we see from his critique of Locke that in Wolterstorff's view, doxastic deontology—morally significant doxastic duty and obligation—requires some measure of doxastic volition. Wolterstorff also notes that since both Reid and Alston deny that the will plays a significant role in belief formation, neither emphasizes doxastic deontology.[12] Locke tries to have his doxastic deontological cake and eat it too: he affirms that we are religiously and socially accountable for right doxastic conduct *and* that our belief-forming psychology never escapes the doxastic corruptions of education, tradition, and self-interest.

Intentional action is essential to doxastic deontology; but so is the availability of beliefs. One cannot be held accountable for beliefs unavailable in one's situation. But not all beliefs available to one are such that one can

---

9. See Wolterstorff, *John Locke*, 1–12; "Evidence, Entitled Belief, and the Gospels," 429–30; "Once Again, Evidentialism—This Time Social," in *Practices of Belief*, 270.

10. Of Locke's reversal on this point Wolterstorff says, "There is no better example of 'deconstruction' in the history of Western philosophy" (*John Locke*, 97).

11. According to Wolterstorff, Locke rejects direct doxastic voluntarism: "[I]t is of fundamental importance for understanding Locke to realize that he regarded belief and assent as formed by some faculty or faculties and not by the will." "But," according to Locke, "the workings of our assent- and belief-forming faculties must be governed . . . We are to monitor and intervene" (*John Locke*, 61). We intervene, Locke thought, directly into the belief-forming process, when necessary. The problem, Wolterstorff explains, is Locke's admission that there are such "wounds of the mind" as to "have a devastating effect on Locke's vision," on his vision for doxastic good conduct and doxastic socio-religious accountability (ibid., 94). In other words, his very noble hope for doxastic urbanity is, by his own admission, undone by the pervasive influence of ungovernable bias.

12. See n4 above.

be held accountable for them. This latter distinction depends upon whether the available beliefs are subject to intentional action.

Along these lines, in his *Divine Discourse*, Wolterstorff argues that sentences have meaning apart from and prior to utterance, and most sentences offer a menu of potential meanings, some more direct, some more ambiguous or metaphorical.[13] The intentional action by which a speaker employs a sentence in a particular speech act leads an interlocutor to the intended meaning—one (or more) among several possible meanings—and accurate interpretation. The author or speaker actualizes or intentionalizes, we might say, a particular applied meaning of a sentence by means of his intentional use of a sentence in a particular speech act.

What Wolterstorff has in mind throughout this discussion is the employment of human language structures as a mode of divine speech. Language units 'already there' are adapted to divine use by divine authorial intention, giving rise to a distinct instance of speech and meaning. The example which launches his study is the story of Augustine overhearing the child who sang, "*tolle lege, tolle lege*"—speech which Augustine took to be from God to himself, then and there. It is in this sense that it may be said of some piece of human discourse that God is the speaker or the author: by virtue of intentional action, the divine subject becomes the author or the speaker or the party responsible for a piece of discourse.[14]

In an analogous manner, Wolterstorff's understanding of the doxastic situation is one in which some beliefs are, in a sense, out there. They are situationally available. For example, perceptual beliefs surround the doxastic subject like a vast menu of propositional-doxastic possibilities. Perceptual beliefs are actualized in us by turning one way or another, by touching some things and not others, by turning on the light, by opening a door, or by looking out a window. Wolterstorff says, "If I look to the left, I'll perceive certain things and my perception will ineluctably evoke certain beliefs in me; if I look to the right, I'll perceive other things and my perception will ineluctably evoke other beliefs in me."[15] It is a necessary condition of a person's being held morally accountable for particular believings that those beliefs are situationally available in this way.

No such beliefs pertaining to today's weather are available to me at this precise moment, since the view out the window to my right is blocked

13. *Divine Discourse*, 51–57.

14. See *Divine Discourse*, esp. chapters 11–12.

15. He continues, "So even though my beliefs do get formed by the activation of dispositions, yet it's to a considerable extent the consequence of intentions I form that such-and-such activations occur" ("Ought to Believe—Two Concepts," in *Practices of Belief*, 67–68).

by closed blinds. But I do perceive the rather cluttered state of my desk; the ineluctable perceptual belief that my desk is cluttered is both available to me in my present doxastic situation and actual, since I cannot help but see it. But it would be neither available nor actual were I in another room or outside. Am I accountable for my beliefs about the weather? Only insofar as I can influence those beliefs. Since I could easily walk over to the window and open the blinds or look up the weather forecast on the internet, I am indeed accountable. If I dressed for summer weather but upon walking out the door found myself in a snow storm, dereliction of doxastic duty would be the source of my problems.

If ought implies can, one cannot always be held accountable for one's coming to hold immediately formed, ineluctable beliefs. But to the extent that one can govern the faculties responsible for the formation of ineluctable beliefs—as I would be doing were I to look out the window—to that extent, one may certainly be held accountable. And to these rather simple, intentional actions, such as making an effort to look out the window, we may add more complex ones: "Because I find Anton Webern's music fascinating but baffling I enroll in a course on classical music of the early twentieth century in the hope of learning how to listen to it."[16]

While a person's core doxastic faculties may not be directly controllable, to some extent they are often governable. Thus, the doxastic life is rife with intention and deliberative choice, the activity of belief formation being constantly manipulated, guided, or directed in various ways. In sum, belief-formation on some level is involuntary, particularly in the case of the immediate formation of ineluctable perceptual beliefs. But belief-formation is also governable. If we may think of a person as capable of governing belief-formation, to that extent we may speak of his being responsible for his believings.

If doxastic intention is limited, so is accountability, or the reach of ethical significance into the realm of believing and belief formation. There is a role for intention in the holding and forming of beliefs, and so, as we have seen, understanding where and how the will may function in the doxastic life is necessary for understanding doxastic responsibility and for understanding what, we hope to be able to say eventually, makes a belief ethically significant in Wolterstorff's view. As it turns out, the contours of doxastic volition are situational.

As noted, there are many ways in which belief-forming dispositions may be governed, at some distance removed from direct doxastic voluntarism. This is true for the immediate and irresistible beliefs of perception,

---

16. "Entitlement to Believe and Practices of Inquiry," in *Practices of Belief*, 87.

which can be governed by simple actions such as looking more attentively at something. Just as I could choose to look attentively at an object, I may consult an expert on an issue which puzzles me (Webern's music, for example). I could also avert my eyes or disregard expert opinion.

This means that no two people stand in identical spheres of objective doxastic possibility. Even a person sitting only a short distance from me as I work has within his realm of doxastic options no beliefs about what I am writing or exactly what I am seeing. Similarly, the doxastic options available to a person in a large university library in the twenty-first century are particularly vast in some regards—in comparison, say, to a potato farmer in Idaho one hundred years ago—but dramatically more narrow in other ways. In an instant I could have a clear understanding of the geography of a distant land by looking it up on the internet, but I will never, sitting in a library, learn how to drive a tractor or to predict the weather by observing cloud patterns, sensing the humidity, or gauging the speed and direction of the wind.

Intention enters in such a way that, trusting my faculties to operate as they were made, designed, or conditioned to operate (as discussed in chapter 2), I may so manipulate a doxastic situation as to achieve a desired outcome—that I observe the distance from here to there, or that I have a better understanding of this or that. Doxastic intention invites and provides for doxastic accountability, within a particular context of doxastic possibility. The reason that there are such things as doxastic responsibility and obligation, is that there is such a pervasive role for the intentional governance of the formation and holding of beliefs; and that role always takes shape according to the subject's particular situation.

We have been able to articulate a role for purposeful governance of belief-forming faculties and dispositions, and thus to outline the situational domain of the ethical in the doxastic life. But there is more to say about the ways in which these volitional aspects of belief formation help us to understand the constitution of doxastic situations. As Wolterstorff explains, "[w]hich obligations of this sort apply to a given person depends for one thing, on the doxastic practices available to that person, and what he entitledly believes and doesn't believe about them. . . . Secondly, it depends on the abilities of the person. . . . Thirdly, which obligations of this sort apply to a given person depends on the totality of that person's other obligations."[17] I now discuss the latter two points, and I will afterward introduce the first—doxastic practices—but treat it more extensively in section §3.2.

---

17. *Divine Discourse*, 272–73.

What might Wolterstorff have in mind when he says "the abilities of the person"? On the principle outlined above, that ability delineates the sphere of obligation, such that the constitution of a doxastic situation must take into account an individual's unique natural abilities. Only that which a person has the capacity to believe or understand falls within the range of doxastic possibility and consequently, more narrowly, of doxastic intention; and since no one can intentionally come to know something too complex for him to understand, no one can rightly be held accountable for what is thus beyond his natural intellectual ability. For example, it is simply not within the range of possibility for the average person to arrive at clear and confident beliefs about the harmonic structure of a complex musical composition. For most people, as for myself, the immediate aural discernment of complex harmonies is simply not a possibility, and for most people, particularly in comparison to folks more gifted, rigorous training would augment those abilities relatively little. There are people, however, who have such ability naturally. Upon hearing even very complex musical compositions, such a person would acquire beliefs, in many cases immediately, as to the harmony, formal structure, and so on, of the piece. Due to a naturally uneven distribution of these capacities, there cannot be a generic distribution of morally heavy doxastic accountability: it cannot be the case that all people are held responsible for the rapid apprehension of things which are beyond their natural abilities to apprehend. Raw ability is therefore a limiting factor in terms of doxastic intention and accountability. No two people possess identical intellectual capacities, and moral accountability ends where ability ends.

Wolterstorff speaks at times of a person's "place" or "location" within the "space of moral obligation."[18] What he has in mind, I gather, is the situational (including social) nature of obligation in general, coupled with the claim that doxastic obligation is a function or species of the broader ethical aspects of situationality. Responsibilities and expectations weigh on a person not only in terms of that person's natural capacities, but also in terms of a person's social roles and relations, and his personal convictions.

So the scope of doxastic accountability is also shaped by social factors in both subjective and objective dimensions. A person's social role, whether he is a teacher, a restaurant worker, a bus driver, or a politician, conveys to that person a set of responsibilities and obligations, and moral obligation begins to take shape. It is the teacher's socially constituted responsibility to know her subject matter thoroughly, the waiter's responsibility to know the

---

18. "Entitlement to Believe and Practices of Inquiry," in *Practices of Belief*, 105; cf. "On Being Entitled to Beliefs about God," in *Practices of Belief*, 315, where Wolterstorff refers to "where I am situated in the total space of obligation."

menu, the bus driver's obligation to know his route, traffic laws, procedures in case of emergency, and so on. In some situations the responsibility is more grave than in others, and the weight of doxastic obligations will mirror that. If I am the pilot of a passenger plane, it is incumbent upon me to be sure that the plane I am about to fly is in good working condition. Responsibility initially comes from the particular social role a person carries, and is proportionate to the social significance of that role. The pilot's responsibility is so serious because so much is at risk—because other people entrust him with so much.

Accountability accrues not only in terms of a social role, but also in terms of the various actions which are considered the proper means of acquiring the beliefs required of a person carrying a particular role. As a pilot, I am responsible for guaranteeing that the plane I will fly is in good working condition. Now I could find out whether it is in good condition by asking the passengers if they noticed anything amiss as they boarded or by inspecting the plane myself. But certainly it would be better to defer to an appointed team of mechanics and engineers before takeoff. It would be more responsible to do so. Considerable obligation to go about acquiring reliable information regarding the condition of the aircraft, and to go about the acquisition of such information according to a standard, socially ordained procedure, weighs on me as a pilot.

As we shall see below, Wolterstorff argues that since relationships introduce morality into the doxastic situation, what counts is not whether, regardless of anyone's beliefs on the matter, doxastic means actually do lead to good information, but whether it is the social and cultural consensus that they do. A pilot will not be blamed so long as he trusts the word of the aircraft mechanics—he has performed his socio-doxastic duty, even if it should turn out that the mechanics' assessment was inaccurate. Which obligations, the weight of those obligations, and, additionally, prescribed avenues of inquiry, are a function of a person's social role and situation.

In sum, what we can say generically about doxastic obligation is that, from Wolterstorff's point of view, nearly every person, certainly every well-functioning person, finds himself working with a set of doxastic obligations, responsibilities, and possibilities, which are the stuff of an objectively and subjectively unique situation: "Whatever be their nature, it's important to realize that the obligations in questions [sic] are *situated* obligations, in that which obligations of this sort actually apply to a given person is a function of various aspects of the particular situation of the person in question."[19]

---

19. *Divine Discourse*, 272. The pilot illustration is my own. Wolterstorff offers an extended discussion of the epistemic merits and situated rationality of a real-life instance of religious experience and the related doxastic states in *Divine Discourse*, 273–80. We

We have also seen that intention and availability are necessary conditions of these obligations bearing any ethico-doxastic significance. Doxastic practices, as intentional actions with regard to situationally available beliefs, are therefore bearers of doxastic deontological value.

We turn now to Wolterstorff's thought on doxastic practices. "The clue to the applicability of deontic concepts to our believings," he writes, "lies in the notion of a *doxastic practice*, as I shall call it . . ."[20]

3.2 PRACTICES OF INQUIRY AND WAYS OF FINDING OUT

We may say that belief-forming faculties are subjective, in the sense that they are aspects of the individual psychology of doxastic subjects. We may say, by contrast, that doxastic practices, as Wolterstorff understands them, are objective, since they are constituents of the situations in which doxastic subjects finds themselves. In this section, we will look at doxastic practices in terms of truth-conducivity: Wolterstorff's distinction between practices of inquiry and ways of finding out. We will also mention the reciprocal relationship in which such practices stand to socio-historical situations: doxastic practices both constitute and reflect socio-historical situations. We will also discuss the issue of social and personal accessibility and acceptability, criteria which determine a doxastic practice's ethico-doxastic value. Finally, we will re-introduce the language of entitlement, since we will have in place at that point the essential components of Wolterstorff's theory of situated rationality.[21]

Not all doxastic practices are at the end of the day actually truth-conducive. Whether my employing a particular doxastic practice is rational depends upon the social consensus, in my situation, as to the effectiveness and appropriateness of it. The deontological aspect of rationality rests

---

also find in this section a succinct description of doxastic practices: "We implement what I shall call *doxastic practices*. We implement ways of finding out about new things. We implement ways of ousting false beliefs. And we implement ways of forestalling the emergence of false beliefs, or rather, of diminishing the frequency of their emergence, so that various components of the flow become more reliable. Some of these ways we learn on our own, from experience. But massively it's the case that we learn them from others. For many are established in our society; they are *social practices*, in Alisdair MacIntyre's sense; and we are inducted into them, by modeling and by explicit instruction" (ibid., 270).

20. Ibid., 269.

21. I discuss Wolterstorff's notions of rationality, justification, and entitlement in section §2.1.

largely upon this consensus relative to a doxastic practice, not upon objective knowledge of its truth-conducivity. What lends a practice positive ethico-doxastic status is the general social consensus that it is truth-conducive, when it may or may not actually be. So, were I to brazenly disregard social consensus regarding the truth-conducivity of a doxastic practice and employ it or not employ it in defiance of that consensus, that in itself would be a violation of the ethical principles which impinge upon doxastic behavior; it would be irrational.

Suppose I have come to seriously doubt the truth-conducivity of trusting the news media, particularly when they report on politically charged matters. Still, generally speaking, turning on the television is an entrenched, socially regarded practice of inquiry. Because it is, I might be blameworthy for not being aware of something which was "on the news." I should have availed myself of the appropriate practice of inquiry. "Culpability in such cases," we shall say, "stems from failure to use some relevant *practice of inquiry*."[22] So, practices of inquiry are socially esteemed doxastic practices.

A "'way of finding out X,'" by contrast, "will always be a sequence of actions . . . such that, for some sort of human being in some sort of situation, were a person of that sort in a situation of that sort to employ that sequence as an action-plan for finding out X, the consequence would ensue that the agent found out X."[23] Or more succinctly, "it's to engage in a means/end project whose goal is that one be in the state of having found out X."[24] A way of finding out is an action or sequence of actions which is doxastically fruitful, or actually truth-conducive.[25] A way of finding out may be

---

22. "Ought to Believe—Two Concepts," in *Practices of Belief*, 83. Not knowing what was "on the news" is an example of failing to avail oneself of a readily available, socially esteemed practice of inquiry. Here is a fictional example Wolterstorff gives of the active use of a practice which is socially suspect, and probably ought to be: "Suppose a person takes a fancy to a proposition and just up and believes it . . . by our criterion he most assuredly is not rational in his belief. The 'mechanism' operative in this imaginary case—one may doubt whether there really is any such 'mechanism' and whether anybody really can believe in this fashion, but let that pass—the 'mechanism' operative is that of believing what one takes a fancy to. But certainly any normal adult human being not only ought to know but also *does* know that this is a most unreliable 'mechanism' of belief formation" ("Can Belief in God Be Rational," in *Practices of Belief*, 258). While I depend here somewhat on this earlier essay ("Can Belief in God Be Rational" was originally published in 1983), it should be noted that Wolterstorff does not appeal to a developed notion of practices of inquiry and the role they play in belief entitlement until much later.

23. "Entitlement to Believe and Practices of Inquiry," in *Practices of Belief*, 91.

24. Ibid.

25. Wolterstorff also says: "And lest there be misunderstanding, perhaps I should mention that one's employment of a way of finding out X will sometimes have the

anything from simply attending with special care to some perceptual matter, concentrating, or intentionally remembering, or more complex actions such as signing up for a course, researching a particular question, consulting an expert, or performing a series of experiments.[26]

A practice of inquiry, on the other hand, is a socially recognized doxastic practice which may or may not be truth-conducive; it may or may not in fact be a way of finding out. ". . . people often believe that a certain sequence of actions employed in a certain circumstance is a way of finding out so-and-so when it is not. . . . Thus to participate in a social practice of inquiry may or may not be a way of finding something out." So, "A way of finding something out is an abstract sequence of actions that may function as the content of a social practice of inquiry; a practice of inquiry is socially entrenched and thought to embody a way of finding something out."[27] And he writes: "All practices of inquiry are thought to embody ways of finding things out; some actually are that, some are not."[28]

A way of finding out is some course of action which is, in fact, truth-conducive. So some doxastic actions are effective ways of finding out but not socially available practices of inquiry. Some socially available practices are ways of finding out, and some are not.

Practices of inquiry are important features of a socio-historical context: they both define that context and are defined by it. Practices of inquiry are so central to the definition of such a context that one's 'induction' into those practices represents one's participation in a particular socio-historical situation: ". . . a large component of what it is to become a member of a human community and to become a participant in its culture consists of being inducted into the practices of inquiry extant in that community."[29] So for example, an educated Westerner in the twenty-first century is not likely to practice divination; it is not a practice of inquiry recognized in the modern

---

character of a *critique* of what one already believes rather than *discovery* of something new; one aims to find out whether that which one already believes is really true" (ibid.).

26. "But rather than speaking, all of the time, of *ways of finding out, of attending*, or *of remembering*," he writes, "I propose saving words and calling all three of these, 'ways of finding out'" (ibid., 91–92).

27. Ibid., 92–93.

28. Ibid., 92.

29. Ibid., 96. Elsewhere he says, "[E]ach member of every group of human beings performs actions that affect other members of the group and elicit a variety of responses from them. These we may call *socially significant actions*. In any group there will be complexes and sequences of such actions which, by virtue of their repetition, may be called *practices*. The *fundamental* social practices of a group, along with *pervasive* features of their practices generally, will also be regarded as belonging to the structure of that society of people" (*Until Justice and Peace Embrace*, 23).

West. Because it is not, a person would be a kind of social pariah if he were openly a regular practitioner of divination. Practices of inquiry are essential aspects of what it means for a person to belong to a socio-historical context. On the other hand, inasmuch as a practice is defined by its context, a given context is constituted by doxastic practices.

Consider another example. Only recently has the U.S. federal government begun to post proposed legislation on the internet, making it accessible to the general public. Thus a new practice of inquiry has been introduced which renders others, in comparison, less authoritative. It also changes many people's doxastic deontological situation: since detailed information about proposed legislation, particularly in a public capacity, is readily available to anyone with internet access, there will be a greater expectation that a person commenting on that legislation will have consulted the primary source. In this case, the doxastic deontological situation is redefined to some degree by the introduction of a new practice of inquiry.

Wolterstorff proposes personal and social criteria for the appropriateness of a practice of inquiry. For a practice to enjoy social esteem and to carry deontological weight, it must be socially and personally accessible (or available); but it also must be personally and socially acceptable.

Here is how Wolterstorff defines social availability:

> ... the social availability of ways of finding things out is, for the most part, parochial rather than ecumenical. Social availability comes and goes across time and space with the coming and going of the frameworks of conviction that give rationale to those ways of finding things out and make them interpretable. It comes and goes across time and space with the coming and going of the values that make people prize the knowledge those ways of finding things out promise to those who employ them. It comes and goes across time and space with the coming and going of the skills and habits required for employing those ways of finding things out. And very often the social availability ... comes and goes ... with the coming and going of the technology ...[30]

In terms of accessibility or availability at the personal level, he writes, "... for any member of a given society ... only some of the ways of finding out that are socially available in that society are *personally accessible* to him or her ..."[31] For example, "[m]ost of the ways of finding things out that are

---

30. "Entitlement to Believe and Practices of Inquiry," in *Practices of Belief*, 94.
31. Ibid.

employed in the scientific laboratories of the modern world are personally inaccessible to me," Wolterstorff writes.[32]

Of all the socially and personally accessible practices available to me, only some are socially or personally acceptable. Moral or religious commitments may play a role, or concerns about the propriety of knowing this or that ('some knowledge is dangerous'), or to the moral acceptability of a practice itself which is believed to lead to otherwise welcome insights may be of concern to one individual or to many on some grounds other than truth-conducivity. And so, as Wolterstorff writes, "[a] good many of those ways of finding things out that are socially available and personally accessible are *contested* in society."[33] Though they may be accessible, they may not be acceptable.

For example, opponents of embryonic stem cell research in the United States rarely argue that the practice is unlikely to produce helpful insights. On the contrary, some opponents might even admit that such research stands to be fruitful. But this is not typically their chief concern. They object to the practice itself on moral grounds, arguing that despite the projected truth-conducivity of the practices involved, those practices violate moral precepts they are not willing to compromise. The implication is that a broader morality trumps truth-conducivity, or the moral value of one thing—whatever principle stem cell research violates—trumps the value of the insight such research promises.[34] Doxastic ethics in this case are evidently subsumed under a broad moral context, and not considered with reference solely to truth-conducivity. Indeed, much of the flow of daily human interaction avoids the most direct routes to truth, electing instead to employ the appropriate practices at appropriate times, in order to prioritize relationships, security, and many other things, over an impersonal, single-minded hunt for raw fact.

Just as the acceptability of practices of inquiry is a function prior moral commitments, so also is the intelligibility of practices of inquiry dependent upon prior philosophical commitments. Wolterstorff explains:

> Practices of inquiry . . . acquire their point and plausibility, and their results become interpretable, within a context of ontological and epistemological conviction. Outside that context, employing them makes no sense and their results remain mute.

32. Ibid., 95.

33. Ibid., 96.

34. To be more precise, the debate in the United States has been over *federal funding* for stem cell research. So the question is not so much whether the promised benefits of that work outweigh the moral compromise required by it, but whether this sort of high stakes moral game should be played with taxpayer funds at the federal level.

> To employ them is to presuppose that frame of conviction. And over and over it turns out that many of the ways of finding out ... are unacceptable to him because he does not accept the framework of ontological and epistemological conviction within which they find their home.[35]

In terms of "ontological and epistemological" convictions, what Wolterstorff affirms here regarding the nature of practices of inquiry is that, first, they assume a conceptual framework apart from which they are unintelligible, and, secondly, that the conceptual framework is a collection of convictions about deep structure matters which may not enjoy universal support. Anyone might object to some element of the framework on theoretical or other grounds, and the result is that the practice it endorses itself comes under question. Just as there may be a rift in the moral culture that draws a practice into the heat of social debate, as with federal funding for embryonic stem cell research, so also the intelligibility of a practice may be brought under heavy scrutiny if there is widespread disagreement about prior philosophical commitments. Trust in inscripturated divine revelation or in the veridicality of religious experience are two examples.[36]

Finally, recall that a distinction obtains between ways of finding out—means/end sequences which objectively and in fact yield true beliefs or belief likely to be true—and the sort of practices we have focused on, socially established practices of inquiry. It would appear that this distinction obtains because the social entrenchment of a practice is an unreliable indication of a practice's actual truth-conducivity. There is an important epistemological distinction, to put it more directly, between the two to which the situated subject has little or no ethically significant access. It is for this reason that, as mentioned, the ethico-doxastic status of practices of inquiry rests upon beliefs about their effectiveness, not upon their actual truth-conducivity—even if those beliefs are beliefs about actual truth-conducivity.

---

35. Ibid., 97–98.

36. Similarly, a conceptual framework is assumed in the operation of a Reidian credulity disposition, Wolterstorff says, "I propose the following model: All of us (after infancy) bring along a *framework of beliefs* to our apprehension of someone saying something. And whether or not we believe p on someone's sayso is a function (in part) of what we already believe, of how firmly we believe it, of how we came to believe it, and of whether or not we believe that p and our current framework of beliefs might jointly be true" ("Evidence, Entitled Belief, and the Gospels," "Entitlement to Believe and Practices of Inquiry," in *Practices of Belief*, 450). Then he adds, "All we can do is stand *within* our framework of beliefs, many of them acquired by believing on sayso, and test some of what has been told us by holding it up against other things told us—and now and then test some of it by looking, listening, tasting, calculating, reflecting, recalling, etc." (ibid., 451).

"It's a truism that one has no option, at the time of choosing, but to go by what one believes."[37] So if we ask, what constitutes a person's doxastic situation? Wolterstorff says, "[o]nly in the light of the complete contour of obligation that holds uniquely for a given person at a given time in her life, and in the light of that person's convictions about the accessibility, acceptability, and promise of various practices of inquiry for removing the deficiencies of belief, can this question be answered."[38]

An individual doxastic situation rests ultimately on an individual's understanding—knowledge or belief—of that situation. Wolterstorff affirms therefore that what a person believes about his situation is the only rationally significant view of that situation. In the end, the result may be that a person holds beliefs irrationally because of a blameworthy view of the doxastic situation. "Entitlement is not directly related to truth-conducivity. It has to do with getting one's doxastic house in order; only indirectly does it have to do with how that house is related to the world outside. So much is this the case that one can imagine situations in which one is not even entitled to believe *what one knows*."[39] The pivotal question is, at bottom, whether a person's beliefs about her situation are entitled beliefs. "The situation is this," Wolterstorff concludes:

> often an agent's beliefs about the character of her belief-system and the contour of her obligations are a crucial component in what it is that makes her not entitled to a certain belief or non-belief, or not entitled to hold a certain belief in the manner in which she does. And often that remains true even if the beliefs are false, provided that the ignorance that those false beliefs represent is non-culpable ignorance.[40]

---

37. "Entitlement to Believe and Practices of Inquiry," in *Practices of Belief*, 102.

38. Ibid., 108.

39. Ibid., 107. Elsewhere he says something similar: "It may be that even if one had inquired into what one ought to have inquired into, one would still believe exactly as one does now, having failed one's duties. Being right in one's beliefs doesn't necessarily get one off the hook. When it comes to epistemic obligation, it is not beliefs but activities . . . which are fundamental" ("Evidence, Entitled Belief, and the Gospels," in *Practices of Belief*, 452). And yet, "from the fact that there is the disparity noted between truth and entitlement and between truth and obligatory practices of inquiry, we must not jump to the conclusion that entitlement has nothing to do with truth. Practices of inquiry are ways of finding things out, or believed to be ways of finding something out. And ways of finding things out are ways of getting at the truth of the matter" ("On Being Entitled to Beliefs about God," in *Practices of Belief*, 330).

40. Ibid., 106.

With this in place, we are now able to appreciate more fully Wolterstorff's notion of belief entitlement.[41] A person is constantly forming beliefs. Belief-forming faculties, supposing they are working well, are constantly at work. Furthermore, belief-forming faculties are perpetually developing, both naturally—by 'design'—and in response to personal experience. And as we have seen, those faculties are governable in many ways. A person is able to so direct his belief-forming faculties as to responsibly handle himself in a doxastic situation. In any particular situation, particular sets both of beliefs and of means of doxastic action are available to a person, that availability being shaped by social and personal availability and social and personal standards of acceptability.

But we must also account for faulty belief-forming faculties.[42] A person's responsibility, particularly in light of the potential for non-truth-conducive faculties, is to monitor his doxastic activities toward a goal of getting in touch with reality as best he can, as best as can rightly be expected of him.[43] One should remember, furthermore, that the alethic obligation should not be enforced in isolation from the rest of a person's obligations. And so, our noetic obligation is, relative to relevant propositions, "to do as well as can be rightly demanded of us so as to bring it about that we believe them if they are true and disbelieve them if they are false," remembering that "[o]ur noetic obligations arise from the whole diversity of obligations that we have in our concrete situations."[44]

---

41. As noted in the introduction to chapter 2 and in section §2.1, entitlement is the chief epistemic desideratum of Wolterstorff's theory of rationality. We may often read Wolterstorff denying that "rationality" or "justification" is this or that, and, conversely, affirming that "rationality" or "justification" is something else. I believe that in the majority of cases we may understand him to be speaking of what in other places he calls "entitlement." Andrew Sloane agrees: "Wolterstorff's notion of *entitlement* . . . in fact, is simply a clarification of his prior criterion of *rationally justified belief* which avoids the potentially misleading words *rational* and *justification*, without substantially altering its central tenets . . . *rational justification* is the terminology he uses in his earlier and most extensive published treatments of the issue" (*On Being a Christian*, 96).

42. On the notion of faulty belief-forming faculties, see "Can Belief in God Be Rational," 247–48.

43. In this regard, Wolterstorff makes a distinction important for the deontology he wishes to maintain in his theory of rationality: "Doing one's best may be more than can rightly be asked of one—well beyond the call of duty . . . What seems rather to be the case is that each of us has the obligation with respect to certain propositions *to do as well as can rightly be demanded* of us so as to bring it about that we believe them if they are true and disbelieve them if they are false. Of course, the concept of doing as well as can rightly be demanded of one is, unlike that of doing one's best, a deontological concept" ("Can Belief in God Be Rational," in *Practices of Belief*, 231).

44. "Can Belief in God Be Rational," in *Practices of Belief*, 231.

Responsible doxastic behavior takes the form of rightly monitoring one's doxastic activities and asking, "[w]hich deficiencies in one's system of beliefs is on obligated to remove or forestall, or try?"[45] In other words, "we are looking at the person who already has an array of beliefs, so as to give him and others a criterion for picking out those that are rational for him to hold from those that are not. What we are after is not rules for the direction of the mind but a criterion for separating one's rational beliefs from one's non-rational beliefs."[46]

A belief which is responsibly formed (and thus rationally held) is a belief which is formed using the appropriate practice(s) of inquiry, when a person holds responsibly formed beliefs both about his ethico-doxastic situation and about the appropriateness of the practice(s) in question. Such a belief is an entitled belief. Conversely, "[b]eliefs to which one is not entitled are beliefs that are consequences of culpable negligence."[47] Elsewhere he says, ". . . a person S is *entitled* to his belief that *p* just in case S believes *p*, and there's no doxastic practice D pertaining to *p* such that S ought to have implemented D and S did not, or S ought to have implemented D better than S did."[48] And in another place, "Let us say that someone is *fully entitled* to some belief of theirs if it represents no failure of governance obligations on their belief."[49]

We have come a long way from the abstract, impersonal doxastic subject, and from an abstract, de-personalized view of facts and entitled beliefs. As we have seen, Wolterstorff reconfigures, we might say, the entire ontological and epistemological framework within which theories of rationality are forged. And he goes so far as to point out that situationality is our epistemological starting point: provided a person's beliefs about her doxastic situation are not culpable in some way, that subjective point of view just is the relevant doxastic situation.

In the next section, with this picture of doxastic situationality in place, we begin to pry into the question of moral value. What we find, in effect, is

---

45. "Entitlement to Believe and Practices of Inquiry," in *Practices of Belief*, 103. He continues: "I think John Locke was right when he said that the answer varies from person to person. For The Human Being as Such, there is no answer. It all depends. Only in the light of the complete contour of obligation that holds uniquely for a given person at a given time in her life, and in the light of that person's convictions about the accessibility, acceptability, and promise of various practices of inquiry for removing the deficiencies of belief, can this question be answered."

46. "Can Belief in God Be Rational," in *Practices of Belief*, 245–46.

47. "Entitlement to Believe and Practices of Inquiry," in *Practices of Belief*, 90.

48. *Divine Discourse*, 272.

49. "Evidence, Belief, and the Gospels," in *Practices of Belief*, 453.

3.3 DOXASTIC OBLIGATION AND THE QUESTION OF MORAL VALUE

The subject of this concluding section of chapter 3 is doxastic obligation and moral value. The goal is to raise the question of moral value, specifically, how to account for it. We shall work our way toward this question by, first, examining Wolterstorff's claim that there are no specifically, exclusively, doxastic norms. There are no specifically doxastic norms because epistemic rationality (or doxastic normativity) is parasitic on the broader moral situation of the subject, as we have seen. So Wolterstorff's situated rationality is incorporated within a situated ethic. That ethic is situated, but not relativistic. So even though no two moral situations are identical, all situations are of a moral kind. Wolterstorff appears to believe that all unique moral situations share a single moral foundation, one which goes largely, though not entirely, unnamed in his work on epistemology and rationality. In this section, we will see that similarities between ethico-doxastic situations refute the charge of relativism and lead us toward the question of universal moral value and thus to the biblical ethical vision of shalom, which is introduced in the following chapter.

The platonic epistemological tradition is known by its fruit: universal, super-situational doxastic norms. Take, for example, Roderick Chisholm's description of our doxastic duties:

> Each person is subject to two quite different requirements in connection with any proposition he considers: (1) He should try his best to bring it about that if the proposition is true then he believes it; and (2) he should try his best to bring it about that if that proposition is false then he not believe it.[50]

That one should avoid believing falsehood and pursue truth is relatively uncontroversial.[51] But what about the duty to test *each proposition a person considers* to *the best of one's ability*? Wolterstorff finds this plainly impractical: "Suppose, upon looking at a bean bag, that the thought crosses

---

50. Chisholm, *Theory of Knowledge*, 15, quoted by Wolterstorff, "Can Belief in God Be Rational," in *Practices of Belief*, 228.

51. Wolterstorff says, "[B]oth goals are necessary: the goal of increasing one's stock of true beliefs and the goal of avoiding or eliminating false beliefs" ("Can Belief in God Be Rational," in *Practices of Belief*, 229).

my mind that it contains exactly 2,019 beans. . . . Is not the acquisition of true, and the avoidance of false, belief on this matter so unimportant to my life that I have no such obligation . . .?"[52] Wolterstorff's *reductio* response raises several objections to Chisholm's formulation.

It cannot possibly be the case that all propositions deserve the same level of attention. The situations are rare indeed that rightly formed beliefs about the number of beans in a bag are among the more urgent socio-doxastic duties of any person. Typically, many other beliefs that cross our minds will obviously merit more attention. Consequently, giving all propositions equal attention may result in an unethical imbalance in our handling of our doxastic duty: ". . . doing one's best with respect to some [propositions] may interfere with doing one's duty with respect to others."[53] Furthermore, Wolterstorff adds, "[m]any of the things we believe, and ought to believe, have never been *considered* by us. Considering is involved in only some modes of belief acquisition."[54] Chisholm's formulation of doxastic duty neglects variety in the modes of belief acquisition and crucial distinctions between the relative importance of propositions.

As Wolterstorff notes, "[w]e do not have obligations of rationality concerning reality's entire stock of propositions."[55] The reason we do not, simply put, is that "the ones [the obligations] each of us does have are always situated obligations. They are contextual obligations. . . . each person's configuration of tasks and obligations is unique."[56] To the distinction between the importance of various propositions we must add subjective situationality: no two arrangements of doxastic duty are identical. Rationality is "very much a matter of where that person is situated in the space of moral obligation."[57] Belief obligations, in other words, are simply the doxastic refractions and implications of obligations in general, obligations which are always situationally individualized. "What I have argued," Wolterstorff says,

> is that the 'ethic of belief'—if we wish to speak thus—is grounded in the ethic of practices of inquiry and of ways of finding out. And I have assumed throughout that to discern whether a

---

52. Ibid., 230.

53. Ibid., 231.

54. Ibid., 230. I would suggest that the considered acquisition of beliefs is by far the minority mode of belief acquisition. For example, if I pause to reflect on what, at any single moment, I take to be true—if I pause to inventory my present stock of beliefs—certainly the vast preponderance of propositions I take to be true are so taken without focused consideration or without any consideration at all.

55. Ibid.

56. Ibid.

57. "Entitlement to Believe and Practices of Inquiry," in *Practices of Belief*, 105.

person ought to have employed some practice of inquiry, one does not consult some supposed doxastic obligations but consults his ethical obligations, his legal obligations, his professional obligations, and so forth.[58]

A fair account of doxastic obligations, Wolterstorff argues, must take into account the full scope of obligation in terms of a person's relationships and responsibilities. The implication is that there can be no norms bearing solely and exclusively on the act of believing any more than there can be norms bearing solely and exclusively on seeing, speaking, or locomotion. "My reason for not postulating and appealing to distinct doxastic norms is my conviction . . . that there are no such norms. There is no ethic of belief constituting a distinct realm of normativity analogous to the ethical, the legal, the professional, the ecological, the religious, and so forth." Even though, he concedes, "[t]he supposition to the contrary is tempting . . ."[59] And a few pages later he writes, "[o]bligations to employ practices of inquiry are *personally situated* obligations. . . . And they are moral, legal, professional, ecological, and religious obligations. The whole worried discussion about the relativity or non-relativity of doxastic norms is misconceived. There are no such norms."[60]

Obligation in general, moral deontology, then, is situational and subjectively conditioned. No two people find themselves within precisely identical webs of moral accountability. Given varying personal and sociohistorical factors, and deeper epistemological and ontological pre-commitments, moral obligation is irreducibly situational and subjective.[61]

58. Ibid., 109.
59. Ibid.
60. Ibid., 111.
61. The following rather lengthy summary outlines the full situationality of doxastic deontology along those lines: "The fact that entitlement is a mostly local affair is the consequence of three distinct but interacting factors. For one thing, which features of my system of belief I am obligated at a particular time to try to forestall or eliminate is a function of the whole contour of my obligations at the time, a function of where I am situated in the total space of obligation. Sometimes the fact that I have only an imprecise knowledge of the time of day makes no difference whatsoever; at other times, I am under obligation to remove the imprecision. Second, which features of my system of belief I am obligated to try to forestall or eliminate at a particular time is a function of which practices of inquiry are then socially available to me, which of those are personally accessible and acceptable, and which of those, by my non-culpable lights, show sufficient promise of forestalling or eliminating the offending feature if employed. . . . And third, included under the preceding but worth singling out for special mention is this: which features of my belief system I am obligated to try to forestall or eliminate at a particular time is a function not just of my generically human 'hard-wiring' but also of my personal 'programming' as a belief-former at the time. In short, variations

But if it is subjective, is it subjectivism? Is situationalism relativism? "No," Wolterstorff says unequivocally, "the position I have been defending is not relativism."[62] There are a number of ways to vindicate Wolterstorff's negative response to the charge of relativism.

Wolterstorff himself, at one point, raises "the skeptical question," namely, "how can we ever know whether or not our beliefs correspond to the facts?"[63] The problem, it would seem, is that according to his own Reidian doxastic anthropology, "[b]eliefs are not the outcome simply of reality's impact on our hard-wired dispositions for belief-formation but the outcome of reality's impact on our hard-wiring *plus our programming, with all its glitches*."[64] So, how can we ever be sure that we have true knowledge or even trustworthy beliefs?

Wolterstorff offers two points in response. He says, "First, the skeptical conclusion . . . rests on incoherence. If we have no way of telling where our programmed self leaves off and our presumptively reliable indigenous self takes over, then of course we cannot know that there are glitches in our doxastic programmings."[65] Then he adds, ". . . second, we must not allow our examples to lead us into concluding or assuming that our doxastic programming only functions obstructively; much of it also functions *accessively*."[66] So, in conclusion, "contrary to what our sociologists of knowledge tell us, our programming, though it sometimes constitutes a barrier between us a reality, is often if not usually a means of access."[67]

Elsewhere Wolterstorff explains that "[w]hat may give the impression of relativism is that I have defended a version of *situationalism* with respect to entitlement."[68] Wolterstorff provides, here again, two responses to the charge of relativism. He says, "I have not argued for the truth of situationalism regarding entitlement in general . . . what I have done is argue that, *for*

---

from person to person in available, accessible, acceptable, and promising practices, and variations from person to person in programming and belief-formation—these are the factors that account for the fact that entitlement is a mainly local affair" ("On Being Entitled to Beliefs about God," in *Practices of Belief*, 315).

62. On Being Entitled to Beliefs about God," 331. He also says, "Nothing I have said requires the profession of 'anything goes'" (*Reason within the Bounds*, 56).

63. "Historicizing the Belief-forming Self," in *Practices of Belief*, 137. This essay is a revised version of an essay with the same title that appears in Crisp, Davidson, and Vander Laan, eds., *Knowledge and Reality: Essays in Honor of Alvin Plantinga*, 111–35.

64. "Historicizing the Belief-Forming Self," in *Practices of Belief*, 137. See §2.5 of the present study.

65. Ibid., 138.

66. Ibid.

67. Ibid.

68. "On Being Entitled to Beliefs about God," in *Practices of Belief*, 332.

very many propositions, the situationalist thesis is true for believings *of those propositions*."⁶⁹

What does Wolterstorff mean exactly? If the situational nature of belief entitlement applies to only some propositions—if there is at least one proposition which is *not* situationally entitled—then there is either at least one proposition the believing of which is universally entitled or at least one proposition the believing of which is never entitled (or both). For a defense against the charge of relativism, either option will do (or both). Either way, we may suppose that Wolterstorff is suggesting that there are some propositions the believing of which is always entitled. This is because the proposition that there are some propositions the believing of which is never entitled is itself a proposition the believing of which might be always entitled. The implication clearly is that, while no two situations are identical, there are at least some beliefs that are always entitled. There is some degree of common—even universal—entitlement which links all situations, such as, for example, the ethico-doxastic significance of ethico-doxastic situationality.

He then adds this argument: "What must be distinguished from both relativism and situationalism with respect to entitlement is whether there can be entitled disagreement about whether a case of belief is entitled. I hold that there definitely can be."⁷⁰ If relativism were true, no entitled disagreement would be possible; but Wolterstorff affirms that entitled disagreement is possible.⁷¹

69. Ibid., 332–33; emphasis added.
70. Ibid., 333.
71. I see two ways of reading this argument. First, if he is claiming that entitled disagreement is precisely the thing precluded by relativism, I would have to confess that this is not how understand relativism. Earlier in the same discussion, Wolterstorff says, "[r]elativism in general is a response of a certain sort to a situation in which it's claimed of a given entity at a certain time that it has a certain property and also claimed of it that it lacks that property at the same time . . . It's the response which says that both claims are true because it is two different relational properties that are being attributed to the thing in question. Relative to Mary, Joe is tall; relative to Herbet, Joe is short" ("On Being Entitled to Beliefs about God," in *Practices of Belief*, 331–32). So Wolterstorff says that relativism is the relativizing of a property in order to avoid contradiction. To my understanding, this is not what is meant by relativism. If relativism is, as one standard source has it, "the denial that there are certain kinds of universal truths," then *truth* would be the single property that is relativized (Pojman, "Relativism," in *Cambridge Dictionary of Philosophy*, 799). If that were the case, then the proposition "Relative to Mary, Joe is tall," would be both true and false. So it would seem that entitled disagreement—entitled contradiction, even—is rather a textbook instance of relativism, rather than demonstration that relativism is false as Wolterstorff suggests. But there is a second way of reading Wolterstorff here, which fairs much better, in my view. Perhaps his point is that two people can entitledly hold beliefs which are contradictory because entitlement is not an abstract matter concerning the de-personalized relation between

In another place, Wolterstorff explains his position thus, clearly affirming some universal aspect of justification:

> I hold that in a similar way, there are norms for justified belief which hold universally in theorizing. The classical foundationalist *formulation* of that universal norm is untenable. Likewise the historicist formulation of that universal norm is untenable. But from this I do not conclude that there *is* no universal norm. Further, I hold out the hope of *formulating* it, of formulating a general criterion, not just for rationality in scientific belief, but for rationality—intellectual justification—in general.[72]

He says, more concretely, "[w]hat I in my situation am held responsible by God for doing and believing is not determined by what I and others *believe* on the matter; it is determined simply by what God does in fact hold me responsible for."[73]

And in another place, he affirms directly that similarities obtain between situations:

> This is not to be taken to imply that no generalizations are possible concerning deficiencies in belief that persons are under obligation to remove, nor must it be taken to imply that no generalizations are possible concerning ways of finding out and practices of inquiry that they are obligated to employ. Though each of us occupies a unique position in the space of moral obligation, among our positions there are similarities.[74]

---

beliefs. Entitlement is instead about the relationship of persons to their believings. ("Justification . . . is not a relation between propositions. It is a relation between a *person and some one of his believings*" ["Can Belief in God Be Rational," in *Practices of Belief*, 241].) It would be easier to see then how this formulation avoids relativism: entitlement is not about truth; it accrues to the holding of beliefs only by non-omniscient epistemic subjects. It is purely adverbial to the act of believing, to put it one way. Entitlement and relativism never cross paths.

72. "On Avoiding Historicism," 184. This short piece is a response to a critical review of *Reason within the Bounds* by Edward J. Echeverria, entitled, "Towards a Critique of the Subject." Both pieces were published in *Philosophia Reformata*.

73. Ibid.

74. "Entitlement to Believe," in *Practices of Belief*, 105. He also says, "The fundamental contour of my position on entitlement is thus non-relativism combined with a broad situationalism." Notice, further, "What must be distinguished from both relativism and situationalism with respect to entitlement is whether there can be entitled disagreement about whether a case of belief is entitled. I hold that there definitely can be" ("On Being Entitled to Beliefs about God," in *Practices of Belief*, 333; see also the section entitled "It is Relativism?," in ibid., 331–33).

In addition to these direct denials, there are a number of other ways in which a denial of relativism may be inferred from Wolterstorff's discussion of entitlement. For one, Wolterstorff formulates a universal criterion for situated entitlement.[75] Were he a relativist, no such criterion would be possible.

For another, recall that an important part of Wolterstorff's theory of rationality is a universal alethic obligation, the obligation to get more amply in touch with reality as best as can be expected of one. This obligation is universal, though it is manifest situationally, and even conditioned situationally by other competing desiderata. Sloane notes this as well: "rationality is both situation and person specific, and also generalized, for every individual's obligations-in-general have features that are unique to that individual as well as those that are common to all people." To be specific, "[i]t is because our general obligations require us to become more closely in touch with some relevant aspect of reality that we are obliged to do so."[76]

We may also infer a general metaphysical realism particularly from one feature of situated rationality, Wolterstorff's Reidian doxastic optimism.[77] It is *to reality* that our belief-forming dispositions and the dispositions to form dispositions respond, and upon this interaction with reality Wolterstorff rests a general alethic optimism.[78] Wolterstorff's doxastic optimism also rests upon theological realism: it is because our belief-forming faculties are so designed by God, that we can trust them to be, on the whole, truth-conducive. We might also infer theological realism from what appears in this statement, quoted previously, to be deontological objectivism: "What I in my situation am held responsible by God for doing and believing is

---

75. "Can Belief in God Be Rational," in *Practices of Belief*, 254; *Divine Discourse*, 272.

76. Sloane, *On Being a Christian*, 103. See Wolterstorff, "Can Belief in God Be Rational," in *Practices of Belief*, 228–31.

77. See section §2.5 of the present study.

78. Wolterstorff says, "Nothing I have said requires the repudiation of truth as a legitimate and attainable goal of inquiry," and "[n]othing I have said requires the profession of cosmic agnosticism" (*Reason within the Bounds*, 56). Sloane also discussions Wolterstorff's metaphysical realism: "One of the crucial ways in which Wolterstorff is able to avoid relativism, despite his defeasible person- and situation-specific epistemology is by embracing a (critical) realist stance on the existence of theoretical entities" (*On Being a Christian*, 193). Sloane also offers a defense of Wolterstorff's realism (ibid., 192–99). "Essential to Wolterstorff's metaphysical realism," he argues, "is the assertion that reality has a structure which is largely independent of human beings, which we are nonetheless able to grasp in our believings" (196).

not determined by what I and others *believe* on the matter; it is determined simply by what God does in fact hold me responsible for."[79]

In all situations, the subject is obligated to get as amply in touch with reality—with truth—as can be rightly expected of him. Truth, in situational manifestations, bears universal deontological value. And yet, even the deontological weight of truth is often conditioned by competing concerns. (Recall the issue with one's belief that there are 2,019 beans.) So our obligation to truth is sometimes surpassed or conditioned by the deontological weight of other concerns. And it would be a curious thing if Wolterstorff denied relativism but named no single thing which was not subjectively or situationally defined. Failure to name a unifying concern would test the tenability of his denial of radical subjectivism. So what is it, exactly, which allows Wolterstorff, on the one hand, to deny relativism, but on the other, to maintain universal ethico-doxastic normativity?

John Locke, Wolterstorff observes, grounds the obligation to truth thus: "the temporal and eternal well-being of oneself and others depends on discovering the truth on such matters."[80] Although Locke appears often to preach the categorical value of knowledge of religious truth (or evidentially secure religious belief), he also defends the instrumental value of rightly conducting one's doxastic activities toward religious truth *for the sake of social well-being*. Wolterstorff expresses preference for the second, the instrumental, approach, and adds this clarification: "More than well-being is involved: honoring the dignity of oneself and of the other is also involved." So, he adds, "if Locke's comment, thus modified, is correct, then discovering the truth on matters of morality and religion is not a fundamental categorical duty but an instrumental duty."[81] It is instrumental toward honoring oneself and others.

In another place, Wolterstorff affirms the priority of faithful obedience to the authority of God over the demands of epistemic rationality:

> From the fact that it is not rational for some person to believe that God exists it does not follow that he ought to give up that belief.... Perhaps, in spite of its rationality for him, the person ought to continue believing that God exists. Perhaps it is our duty to believe more firmly that God exists than any proposition that conflicts with this, and/or more firmly than we believe

---

79. "On Avoiding Historicism," 184. Sloane writes, "His central reason for rejection epistemological anarchy, relativism and antinomianism is this: God exists: he has created a real world which exists independently of our observing it: he has created us with the capacity to come to know this world" (*On Being a Christian*, 109).

80. "Entitlement to Believe," in *Practices of Belief*, 109.

81. Ibid., 110.

that a certain proposition *does* conflict with it. Of course, for a
believer who is a member of the modern Western intelligentsia
to have his theistic convictions prove non-rational is to be put
into a deeply troubling situation. There is a biblical category
that applies to such a situation. It is a *trial*, which the believer is
called to endure. Sometimes suffering is a trial. May it not also
be that sometimes the non-rationality of one's conviction that
God exists is a trial, to be endured?[82]

In relationships with God, with others, and with oneself, the obligation to truth is incorporated into a fuller set of relational obligations which are defined not abstractly but according to the persons themselves in relationship. The surpassing standard of doxastic deontology is peace and fulfillment in these relationships. So far as the attainment of true beliefs promotes the well-being of others and of oneself, and of one's social context in general, we are obligated to seek that attainment (as far as can rightly be expected); so far as it is pious to do so, the Christian is to do the best that can be expected of him to believe true things about God. Regarding the proposition that God exists, that obligation is steadfast; regarding the proposition that

---

82. "Can Belief in God Be Rational," in *Practices of Belief*, 263. The use of the term "rational" here is ambiguous. The argument of this section is that, according to Wolterstorff, doxastic normativity never stands alone; it is inextricably woven into the moral fabric of a person's situation broadly understood. In other words, rationality is always practical rationality. Furthermore, this section raises important indications that practical rationality is for Wolterstorff relational duty to oneself, others, and God (as this quotation indicates). Wolterstorff rejects therefore the notion of a purely epistemic rationality in favor of one always linked to relational and practical rationality. So on the one hand, we may say that rationality (doxastic normativity), especially if we take it merely to mean alethic obligation, is trumped by religious or relational practical rationality; on the other, we may say that rationality, as Wolterstorff is redefining the term, is a religious and ethical notion through and through. (We are following Wolterstorff in substituting rational justification for entitlement. See section §2.1.) But both are true if we allow ambiguity in the use of the term "rational." So in this quotation, though it appears that Wolterstorff is arguing that religious duties, personal duties to God, surpass rational obligations, it should be observed that "rationality" here refers to a notion Wolterstorff is rejecting, one that takes universal alethic obligations to be the sole epistemic desideratum. I would rather say that, in this passage, Wolterstorff is redefining rationality by denying that alethic obligations are the sole or even the leading epistemic desiderata. Rationality, for Wolterstorff, is always and everywhere religious and relational; for this reason he speaks of belief entitlement instead of rational justification. Sloane says that for Wolterstorff there is a point at which rationality stops and religious duty continues, so that one may be religiously obligated to believe something that is non-rational. In explaining it thus, he holds fast to the alethically heavy notion of rationality which Wolterstorff rejects. Sloane says, "This 'doing as well as can rightly be demanded of us' means that there are situations in which truth is not our primary concern, and so rationality may need to be sacrificed for the sake of a higher obligation" (*On Being a Christian*, 104).

others and oneself deserve respect and honor, the obligation is again non-negotiable. But these relationships cannot be reduced to alethic obligations. Nor can interpersonal rights and duties against the other simply be traded for epistemic, alethic ones. So for Wolterstorff, epistemic rationality is subordinate to moral rationality; doxastic normativity is incorporated within a relational ethic which honors God and the dignity of persons.

The deontology of the doxastic life serves the deontology of the moral life in general. And what is Wolterstorff's view of the moral life in general? He takes it to be the sum of the religious and social duties of persons, who, in their unique situations, are accountable to God's purpose for humankind, his goal of human fulfillment. "It would seem," Wolterstorff says,

> that human fulfillment is to be found in what we experience when we love God with our whole life, when we love our neighbors as ourselves, when we act as responsible stewards of nature. It would seem that in enjoining us to act thus with respect to himself, neighbor, self, and nature, God is enjoining us to participate in his own cause of human fulfillment . . . immediately at hand in the Christian Scriptures is a better concept for describing God's goal for human existence . . . The concept I have in mind is the concept of *peace*—in Hebrew, *shalom* . . . The goal of human existence is that man should dwell at peace in all his relationships: with God, with himself, with his fellows, with nature.[83]

Shalom is the bedrock notion for situated rationality. Wolterstorff rejects a notion of epistemic rationality which enforces a universal, super-situational alethic obligation. He offers instead a personally and socially defined situationality which brings to bear shalom obligations on a person's entire moral context. Doxastic deontology is merely an aspect of shalom-situated deontology, within which a personally and socially constituted notion of belief entitlement is the chief desideratum. One is entitled to one's believings so long as those believings do not violate any of one's shalom obligations to God, to others, to oneself, or to the world. This, in brief, is Wolterstorff's notion of situated rationality.

In the following two chapters, I examine shalom and its theological roots and religious significance, and then take a look at how it bears on individuals in terms specifically of the life of the mind. Shalom is theologically and biblical drawn, so we begin our analysis of it in chapter 4 by reflecting upon its biblical roots and its place in Christian theology (§4.2). I then compare shalom to its close cousin, the neo-Calvinist creation-order

---

83. *Reason within the Bounds*, 112, 113–14.

tradition (§4.3 and §4.4). Perhaps most informative in terms of the essence and significance of shalom is the final section of chapter 4 in which I examine Wolterstorff's arguments for the integration of shalom into the life of the church both in terms of its worship and liturgy and its engagement with the world (§4.5).

4

The Comprehensive Ethic of Shalom

My thesis in chapters 4 and 5 is that Wolterstorff's concept of "shalom" provides the ethical substance which our analysis of situated rationality still awaits. Shalom is both the ethical foundation of situated rationality and its ethical *telos*. Put differently, shalom is a biblical vision of how the world ought to be which suggests, as a feature of its comprehensive vision, a situational approach to rationality such as the one Wolterstorff proposes. Additionally, situated rationality embodies the ethic of shalom by conceiving of the rational status of doxastic practices in terms of shalom conducivity. Shalom, in effect, is the value theory upon which rests the whole enterprise of doxastic behavior and deontology in Wolterstorff's theory of situated rationality. Chapter 4 presents a study of shalom against its biblical, theological, and neo-Calvinist background, and in terms of the relationship between a shalom ethic and liturgy. Chapter 5 is devoted to drawing the connection between shalom and the ethics of belief.

I devote the second section of the present chapter to defining shalom (§4.1). Wolterstorff has written about shalom in numerous publications over the course of more than thirty years.[1] Most of these treatments are, however, relatively light: there is no single book length analysis to date, and

---

1. From as early as the second edition of *Reason within the Bounds*, published in 1984, and the Kuyper Lectures at the Free University of Amsterdam in 1981 (published as *Until Justice and Peace Embrace*), through to his most recent work, Wolterstorff's thought on shalom and its biblical roots is remarkably consistent. For this reason, I have opted for a synthetic reading of Wolterstorff on this topic.

even though much of his recent work treats relevant topics such as human rights, the nature of justice, and political theology directly and in considerable detail, none of this literature offers an isolated chapter or even a single chapter section devoted to explicating shalom.² Shalom itself, as we will see Wolterstorff himself explain (chapter 5), does not look favorably on the exclusively theoretical life, and so, perhaps for this reason, Wolterstorff himself has not given in to this temptation. That is to say, while there is no book-length analysis of shalom itself, a substantial portion of Wolterstorff's production is in fact both explanatory of it, and driven by its ethos.

The ability to allow the application of shalom, instead of its theoretical exposition, to take center stage is to some extent the blessing of precedent. Shalom is consistent with many themes in North American and Dutch neo-Calvinism in the tradition of Abraham Kuyper, such as the so-called creation order tradition which has roots in Toronto, Grand Rapids, and ultimately Amsterdam. But it is also evident that Wolterstorff believes shalom to be the plain teaching of the Christian Scriptures and so ought to be a mainstay of Christian theology (and corrective of specific shortcomings of the creation order tradition, to be discussed below). If indeed it is so plain, merely drawing attention to the relevant themes and most telltale passages of Scripture along with the most salient theological topics should save Wolterstorff the trouble of inventing shalom out of thin air or building it from the ground up, and relieve him of the burden of defending it at great length. And in fact, Wolterstorff's writing on shalom features precisely these emphases on scripture, theology, and ethical self-consciousness. Here I address them in the following order: indications that shalom is the central or governing theme of the biblical narrative and biblically grounded theology (§4.2), a give and take with neo-Calvinism (§4.3), and an argument for the integration of shalom into the life of the church in its theology and its worship (§4.4). Careful attention to each of these themes will produce a well-rounded picture of Wolterstorff's notion of shalom.

The burden of the fifth chapter will then be to re-introduce situated rationality and to articulate in detail the connection between it and shalom. Examining Wolterstorff's view of the implications of shalom for theorizing and scholarship, we are perhaps not surprised to discover his view that theorizing and scholarship, both in theory and in praxis, should advance and embody the ethic of shalom. We see, furthermore, that Wolterstorff's

2. Examples include *Justice: Rights and Wrongs*; *Justice in Love*; *The Mighty and the Almighty: An Essay in Political Theology*; and *Understanding Liberal Democracy: Essays in Political Philosophy*. On the other hand, one might argue that the subject matter of most of this literature is in fact shalom, in theory and in practice. That none of these books has the word "shalom" in the title certainly does not preclude that possibility.

insistence that theorizing is not an exclusively academic, ivory tower undertaking. On the contrary, everyone theorizes. From this point it becomes clear that what Wolterstorff says in terms of shalom theorizing and scholarship applies more broadly in terms of shalom believing, belief-formation, monitoring doxastic behaviors, and so on; we thus find ourselves before a shalom ethic of belief and the fundamental moral aspects of situated rationality which were until this point only implicit. The value of this apparently circuitous approach to my thesis should at that point become clear: connecting shalom with situated rationality will be both demanded by the way in which Wolterstorff conceives of scholarly theorizing as through and through a shalom undertaking, and theoretically fluid, since we will begin to see how several shalom categories—the dignity of the human person, the fallenness of the humanity, the moral significance of social institutions and practices, and others—are integral to Wolterstorff's situated rationality. This sort of denouement is the goal of chapter 5.

We may note at this point that the theological underpinnings of shalom are, due to the organic relation between shalom and theorizing and between theorizing and the doxastic life in general, also the underpinnings of Wolterstorff's situated rationality. And if shalom is a theological vision, or a theologically grounded notion, and if situated rationality is drawn from the ethic and vision of shalom, situated rationality is also theologically infused and represents, therefore, a distinctly theistic approach to the ethics of belief. Noting the theological roots of shalom, therefore, raises once again the question I introduced in chapter 1, of the relationship between the truth of Christian belief and the situated rationality of Christian belief.[3] But we are getting ahead of ourselves. What, exactly, is shalom?

4.1 SHALOM: SEEKING A DEFINITION

Shalom is the preeminent ethical vision for all humans as creatures of God. It is both a vision of the way things ought to be and a vision of the way all people ought to conduct themselves, or the end for which all people were meant by God their creator to guide their thoughts, words, and actions. Shalom is a comprehensive ethical vision, drawn from the Christian scriptures, which promotes justice and demands protection for persons:

> To guide our thoughts, we need some vision yet more comprehensive . . . is there some comprehensive vision that can serve to orient those reflections and thereby keep us from losing our

---

3. See section §1.3.

way? . . . I think there is. It is the vision of *shalom—peace—*first articulated in the Old Testament poetic and prophetic literature but then coming to expression in the New Testament as well. We shall see that shalom is intertwined with justice. In shalom, each person enjoys justice, enjoys his or her rights. There is no shalom without justice. But shalom goes beyond justice.[4]

"Shalom is," first, peace: "the human being dwelling at peace in all his or her relationships: with God, with self, with fellows, with nature."[5] Shalom is more than the mere absence of conflict, however. Wolterstorff insists that justice is necessary but not sufficient for the realization of shalom. It is conceivable that, even given the establishment of perfect justice, human life and enjoyment may yet be stifled, and cultural flourishing stagnant. So shalom requires justice, and freedoms of different sorts, but, in its full and true realization, it goes beyond justice: shalom is "enjoyment" of the relationships constitutive of human life in the world.

But the peace which is shalom is not merely the absence of hostility, not merely being in right relationship. Shalom at its highest is *enjoyment* in one's relationships. A nation may be at peace with all its neighbors and yet be miserable in its poverty. To dwell in shalom is to *enjoy* living before God, to *enjoy* living in one's physical surroundings, to *enjoy* living with one's fellows, to *enjoy* life with oneself.[6]

Evidently, to some extent Wolterstorff envisions a web of organically connected relationships. One's relationships to God, to others, to nature, and to one's self weave together and, ideally, resonate in concert a realized shalom harmony and creational flourishing. And yet he affirms a particular economy among these relationships: Shalom requires peace and enjoyment within human relationships and within man's relationship to nature, but "shalom," Wolterstorff says, "in the first place incorporates right, harmonious

---

4. *Until Justice and Peace Embrace*, 69. This section is republished in *Hearing the Call: Liturgy, Justice, Church, and World: Essays by Nicholas Wolterstorff*, 109–13.

5. Ibid. One often encounters a threefold relational context for shalom in Wolterstorff's writing: God, society, and nature or world. The addition of the "self" in this quotation is unusual, and in a sense redundant. In section §4.3, I discuss the Kuyperian origin of this formulation.

6. Ibid., 69–70. Notice in the quotation that being "miserable" in "poverty" is inconsistent with shalom. Misery per se, *simpliciter*, is, it is clear enough, an impediment to shalom. Wolterstorff gives particular attention to issues of poverty in a number of places. See, for example, chapter 4 of *Until Justice and Peace Embrace*, "The Rich and the Poor," and the brief article "The Moral Significance of Poverty." An expanded version of the latter essay was published in *Hearing the Call*, 287–96.

relationships to *God* and delight in his service.... Shalom is perfected when humanity acknowledges that in its service of God is true delight."[7]

Wolterstorff adds that shalom cannot be achieved simply by convincing people that they enjoy peace, nor is shalom truly realized if some people feel as though they have all the relational enjoyment they could ask for, when in fact they do not. Shalom requires objectively realized justice. "Shalom cannot be secured in an unjust situation by managing to get all concerned to feel content with their lot in life," lest deception open the door to oppression: "Shalom would not have been present *even if* all the blacks in the United States had been content in their state of slavery; it would not have been present in South Africa *even if* all the blacks there felt happy. It is because shalom is an ethical community that it is wounded when justice is absent."[8]

Wolterstorff speaks here of shalom objectively obtaining; he speaks from what we may call a 'God's eye point of view,' and he does so because shalom is basically theological and drawn from the authoritative revelation in scripture of the God of creation. Wolterstorff indicates what will become clear shortly, that shalom is not the flowering of a contrived and subjective inspiration or of a humanistic or political sublime, but shalom is, ultimately, the real presence and fruition of divinely created design and intention in the created order. The provenance of shalom is the mind and character of the creator God of the Bible. The fact that shalom is grounded in theological ontology warrants Wolterstorff's appeal to shalom as an objective state of affairs.

Wolterstorff will often speak of human "flourishing" as an important aspect of shalom, indicating that he has in mind more than the elimination of impediments to the full enjoyment of life. And so the "Kingdom of Peace" is one in which every human being is not only free to, but actually does enjoy the realization of the full potential of his natural abilities.[9] "What God

---

7. He writes: "Secondly, shalom incorporates right harmonious relationships to other *human beings* and delight in human community. Shalom is absent when a society is a collection of individuals all out to make their own way in the world." And: "Thirdly, shalom incorporates right, harmonious relationships to *nature* and delight in our physical surroundings. Shalom comes when we, bodily creatures and not disembodied souls, shape the world with our labor and find fulfillment in so doing and delight in its results" (ibid., 70).

8. Ibid., 71.

9. Though at times shalom sounds like "the good life," or the Greek ethical ideal of eudaimonia. Wolterstorff prefers not to see it this way. See "Why Eudaimonism Cannot Serve as Framework for a Theory of Rights," in *Justice: Rights and Wrongs*, 149–79. I rather think that the notions of biblical proctology or eschatology might do a better job of connecting shalom with the biblical narrative, but both raise theological questions which could not be adequately addressed here.

desires for God's human creatures is that comprehensive mode of flourishing that is shalom."[10] In brief: shalom requires but is more than justice, and shalom means the enjoyment of relationships and the flourishing of the God-given design and potential of all people.

If shalom as the way things ought to be is given in the natural or created constitution of things, and is thus no ungrounded utopian fantasy, what follows is a theologically informed and rather demanding notion of natural rights. What a person naturally deserves or holds claim to, from the shalom point of view, goes beyond what we might call negative freedom, the absence of impediments to self-fulfillment and life enjoyment. It is rather the actualization of fulfillment and enjoyment of life and self. A person is entitled to and possesses a natural claim to the fulfillment and flourishing of his God-given potential, so that on the relational level, the public aspects of realized shalom are every person's full and harmonious enjoyment of himself and others and the world. Wolterstorff says, for example, "I have a right to a polite answer when I arrive at the clinic and ask where the internal medicine department is located."[11] Clearly there is no such *legal* right, nor does the legal enforcement of such rights bode well for a free society. Shalom-rights are implied in the God-createdness of people and things, and they merely begin—not end—with justice.[12] Shalom rights are the implicit divine intention in the world, in people, and in created things, and they have as their *telos* the full flourishing and enjoyment of creational potential.

What is implied, conversely, by the universality of this claim to fulfillment and life, is the duty of all people, not only not to impede, but to honor, encourage, and to promote the flourishing and enjoyment of others. "[R]ights are always grounded in duties, in responsibilities, in obligations."[13] For a "structure of rights requires, as its correlative, a structure of duties—if I have a right to something, then some person, group, or organization has a duty of some sort. The right grounds account for the duty; someone has a duty on account of my having the right."[14] If one person has the shalom-right to fulfillment and life, it is his neighbor's shalom-obligation, to the

---

10. "Why Care about Justice?," in *Hearing the Call*, 99; originally published in David A Fraser, ed., *Evangelicalism: Surviving Its Success*, 156–67; another version appeared in *The Reformed Journal* in 1986.

11. *Justice: Rights and Wrongs*, 246.

12. The term "shalom rights" is my own. Wolterstorff might say that when someone's rights are honored, that is an aspect of shalom.

13. *Until Justice and Peace Embrace*, 124.

14. "The Moral Significance of Poverty," 9. As noted, an expanded version of this article has been republished in *Hearing the Call*, 287–96. Hereafter I quote from the later publication unless otherwise indicated.

best of his abilities and means while balancing other concerns, to see to the enjoyment of those things for the other. Furthermore it is the shalom-obligation of institutions, or of corporate social bodies, just as well, to advance the shalom of individuals and groups of individuals and of society generally, according to their capacity and design.[15]

More should be said here with regard to Wolterstorff's notion of rights. In chapter 10 of *Justice: Rights and Wrongs*, Wolterstorff seeks a non-circular account of the goods to which one has rights. He says that he wants to "find some character that all these states and events share, a character such that their having that character is not analytically implied by their all being life- and history-goods . . ."[16] In other words, Wolterstorff is interested in an account for basic goods, for those 'aspects of well-being' which constitute the objects or content of rights.[17]

Utilitarian accounts, focusing on desire-satisfaction, and natural law accounts, which depend upon a notion of the good anchored in proper-function, both disappoint. The utilitarian attempt cannot shake the disastrous "stance of the amoralist in judging the worth of person's lives," while surely "some desires . . . are malformed" and surely "those afflicted with

---

15. Wolterstorff attributes his consistent interest in the moral status and spiritual health of institutions to the same historical tendency in Calvinism. He mentions this specifically in an interview published in *Hearing the Call*, entitled, "It's Tied Together by Shalom," where he says, for example, "Growing up in an Americanized version of the Dutch Reformed tradition, as I did, I absorbed the idea that being loyal to, and supportive of, institutions is a fundamental Christian responsibility" (425). Wolterstorff's interest in the morality of institutions extends even to speaking as though impersonal cultural or social institutions are moral agents before God—they are sinful, they promote evil, are accountable and thus 'guilty,' and stand in need of reform. He says, "A fundamental thesis in our discussion is that not only are the individual members of society fallen and in need of reform, but that this is true as well of the structures of society . . . our fundamental social institutions often do things they should not do . . . there are large-scale social practices and a whole system of social roles . . . that cause or perpetuate injustice and misery." *Until Justice and Peace Embrace*, 24. Social institutions are part of the created design for the way things ought to be, perhaps not in themselves—Wolterstorff distances himself from the ontological integrity of institutions characteristic of neo-Calvinism (to be discussed in greater detail in section §4.3 below)—but the ethic of shalom governs institutions and holds them accountable no less than it does persons.

16. *Justice: Rights and Wrongs*, 227. Part II of *Justice: Rights and Wrongs*, comprising chapters 6 through 10, is devoted to "identifying the sorts of goods to which one can have a right" (ibid., 135). Generally speaking, "[r]ights are to states of affairs," which are composed of states and events or, when all goes well, "life- and history-goods" (ibid., 137).

17. Wolterstorff draws a sharp distinction between this locating some essential characteristic and the epistemology of moral goodness: "A characterization of the human good implies next to nothing about an epistemology of our awareness of the human good" (ibid., 237).

irrational, addictive, and immoral desires often have strong higher level desires to be rid of those desires."[18] The natural law account, alternatively, cannot substantiate moral distinctions either: "human beings are capable of making free decisions." So the difference between the person who makes decisions for a supposed "aspect of well-being" and the person who fails to do so or even acts against moral goods is not the distinction between proper and mal-function. "The difference between them is to be tracked not to some malfunction in the latter person but, in both cases, to the person's decision," where that decision-making is always in accord with nature—it is a proper function of the human being.[19]

Alternatively, Wolterstorff proposes as "an example of fantasy realism" an account of goods as those things which God desires for his creatures. Wolterstorff trades the subjective desire-satisfaction of utilitarianism in terms of the desires *of* a person for a divine-desire characterization in terms of God's desire *for* a person or *for* God's creatures: "the goods constitutive of a person's well-being are what God desires for that person's life and history."[20] And "God's overarching desire is that this creature not be treated by other members of its species as if it had less worth than it does have . . ."[21] (More on this worth in a moment.) What God desires for his image-bearers is, in a word, flourishing.[22]

For Wolterstorff, "rights are claims to the good of being treated in certain ways." Those "certain ways" are understood in terms of what promotes and protects flourishing. Additionally, "rights are normative social relationships."[23] In this sense, Wolterstorff says that where there are no social relationships, there are no rights nor violations of rights. A right to some good, he says, is properly defined as a right against other persons' culpably denying me that good which I would otherwise enjoy. There are goods which it would enhance my life to have: I do not have the ability to speak all the languages I would like to be able to speak, and my life would certainly be enhanced if I could. But no person has culpably denied me this good, and so no right has been violated. "The reason the lack of such goods in my life does not represent a violation of my rights is that . . . the lack cannot be traced to the agency of someone who deliberately impaired me." So Wolt-

---

18. Ibid., 232.
19. Ibid., 234.
20. Ibid., 236.
21. Ibid., 235.
22. Wolterstorff explains, "by 'the flourishing life' I mean the life that is both lived well and goes well" (ibid., 145).
23. Ibid., 263.

erstorff says, "[j]ustice and injustice are inherently social. Enjoying what one has a right to, and being deprived of what one has a right to, are social engagements." More expansively, then, "the fundamental structure of a right is that it is a right to the (. . .) good of some action or restraint from action on the part of some person or social entity."[24] In *Justice in Love*, a companion volume to *Justice: Rights and Wrongs*, Wolterstorff brings together this socially constituted notion of justice and rights attendant to inherent worth with a notion of love as care: seeking the shalom of another person is to love that person in the sense of caring about that person.[25] Wolterstorff adds to this the notion that, ultimately, rights are grounded in the inherent worth of human beings as bearers of the divine image.[26]

So, rights and obligations, duties, and responsibilities, are integral to shalom. In shalom, all crooked paths are made straight. And indeed, shalom is even soteriologically significant. Wolterstorff will at times associate salvation itself with shalom renewal and flourishing: "The scope of divine redemption is not just the saving of lost souls but the renewal of life—and more even than that: the renewal of all creation. Redemption is for flourishing."[27]

In sum, "shalom is more than an ethical community. Shalom is the *responsible* community in which God's laws for the multifaceted existence of his creatures are obeyed."[28] "It follows, then, that happiness must be understood in such a way that the enactment of responsibilities is one of its fundamental components." And again, "[a] community of shalom, for one thing, is a responsible community: where shalom exists, there we enact our responsibilities to one another, to God, and to nature."[29]

Shalom is constituted by objectively realized, human flourishing. It is the teleological, cultural realization of all that the human creature is. This realization serves as a governing telos for social ethics and justice here and now. We turn now to shalom and theology.

---

24. Ibid., 286.

25. *Justice in Love*, esp. part 2.

26. See *Justice: Rights and Wrongs*, chapters 14 and 16.

27. "The Grace That Shaped My Life," in *Hearing the Call*, 8–9. This brief autobiographical essay was originally published in *Philosophers Who Believe: The Spiritual Journeys of 11 Leading Thinkers*. He also says, "the Christian gospel, at bottom, is an answer to the question, how can we human beings flourish?" ("It's Tied Together by Shalom," in *Hearing the Call*, 424).

28. *Until Justice and Peace Embrace*, 71.

29. Ibid., 124.

4.2 SHALOM AND THEOLOGY

We have already seen indications that shalom is a theologically rich concept. I propose now to have a closer look at the theological issues surrounding shalom. Wolterstorff distinguishes shalom from what he calls "theo-monistic" views of the Christian life and of the chief end and calling of man. "An ever-beckoning temptation for the Anglo-American evangelical," he warns, "is to assume that all God really cares about for God's human creatures here on earth is that they are born again and thus destined for salvation—to assume that the only kind of lostness God cares about is religious lostness."[30] Wolterstorff believes, first of all, that this view is guilty of a selective hermeneutic: "if we understand the shalom for which God longs in this narrow, pinched way, then all those biblical passages about God's love for justice must remain closed books to us."[31] Reading scripture in this way gives Christianity what Wolterstorff calls an "avertive" orientation.[32] Such an intense focus on transcendent, other-worldly matters allows more immediate and, indeed, biblically central concerns to recede, and the injustice of neglect to take shape. "On this view, God leaves the ninety and nine and goes out in search of that one who is not a believer; but God does not go out in search of the one who is poor, does not go looking for the one who is oppressed."[33]

This unfortunate tendency has, however, not been unique to American Evangelicalism. The medieval or traditional Roman Catholic doctrine of the beatific vision may also be taken in such a way that it undervalues the present order and life in the world, as do the historic Reformed confessions which judge the *telos* of human life to be the glorification and enjoyment of God in eternity.[34] The other-worldliness of these formulations has garnered

---

30. "Why Care about Justice?," in *Hearing the Call*, 99.

31. Ibid.

32. In *Until Justice and Peace Embrace*, Wolterstorff draws a contrast between two basic forms of "salvation religions" in terms of what he calls "avertive" religions, including a "vast array of religions," and "formative" religions, such as historic and neo-Calvinism. He describes the former as maintaining the fundamental value of averting interest in this, "our ordinary existence," and turning toward "a reality outside oneself which is higher, better, more real." In formative religions, "there is also the apprehension of something inferior in our ordinary existence, but in which, rather than acquiescing in this inferiority and then turning away, one seeks its reformation" (5). He later affirms that "It is obvious that Calvin's formulation of the true goal of human existence as the acknowledgment of God in one's life constitutes a profound turn toward this world and a repudiation of avertive religion," and that "The reformation of society according to the Word of God: this was the Calvinist goal" (ibid., 14, 18).

33. "Why Care about Justice?," in *Hearing the Call*, 99.

34. Namely, the *Westminster Shorter Catechism*, Q.1, which teaches that "man's chief end is to glorify God, and to enjoy Him forever."

in some corners of the Reformed community an ethos of quiet remove, even self-content piety. Wolterstorff saves his harshest words for this kind of Christian culture.[35]

Wolterstorff's first contention with the avertive strand of Christian thought is not that the world is not thereby served, although it is not, nor that the cause of shalom is not thereby advanced, although for the most part it is not—at least neither of these is his primary contention. That sort of piety, he argues, is insufficiently biblical: "... the ultimately decisive reason for rejecting the theo-monistic understanding of true happiness is that it is not adequately biblical; so far as I can tell, *shalom* is more genuinely the content that the biblical writers give to the destiny appointed to us by God: our appointed destiny incorporates living in human community in the midst of nature."[36] Wolterstorff frequently explicates his vision of shalom by drawing not only from standard passages such as Isaiah 11, but from the entirety of Scripture, though with, no doubt, an emphasis on Old Testament prophetic literature.[37] He argues that the dominant trends in the theological tradition have been almost exclusively given over to contemplative and avertive, theo-monistic visions of the Christian life. On the contrary, Wolterstorff contends, "the Christian gospel, at bottom, is an answer to the question, how can we human beings flourish?"[38]

There is as well a theological component to the confusion Wolterstorff spies in the tradition, specifically in terms of theology proper. While theologians have traditionally conceived of God as simple, *a se*, immutable, impassible, and outside of time, the Scriptures, Wolterstorff explains, portray God as within time and active in history—as passible and temporal.[39]

---

35. Wolterstorff mentions "that most insufferable of all human beings, the triumphalist Calvinist, the one who believes that the revolution instituting the holy commonwealth has already occurred and that his or her task is now simply to keep it in place" (*Until Justice and Peace Embrace*, 21).

36. *Until Justice and Peace Embrace*, 126. By contrast, Wolterstorff, he himself recalls, was raised in a more world-engaged strand of Calvinism: "In the tenth book of his *Confessions* Augustine imagines the things of the world speaking, saying to him: Do not attend to us, turn away, attend to God. I was taught instead to hear the things of the world saying: Reverence us; for God made us as a gift for you. Accept us in gratitude" ("The Grace That Shaped My Life," in *Hearing the Call*, 266).

37. See, for example, *Justice: Rights and Wrongs*, chapters 3–5, or the shorter, "Why Care About Justice?," in *Hearing the Call*, 95–108.

38. "It's Tied Together by Shalom," in *Hearing the Call*, 424.

39. Wolterstorff takes this dichotomy for granted and does not, to my knowledge, entertain the possibility that God may be transcendent or "most absolute" *and* immanent, both sovereign over *and* active within creation history, though some such balance is affirmed in many corners of historic Reformed theology. *The Westminster Confession of Faith* (WCF), chapter 3, upholds both the aseity of God and the integrity of the will of

Wolterstorff does not deny that there may be scriptural passages which appear to favor the traditional understanding of God as eternal and outside of time, but the vast preponderance of biblical testimony, and the basic activity underlying biblical religion—redemption itself—is indicative of God as "past and future as well as present because his *actions* are past and future as well as present: his actions are located in our history. . . . the God worshiped is apprehended as engaged in a history that is both his and ours . . ."[40] The doctrine of simplicity, Wolterstorff argues, is adopted from neo-Platonism, from Plotinus specifically, and is inconsistent with and alien to the biblical sources: ". . . in fact the doctrine [of divine simplicity] was not the product of scrupulous biblical interpretation. It was philosophical considerations that led everybody at the time to find the doctrine utterly compelling."[41] Specifi-

---

the creature and, in fact, affirms that on no other grounds but the full sovereignty of the eternal, *a se* God can there be true creaturely freedom: "God, from all eternity, did, by the most wise and holy counsel of his own will, freely, and unchangeably ordain whatsoever comes to pass: yet so, as thereby neither is God the author of sin, nor is violence offered to the will of the creatures; nor is the liberty or contingency of second causes taken away, but rather established" (WCF 3.1). And again, "Although, in relation to the foreknowledge and decree of God, the First cause, all things come to pass immutably, and infallibly; yet, by the same providence, he ordereth them to fall out, according to the nature of second causes, either necessarily, freely, or contingently" (WCF 5.2). The divine act of entering into a historical, time-bound relationship with the creation and with creatures, without, these excerpts claim, compromising or qualifying the divine nature, is given the name "voluntary condescension" later in the Confession: "The distance between God and the creature is so great, that although reasonable creatures do owe obedience unto him as their creator, yet they could never have any fruition of him as their blessedness and reward, but by some voluntary condescension on God's part, which he hath been pleased to express by way of covenant" (WCF 7.1), the supreme illustration of which and fulfillment of which is the incarnation and the work of Christ. In other words, the hypostatic union itself presents the unmixed union of the fullness of deity (Col 1:19; 2:9) with a created, human nature (Heb 2:17; 4:15). An example of recent work on covenantal condescension, distinguishing covenantal from the kind of ontological condescension Wolterstorff opts for, is Oliphint, *God with Us: Divine Condescension and the Attributes of God*. For Wolterstorff on what we might call God's voluntary ontological condescension, see the introduction to *Inquiring about God*, where he says the following: "In creating us as the sort of creatures we are, creatures of great worth but capable of wronging God, and in permitting us to wrong God, God chose to be passible, thereby also choosing to give up aseity" (16).

40. *Until Justice and Peace Embrace*, 151–52. For Wolterstorff's rejection of the doctrine of eternity and his argument for divine temporality, see "Unqualified Divine Temporality," republished in *Inquiring about God*, 157–81; his other contributions to *God and Time: Four Views*; "God Everlasting," in *God and the Good*, 181–203; and his "Divine Simplicity," which originally appeared in *Philosophical Perspectives*, 5 and was reprinted in *Inquiring about God*, 91–111. A succinct account of Wolterstorff's view of God's relation to time appears in "God in Time."

41. "Is It Possible and Desirable for Theologians to Recover from Kant?," in *Inquiring about God*, 40. The essay was originally published in *Modern Theology* in 1998.

cally, "the doctrine was bequeathed to theologians by philosophers, Plotinus preeminent among them."[42] "Why," Wolterstorff asks, "would anyone ever embrace and propound so arcane a doctrine as this?"[43] Real historical presence and activity are what at once represents continuity with ancient Israelite religion, experience, and revelation, and what distinguishes the Christian religion from other religions.

42. "Is It Possible and Desirable for Theologians to Recover from Kant?," in *Inquiring about God*, 38.

43. "Is It Possible and Desirable for Theologians to Recover from Kant?," in *Inquiring about God*, 40. Wolterstorff describes the influence of Plotinus on Christian theology proper as follows. "On most Christian theologians this deliverance of Plotinus has had the grip of obvious and fundamental truth. From it has been extracted a truly astonishing list of conclusions: that God is simple, thus having no nature as we would nowadays understand 'having a nature'; that God is immutable; that God is eternal; that God is entirely lacking in potentialities, thus being pure act; that God exists necessarily, since God's essence and God's existence are identical; that no predicate correctly predicated of something other than God can with the same sense be correctly predicated of God; and—to break of the listing—that God has no passions . . . the classic argument for God's simplicity, in turn, came from Plotinus, whose key premise was that reality must comprise a being that is entirely unconditioned" ("Suffering Love," in *Inquiring about God*, 208–9). Since Wolterstorff rejects the neo-Platonic intrusion he attributes to Plotinus, he rejects each of the divine attributes listed here. He says, "I argue that God is not simple, not outside of time, not ontologically immutable, not impassible." And "[i]f simplicity, eternity, ontological immutability, and impassibility all have to go, then aseity also has to go" (Introduction to *Inquiring about God*, 15). Wolterstorff has also denied that God exists necessarily. See *On Universals*, 292. On simplicity, the influence of Plotinus, and Wolterstorff's rejection of simplicity, aseity, immutability, impassibility, and eternity, see "Is It Possible and Desirable for Theologians to Recover from Kant?," in *Inquiring about God*, 37–42; "Divine Simplicity," in *Inquiring about God*, 91–111; "Suffering Love," in *Inquiring about God*, 182–222; "Is God Disturbed by What Transpires in Human Affairs?," in *Inquiring about God*, 223–38; and "Does God Suffer? An Interview with Nicholas Wolterstorff." In *Until Justice and Peace Embrace*, he says, "The picture of God constructed by the classical theologians was that of a God outside of time, dwelling in eternity, ever-present, with no past and no future, impassive, immutable. The picture of the biblical writers is profoundly different" (151). Wolterstorff's view is, however, open to question. Certainly metaphysical simplicity is largely a Greek notion, but the theological employment of Greek metaphysics is not *per se* unbiblical. Furthermore, few if any of those theologians who held to the traditional doctrine of divine simplicity felt obliged thereby to deny the divine passions or personhood we find in scripture. We may certainly scrutinize the literature, asking how well various writers (Augustine, Anselm, Aquinas, Luther, and Calvin, to name a few) were able to balance the simplicity and impassibility of God with the incarnation and the history of redemption and so on. But to assume that divine simplicity is incompatible with the Scriptures is a vast oversimplification of the historical data and of the question itself. For a recent restatement of the traditional Thomistic approach, see Dolezal, *God without Parts*; and for a samples of contemporary research, see Lister, *God Is Impassible and Impassioned*; and Oliphint, *God with Us*.

Wolterstorff interprets the institution of the Sabbath as paradigmatic of this entire picture.[44] The rhythm of daily life hangs on regular Sabbath observance; thus the living of life in the world is reflective of, and carried out in remembrance of, the lordship of God and his saving activity in history. Worship, even specifically liturgy, and shalom-guided action, as we will see below, are distinct but inseparable, since at a fundamental level the worship which God enjoins is grounded in his own involvement in history in the activities of liberation and real, historical deliverance. The willingness of Christian theologians to adopt the neo-Platonic doctrine of simplicity is a symptom of the avertive orientation of their theological thinking in the first place. Wolterstorff offers this view of ancient Hebrew and Christian worship, reflective of an active and historically engaged God, as a corrective to the cold and contrived abstractness of theo-monism.

What distinguishes Christianity from Judaism, finally, is the climactic historical act of God, the inauguration of the kingdom of shalom in the resurrection of Jesus Christ:

> . . . Christian worship represents a continuity of structure, though an alternation of content, when compared to the worship of old Israel. The church conducts its worship within the context of remembering and expecting as well, but the great event at the center of its remembering is now the resurrection of Jesus, and the great event at the center of its expecting is now the full arrival of God's Kingdom, the Kingdom whose content is shalom.[45]

The proximity of God, and God's historical involvement in and commitment to human flourishing has now, in the incarnation and the redemptive work of Christ, reached its fullest expression, an achievement anticipated in the Hebrew Scriptures and realized in the coming of the messiah. The resurrection of Christ is the inauguration of the kingdom of God, understood as a kingdom of peace, justice, enjoyment, and flourishing. The resurrection of Jesus Christ is not the consummation of the expansion of this kingdom, but the charter of its establishment and mission. With Christ then we have both the fulfillment of Old Testament anticipation—an indicative, 'it now is'—and the definitive establishment of a new kingdom which raises the shalom standard—an imperative, 'and now thus we must be.' It is both in some sense a definitive moment of fulfillment and in another sense the inauguration of the task of realizing shalom; and with the death and resurrection of the kingdom's firstborn, that task is taken up by his followers.

---

44. See *Until Justice and Peace Embrace*, 151–61.
45. Ibid., 156.

Christians are not only recipients of God's love in Christ, but adopted as sons and called to likewise take up their crosses, proclaiming shalom and claiming new ground for the cause of peace and restoration and the full realization of justice and flourishing. Attendant to the suffering of Christ for others is the commission for those in Christ to likewise suffer for their neighbors and to put others and their needs before their own (Philippians 2:3–4 and following), a call distinctive of the new covenant.

Shalom is deeply biblical and theological in its source and inspiration, as this brief survey demonstrates. Wolterstorff proposes shalom both as a theological corrective and as a constructive application of what he understands to be the core of biblical religion. Wolterstorff has not completely re-invented theology, of course; in a manner demonstrative of the scientific eclecticism mentioned above, he has benefited a great deal from his own theological tradition and from others.

Especially in terms of the comprehensive ethical and soteriological vision of shalom, Wolterstorff has inherited a great deal from Kuyperian neo-Calvinism. He has also, however, raised a number of concerns, and distances himself from a particular strand of Kuyperian thought called the "creation order" tradition, in some respects. A brief look at Wolterstorff's interaction with relevant aspects of neo-Calvinism, at some points appreciative and at others critical, will enrich our analysis of the nature and function of shalom as we seek to clarify its relevance to situated rationality.

4.3 THE NEO-CALVINIST CREATION ORDER TRADITION

Wolterstorff has a strong affinity for neo-Calvinism.[46] And much of (cultural) neo-Calvinism is overtly and actively world-formative. It represents, we might say, a welcome corrective to the pietistic and avertive habits of historic Calvinism or other similarly stoic strands of Reformed Christianity. But Wolterstorff finds the creation order approach, a framework characteristic of some forms of neo-Calvinist thought, unsatisfactory in several ways. He is concerned that creation order theory conceives of the world as an exclusively nomological entity composed entirely of law and no gospel. He also finds the Kuyperian idea of the sovereignty of spheres to be dangerously

---

46. Wolterstorff's connection to this tradition is described in chapter 1 of this study. He writes about growing up in the Dutch neo-Calvinist tradition in a number of places. Representative is his "The Grace that Shaped My Life." See also "How My Mind Has Changed: The Way to Justice," in *Hearing the Call*, 430–38, originally published in *The Christian Century*.

Platonic and thus a distraction from shalom. Ideas such as Kuyper's 'true state' reveal an unwarranted, unnecessary and, indeed, less than confidently Christian emphasis on law, when, in light of the resurrection, the emphasis should be on justice, peace, and flourishing—in other words, on shalom. Shalom is our higher and transcendent end for which there is ultimately no lasting need of the ideal structures of spheres.

Though not without reservations, Wolterstorff has indeed benefited from the work of Abraham Kuyper. A detailed study of the influence of Kuyper's thought on Wolterstorff's writing would take us too far afield, though certainly there are sufficient connections to reward richly such a study. Here I shall draw attention to only two Kuyperian features of Wolterstorff's thought: the moral significance of institutions and the threefold relational formula of God, neighbor, and world.

Regarding the threefold relational formula, two features are worth noting: its history and its theoretical import. The central thrust of Kuyper's *Lectures on Calvinism* is a presentation of the Calvinistic worldview and a vision for Christian living in terms of the totalizing dimensions of Calvinist doctrines.[47] Kuyper claims that essential to defending such a comprehensive view of Calvinism is a demonstration of precisely this threefold relationality. What he actually suggests is that development of this tripartite recipe is essential to any true "life-system." Thus his interest in explaining Calvinism along these lines is, by implication, Kuyper's own acknowledgment of an extra-biblical theoretical framework incumbent on Calvinism given its desire to stand against movements of global proportions such as Hegelianism. The concept of "worldview," subsequently, well into the twentieth century, came under heavy criticism from within Calvinist circles, because of this implication of formal parity.[48]

47. Kuyper, *Lectures on Calvinism*, originally the Stone Lectures Kuyper delivered at Princeton University in 1898.

48. See, for example, Marshall, Griffioen, and Mouw, *Stained Glass*. An insightful analysis from outside the Reformed tradition appears in Horwitz, "Churches as First Amendment Institutions," esp. section III. Horwitz borrows Kuyper's idea of sphere sovereignty for the purpose of shedding fresh light on church state relations. He anticipates the question, "[D]oes it matter that Kuyper's theory of sphere sovereignty is a Christian, and specifically Calvinist, theory of the social structure?" His response is, essentially, no: "This article shows that sphere sovereignty is a useful way of thinking about both First Amendment Institutionalism and the constitutional relationship between state and non-state entities in general, even if the religious super-structure is striped from the theory" (93). From a Kuyperian point of view, we might say that this is precisely correct: the spheres are *creational* and thus *should be* recognized by all. However, human behavior relative to spheres and creational norms more often demonstrates destructive, sinful autonomy than creational flourishing. For a very readable discussion of these themes from a Kuyperian-Dooyeweerdian point of view, see Wolters, *Creation Regained: Biblical Basics for a Reformational Worldview*.

Nonetheless, Kuyper himself began to codify a Calvinist interest in worldview structures in terms of relationships with God, with other people, and with the world. He writes,

> The supreme interest here at stake, however, forbids our accepting without more positive proof the fact that Calvinism really provides us with such an unity of life-system and we demand proofs of the assertion that Calvinism is not a partial, nor was a merely temporary phenomenon, but is such an all-embracing system of principles, as, rooted in the past, is able to strengthen us in the present and to fill us with confidence for the future. Hence we must first ask what are the required *conditions* for such general systems of life . . . These conditions demand in the first place, that from a special principle a peculiar insight be obtained into the three fundamental relations of all human life: viz., (1) our relation *to God*, (2) our relation *to man*, and (3) our relation to *the world*.[49]

This theme has borne fruit in Wolterstorff's work, and conspicuously so. Increasingly in recent years, Wolterstorff's productivity has turned toward liturgy and worship, evincing a clear interest in man's active relationship to God.[50] Much of his work on justice and human rights is also theologically informed and links this religious strand of Wolterstorff's thought to his interest in shalom in its social dimensions—man's relationship with man.[51] Interest in a right relationship to the world drives Wolterstorff's interest in beauty and aesthetics, not only in terms of the nature, production, and function of art, but also in terms of active concern for the health and beauty of the world itself.[52]

The claim that Kuyper saw the reformation of social institutions as a biblico-moral imperative needs no defense. Kuyper's own career, as founder of the *Vrije Universiteit* and as politician on the national stage in the Netherlands, is a clarion witness to that interest. Wolterstorff too believes that

---

49. Kuyper, *Lectures*, 19.

50. The volume of collected essays entitled *Hearing the Call* is one example.

51. Much of the material in *Hearing the Call* also points in this direction, but more substantial are *Justice: Rights and Wrongs, Justice in Love*; and *The Mighty and the Almighty*.

52. Wolterstorff has published several shorter pieces on art and aesthetics and regularly lectures on related topics. His two book length pieces are *Art in Action* and *Works and Worlds of Art*. In *Until Justice and Peace Embrace*, he says that Christians and non-Christians alike are concerned about "mass poverty, about the effects of nationalism, about urban blight" (146), and in the introduction to *Educating for Shalom*, he laments the fact that "[u]rban decay seems to be an intractable and permanent feature of American society" (xi).

an interest in social institutions and in the reformation of them is essential to and distinctive of neo-Calvinism. When asked about it in an interview, Wolterstorff stated that it is "typical of the Reformed tradition to care not only about individuals but also about institutions." Wolterstorff himself was "reared," he recalls, "to think in terms of church and not just in terms of a group of Christian individuals. The health of institutions . . . has been a crucial concern of the tradition."[53]

In Wolterstorff's view, institutions deserve the reforming attention of Christians and the shalom driven efforts of all people, because they are socially significant and socially formed. With specifically educational institutions in mind, he enjoins, "reflect now for a moment on the fact that culture is something different from *society*. Culture, as I understand it, consists of *works* of culture. Society, by contrast, consists of *persons* who interact in various ways. From that interaction arise social roles, social practices, and social institutions." We ought not, therefore, to "ignore society and concentrate on culture."[54]

Implied in the distinction Wolterstorff makes here are both continuity with Kuyper and some corrective qualifications. Wolterstorff remains loyal to Kuyper's concern for right social relationships, and evidently the threefold relational formulation undergirds his concern for institutions, but he wishes to distinguish this from, and to distance himself from, a concern for culture itself, understood as impersonal objects. The latter tendency is implicit both in Kuyper's idea of sphere sovereignty[55] and in the creation order

---

53. "It's Tied Together by Shalom," in *Hearing the Call*, 425. He continues, "Growing up in an Americanized version of the Dutch Reformed Tradition, as I did, I absorbed the idea that being loyal to, and supportive of, institutions is a fundamental Christian responsibility. The loyalty involved criticizing them when they deserve criticism." See also *Justice: Rights and Wrongs*, 362–68.

54. "The Mission of the Christian College at the End of the Twentieth Century," in *Educating for Shalom*, 32. "Social practices and social institutions"—Wolterstorff uses very similar language to articulate the moral significance of practices of belief.

55. In the *Lectures on Calvinism*, Kuyper justifies a distinctly Calvinistic interest in politics by arguing that the sovereignty of God over the entire created order is expressed through the vice-regency of man and realized in three worldly structures: the state, society, and the church. "In order that the influence of Calvinism on our political development may be felt, it must be shown for what fundamental political conceptions Calvinism has opened the door, and how these political conceptions sprang from its root principle. This dominating principle was not, soteriologically, justification by faith, but, in the widest sense cosmologically, *the Sovereignty of the Triune God over the whole Cosmos*, in all its spheres and kingdoms, visible and invisible. A *primordial* Sovereignty which eradiates in [radiates through?] mankind in a threefold deduced supremacy, viz., 1. The Sovereignty in the *State*; 2. The Sovereignty in *Society*; and 3. The Sovereignty in the *Church*" (*Lectures*, 79). The word "sovereignty," used here at the outset of the third lecture, refers to the governance of God. Elsewhere Kuyper, and neo-Calvinism after

tradition, which will become clear shortly. All that is to say that there are clear lines of continuity between Wolterstorff and Kuyper, and at least these two are worth noting: the threefold relational concern and the interest in the perhaps moral significance of institutions. This consonance continues, and expands, when we consider developments in cultural neo-Calvinism in the generations following Kuyper.

Although neo-Calvinism is, as any such entity, characterized only by a limited number of core beliefs held loosely in common among the people and institutions which constitute its base, the idea of design or purpose or intention—and post-fall, of 'ought to have been'—implicit in the creation which is to some degree discernible by humans is closely paralleled in Wolterstorff's writing on shalom. It is evident most conspicuously in the theoretical and ethical significance of the design implicit in the createdness of things in the world: if that ethic is normative for human action, at least Wolterstorff himself has understood its nature, and he has begun to spell it out in detail. There is no indication that he views himself as unique in his ability to discern the mandates of creation. For Wolterstorff, shalom itself is "the way things ought to be," the way things were intended, or the way life and things would be were it not for the fall.

As evidence that Wolterstorff's idea of shalom has both this embeddedness in the created order and the (epistemological) availability of the nomological structure of shalom in common with neo-Calvinism, one may point to Wolterstorff's writing on natural human rights. Wolterstorff believes that natural human rights are universally assumed but only defensible on Christian grounds.[56] Specifically, a right is a "normative social relationship," he explains, and that normativity flows from worth: "human beings have worth," and "rights are what respect for worth requires."[57] The worth of human beings is ultimately attributable to their being created in the image of God.[58] Wolterstorff thus assembles a socio-political, ethical structure based on an anthropology of createdness. From the created worth of individual image-bearers he is able to hypothesize what sort of relations the creator intended there to be between human persons, and from there

---

him, uses the phrase to refer not to the sovereignty of God but to the integrity of created things, at least by implication: the sovereignty *of spheres* appears to be the sovereignty exercised in those spheres according to the innate nature of the spheres themselves.

56. See sections §6.2 and §6.3 of the present study.

57. "Can Human Rights Survive Secularization? Part I," 10, 11.

58. In "Can Human Rights Survive Secularization? Part II," he adds, "Christianity locates the basis of that worth in the fact that each of us bears God's image and is redemptively loved by God; that's what gives each and every one of us the worth that grounds human rights" (16).

to what kind of society would reflect the intentions and character of the creator God. What is of special importance is the fact that there is a *telos* implicit in created things, and that this *telos* has been stalled or disrupted by the intrusion of sin. Theologically speaking, eschatology is implicit in this semi-creation order protology. Thus Wolterstorff will speak in terms of the "reform" or "restoration" of society and social institutions toward shalom, language reminiscent of neo-Calvinism and cultural transformationalism. Let us look briefly at representative neo-Calvinist creation order thought in order to clarify this connection.

In an essay outlining the features of (cultural) neo-Calvinism, Albert Wolters writes, "[t]o create is not only to bring into existence, but to bring into existence different kinds of things, kinds which are ontologically separate from each other, each with its own creationally guaranteed nature."[59] The ontological distinctives of things, as created by God, are interpreted by the neo-Calvinists as, from the worshipful and obedient creature's point of view, a kind of implicit law, order, or creation order (sometimes called "creation ordinance"). Within things—within individual things and within the relations between things, since they are cumulatively *one* thing, the creation—there is an implicit blueprint, we might say, of the way the creator intended things to be, of the way things therefore ought to be. Sander Griffioen calls this "deep respect for the God who commands, who through his law-words calls things into being" a "real hallmark of Calvinism."[60] The discernment and articulation, the making explicit, of the implicit law-structure of created things and the active pursuit of its realization falls to the follower of Christ, the prince of shalom, and is characteristic of and even constitutive of the Christian life. Created design or law-structures represent the gold-standard for human conduct and fulfillment in this life, from the point of view of this creational doctrine, for all people. Carroll Guen Hart writes, "[o]n the basis of this creation order, we make the distinction between *wisdom*—conformity to the created order and *folly*—violation of the created order."[61] And Wolters, with more grandeur, writes,

> From the beginning of human life on earth, the human race is mandated to work toward a great future goal: the development of creation in accordance with God's design. That development

---

59. Walsh, Hart, and Vander Vennen, eds., *An Ethos of Compassion*, 42. Wolters's contribution is entitled "Creation Order: A Historical Look at Our Heritage."

60. Griffioen, "Creation Order and Transcendental Philosophy," in *An Ethos of Compassion*, ed. Walsh, Hart, and Vander Vennen, 52.

61. Hart, "The Doctrine of Creation: Judging Law and Transforming Vision: Response to Albert M. Wolters," in *An Ethos of Compassion*, ed. Walsh, Hart, and Vander Vennen, 58.

has been disrupted, but not annulled, by the fall into sin, and is reaffirmed in salvation. The goal toward which history moves is therefore not a return toward to the garden of Eden, but an eschatological fulfillment of creation pictured as the New Jerusalem, into which the glory and honour of the nations will be brought . . .[62]

Wolters delineates Kuyper's particular contributions, saying, "[t]his general theme is worked out by Kuyper in his principle of 'sphere sovereignty,' the principle that different spheres in society . . . have their jurisdiction limited by their created nature."[63] For Kuyper, sphere sovereignty was both rooted in the theology of creation and important for anti-revolutionary politics. Ontological diversity is both a kind of creational essentialism and intrinsically anti-revolutionary, since it is naturally opposed to the synthesis of a Hegelian view of history, and thus stands as a bulwark against political totalism of any kind. As Wolters explains,

> It was Kuyper who first emphasized . . . that sphere sovereignty should be understood as a *creational* principle, and it was Dooyeweerd who expanded the notion of sphere sovereignty to mean ontological irreducibility in general, including the irreducibility of such modal aspects as faith and feeling. Ontological diversity, whether sociological or modal, was grounded in creation and creational law, and provided a criterion for criticizing various kinds of societal totalitarianism and theoretical reductionism.[64]

---

62. Wolters "Creation Order," 42. Evident in this statement are a few of the dangers that haunt neo-Calvinist eschatology. Notice the subtle renunciation of an eschatology of restoration; a return to Eden is not generally favored in Calvinist thought. Wolters shows that the tradition is caught between its aversion to restoration as truncating or immanentizing biblical eschatology and a desire to preserve concern for the present order and to avoid the embarrassment of an avertive orientation and pietistic religiosity. He indicates this latter concern by associating the New Jerusalem with fulfillment of, rather than the destruction and replacement of, the world.

63. Ibid., 43.

64. Ibid. Again, there appears to be some ambiguity in the use of the term "sovereignty." Wolters here means by it the ontological integrity of created things, and he says that this is what is meant by the use of the term in Kuyper's writing. However at least Kuyper's primary use of the term, if not his only use of it, refers not to the sovereignty of created things, but to the sovereignty of God as exercised by human beings through institutions belonging to the created order—through "spheres" such as the state and the university. The sovereignty of spheres is the sovereignty belonging to God, exercised through the spheres. I am not aware of Kuyper's having used the term as Wolters suggests he does, but no doubt speaking that way about the ontology of created things, in terms of a kind of created essentialism, is part of the main stream of neo-Calvinism. In his mention of Dooyeweerd, Wolters may be indicating that it was he who first began to use the term in this way.

The existence of creationally embedded prescriptions for enjoyment and fulfillment, especially in terms of human flourishing and society, is essential for Wolterstorff's writing on shalom, and of deep theological significance. An additional excerpt from Wolters summarizes these neo-Calvinist themes:

> Undergirding the neo-Calvinist understanding of biblical religion is the theme which was so often stressed by Herman Bavinck: grace restores nature. That is to say, the meaning of the Christian religion is the restoration of the fallen world. And because creation was understood in such comprehensive terms, embracing all of history and culture, the neo-Calvinist view of grace, of the Christian religion, and of the kingdom of God, was equally comprehensive. Redemption is a cosmic salvage operation whereby the entire created order is reclaimed by God in Jesus Christ. In this expansive vision of the Christian religion, it is throughout the good creation of God which is at stake in the world-historical drama of salvation, and it is creational normativity which is an ever-present factor in the questions of Christian ethics.[65]

Clearly, Wolterstorff's notion of shalom is related in many ways to creation order thought. I further develop those connections in chapter 6. Before moving on, we should also note that Wolterstorff's reception of the neo-Calvinist creation order tradition was a cautious one. He is in fact quite critical of it.

---

65. Ibid., 44. Here, as elsewhere, Wolters stresses continuity with the theology of historic Calvinism as he finds it in the work of Herman Bavinck. Wolterstorff also stresses continuity with the history of Reformed theology, although, at least in publication, his attention has focused more on Calvin and early Calvinists. He writes, "We have been considering what it was in the thought of the early Calvinists that made their turn toward the world take the shape of world-formative Christianity. I have argued for the importance of two convictions on their part: first, the conviction that the obedient gratitude that constitutes the basis of this turn ought to be exercised within our occupations; and second, the conviction that the occupational structures as presented to us are corrupted and would not serve that goal" (*Until Justice and Peace Embrace*, 17). See also his "The Wounds of God," originally published in *The Reformed Journal* (1987), republished in *Hearing the Call*, 114–32; "Can a Calvinist Be a Progressive?," originally published in *Gereformeerd Theologisch Tijdschrift* (1988), also appearing in *Hearing the Call*, 275–86; and "The Political Ethic of the Reformers," first published in *Hearing the Call*, 328–45 (Wolterstorff writes in the acknowledgments that this essay was probably written in the 1970s [440]). Wolterstorff draws some connections between Bavinck, Reid, and Reformed Epistemology in his article, "Herman Bavinck—Proto-Reformed Epistemologist." Whether there is any connection between the neo-Calvinist doctrines of creation and restoration and Bavinck's Reidian naïve realism, as it is sometimes called, is an interesting and important question, but it cannot be explored here.

4.4 WOLTERSTORFF'S RECEPTION OF THE NEO-CALVINIST CREATION ORDER TRADITION

We have clarified sufficiently those aspects of cultural neo-Calvinism which most positively inform shalom. Let us look more carefully now at where Wolterstorff parts ways with this tradition. Wolterstorff distances himself from the creation order tradition listing four points, he says, of "unease." The first is the legalistic tone of creation order thinking.[66] The creative activity of God "comes close to being reduced to God's making things for which God lays down laws, including, in the case of us human beings, laws requiring obedience. God the lawgiver," in effect, "almost completely occupies the space of God the Creator."[67] But "there's more to creation than legality."[68] Instead, says Wolterstorff, "[i]n my own thinking I have found it more fruitful to think in terms of shalom than in terms of creation-orders . . . shalom pertains to delight, fulfillment, flourishing of the creatures of the world."[69]

Secondly, Wolterstorff wishes to sharpen the accompanying neo-Calvinist view of the fallenness of the world. Conceiving of created design as implicit law or mandate has narrowed the neo-Calvinist conception of what is wrong with the world to only intentional, and thus only human, violations of those mandates. But if created design is what is right, then any divergence from it, any 'should-not-be' whatsoever, is equally an aspect of the brokenness of the world, whether it is the direct result of human agency or it is not. "A great deal of our human pain is connected with such should-not-be's," should-not-be's, he means, which are not the result of deliberate human wrongdoing, not the result of personal agency. "Disabling long-term diseases, early deaths of promising children . . . feminine persons who find themselves in male bodies and male persons who find themselves in female bodies,"[70] and "involuntary, preventable poverty."[71] Such aberrations are, in most cases, not attributable to human intention, but clearly they are out of accord with the intended nature of things. Thus Wolterstorff sees in neo-

---

66. Wolters also, if only in passing, gives voice to this concern: "The ethical problem I see is the danger of legalism. A tradition which emphasizes the ubiquity of law, and the broadness of the call to obedience, is in constant danger of losing the joyful spontaneity and the willingness to make or tolerate mistakes which the redeemed life calls for" ("Creation Order," in *An Ethos of Compassion*, ed. Walsh, Hart, and Vander Vennen, 45).

67. "Points of Unease with the Creation Order Tradition," in *An Ethos of Compassion*, ed. Walsh, Hart, and Vander Vennen, 64.

68. Ibid., 65.

69. Ibid.

70. Ibid.

71. "The Moral Significance of Poverty," 287.

Calvinism a view of brokenness focused too narrowly on sinful human intentions which he would rather put in terms of brokenness *per se*.

A third concern Wolterstorff raises is the rather conspicuous absence of the savior. "Did it strike you that Kuyper, in that passage . . . on our means of knowing God's law, mentioned creation, history, self-awareness and scripture—but not Jesus Christ?"[72]

The fourth critical point Wolterstorff makes targets the creational essentialism of creation order thought. Those essences are often arbitrary, he says. "I think it misleading to talk, as the neo-Calvinists do, about *the* nature of states, and . . . *the* norms for states . . . Our present-day *concept* of a state has an essence, but it doesn't follow that states do . . ." Later he says, "I see no reason not to think that two hundred years from now states as we know them will have disappeared." And if the metaphysics of the thing is questionable, so is the ethic of it: ". . . nor does it follow that we have an obligation to struggle to arrange social reality so that our concept has application."[73]

On the contrary, the Christian ethos, in Wolterstorff's mind, comes down from heaven as much as it is implicit in the creation, and a myopic focus on essences, even more so when they are arbitrarily conceived, forces enjoyment, fulfillment, and flourishing to recede into the background and law for law's sake to take center stage. "Our political obligations," as all others, "are to be determined fundamentally by considering what, given the states that we actually have, conduces to shalom, rather than by considering what will serve to instantiate *the* nature of *the* state," or of anything else, "and *the* norms supposedly attached to that nature." Shalom is, we recall, Wolterstorff's comprehensive and governing vision, which serves to orient our reflections. Wolterstorff does not categorically reject creational designs; on the contrary, divine, we might say, authorial intention is fundamental to just what will constitute the nomology of shalom. It must be remembered therefore that the design and order implicit in the creation and in created things is the design and order of the God of love and forgiveness, the good God who reveals himself as given to and as bound by a historical covenant with a historical people, and ultimately, the God who had no place to lay his

---

72. Wolterstorff, "Points of Unease with the Creation Order Tradition," in *An Ethos of Compassion*, ed. Walsh, Hart, and Vander Vennen, 65. Of the four points Wolterstorff brings against the creation order tradition, this third—the absence of the savior—receives the shortest treatment. He devotes a single paragraph to it, composed largely of rhetorical questions, whereas each of the other four points occupies a half to a full page. My interpretation of this oddity is that, in Wolterstorff's mind, shalom is through and through *about* Jesus Christ and expository of his redemptive work. If this is the case, vast swaths of Wolterstorff's writing are in an expository sense about Christ and a resurrection-driven ethic.

73. Ibid., 66.

head, and died forsaken on the cross. Shalom is God's cause and our cause, and it is itself the *telos* and essence of things—rather than the *telos* and essence of things themselves constituting the Christian ethos. The shalom ethic is prior to, or governs, or is determinative of, the essence of institutions or spheres; the spheres are not eternal givens. The grass withers and the flower falls, we might add, but the word of the Lord—principally, the word "shalom"—remains forever.

Wolterstorff's doctrine of shalom has deep roots in the neo-Calvinist tradition, and even in aspects of creation order theory. Shalom is an ethical—a love, peace, and flourishing-directed—creation order, toward which Christian thinking and action regarding spheres or created essences should be oriented, by which these should be governed. While having benefited so much from neo-Calvinism, Wolterstorff has discovered thoughtful appreciation for shalom in other traditions as well. As far back as *Until Justice and Peace Embrace*, he took up the theme of liturgy and shalom, another theme which has enjoyed his sustained interest for many years.[74] And it was not a Calvinist but an Eastern Orthodox theology of worship which inspired Wolterstorff's interest in the natural connection of worship and liturgy to shalom.

The connection between liturgy and shalom which Wolterstorff envisions represents a path between the horns of an avertive and worldly dilemma. Wolterstorff's discussion of the connection between shalom and liturgy also brings into clearer focus some of the anthropological aspects of shalom and offers additional clarification of the public and social significance of it.

4.5 SHALOM AND LITURGY

The shalom calling, or the calling to foster or promote shalom, is embodied in Christian worship and is therefore central to the life of the church. Wolterstorff explores this observation by emphasizing a deep symbiosis of worship and the active pursuit of justice and shalom in the world. He also argues that a connection between worship and practice grounds the uniqueness of the Christian interest in justice and flourishing.

On the one hand, Wolterstorff concedes that "there are others in the modern world concerned about mass poverty, about the effects of nationalism, about urban blight," and that "not only is there no distinctiveness" to the Christian "struggle for the reform of a corrupt social order . . . there does not even seem to be distinctiveness in the particular goals" of the Christian shalom program for social engagement. Indeed, "[i]t appears that Christians

---

74. Examples include many of the essays included in *Hearing the Call*.

insert themselves into the social world in fundamentally the same way as the secular socialists" and "the secular progressives."[75]

On the other, Christian interest in justice and flourishing is distinguished from the secular interest, or from any other, by the intricate and organic relationship between shalom-driven involvement in the world and Christian liturgy. Wolterstorff argues that the symbiosis of Christian worship and Christian participation in the world toward shalom effectively constitutes a mutual authentication of both worship and social engagement.

In *Until Justice and Peace Embrace*, Wolterstorff hints that shalom-driven activity in the world which lacks grounding in Christian liturgy (secular socialism being the obvious example) ultimately lacks authenticating grounds. But he nuances this implication in a footnote: "I am not suggesting that the *sincerity* of those performing such works is brought into question—a person can sincerely work for justice without engaging in Christian worship, after all—but rather that their (Christian) *authenticity* is brought into question."[76] In *Justice: Rights and Wrongs* and in the brief "Can Human Rights Survive Secularization?," he is more forthright: no secular argument has been offered which successfully accounts for natural inherent human rights. He writes, "I know of no other argument for this position," one which defends natural inherent human rights, "than one that employs those very theistic premises that I will use in grounding my proposal."[77]

Wolterstorff anticipates Christian concern for the distinctiveness of Christian creed and praxis: wherein lies the distinctiveness of Christian existence? That concern arises from a wariness of adopting a social vision which is indistinguishable from a secular one.[78] Wolterstorff addresses the

75. *Until Justice and Peace Embrace*, 146.
76. Ibid., 157.
77. *Justice: Rights and Wrongs*, 341.
78. Wolterstorff occasionally hints at the economic side of shalom. Here for example are a few comments he makes in *Until Justice and Peace Embrace*: "Behind the concentration of capital in Europe and the United States is the use of much gunpowder, elaborate torture, and many prisons" (32), and "[i]t has been said that the principal advantage of the Europeans in their initial contact with the Orient was that they had better ocean-going ships—and better artillery" (38). Elsewhere he indicates that the "fundamental features of the economic arrangements of humanity are duress and domination" (*Educating for Shalom*, 167) and he argues that "possessive individualism and the Christian gospel do not mix" ("Can Human Rights Survive Secularization? Part 1," 13). See also "The Moral Significance of Poverty," where Wolterstorff argues that a distinction should be maintained between two features of Latin American Liberation Theology: preferential treatment of the poor and a "naive" and "perhaps desperate" affinity to Marxism. "Marxism as a social movement has been a disaster in our century," he says. "[I]nsofar as the liberation theologians have defended it, they have been naïve . . . They saw the impoverishment of their people as intimately related to the capitalism

question shortly following an enthusiastic endorsement of the activistic emphasis of Latin American liberation theology and a sharp, morally ponderous condemnation of nationalism.[79] A complementary danger he also hopes to avoid is the depreciation and even neglect of the Christian practice of social engagement in favor of quiet piety and "avertive" religiosity, which is typical, Wolterstorff laments, of contemporary Calvinism.[80]

He makes it clear that "contemplation, spirituality, piety . . . in my judgment . . . belong to authentic shalom." And he says, "one way to deal with our concerns is to confront them forthrightly and say: the inward life is important; not *all*-important, but important."[81] He proceeds to commend the pious and contemplative emphases of the Christian tradition as grounding or even validating the socially active and engaged elements of Christian living. "Could it be that when participation in the Sunday liturgy of the church is missing, then life as a whole is altered in a certain way? Is it not possible that the liturgy *authenticates* our action in the world?" Conversely, ". . . the authentication of liturgy requires that its participants struggle for justice and peace in the world . . ."[82] And again, "can we not also say that if the works of mercy and justice are performed but the worship is missing, then a shadow is cast over those works, and *their* authenticity is brought into question? . . . work and worship are mutually authenticating."[83]

Shalom enjoins active concern for justice and flourishing. But this concern is a shalom concern because it is grounded in worship of the

---

and wealth of North America, and they turned in desperation to Marxism as the only visible alternative. Their defense of a preferential option for the poor is quite a different matter" (287). Within the same article, Wolterstorff returns to say: "The teaching is clear: Those who find themselves in preventable involuntary poverty have a natural human [in the original he adds "unconditional" (11)] right to have their poverty alleviated" (293), whereas he also affirms that "if I have a right to being treated a certain way, then some person or organization has a duty of some sort to treat me that way" (290).

79. The aim of this section of *Until Justice and Peace Embrace* is to appropriate from two traditions what conduces to shalom. In both neo-Calvinism and Liberation Theology, Wolterstorff finds something worth holding on to, while he clearly stops short of full endorsement of either: "An implication of this is that our work will always have the two dimensions of a struggle for justice and the pursuit of increased mastery of the world so as to enrich human life . . . Development and liberation must go hand in hand. Ours is both a cultural mandate and a liberation mandate" (72).

80. As noted above, he distances himself in no uncertain terms from "that most insufferable of all human beings, the triumphalist Calvinist, the one who believes that the revolution instituting the holy commonwealth has already occurred and that his or her task is now simply to keep it in place" (ibid., 21).

81. Ibid., 146–47.

82. Ibid., 148.

83. Ibid., 156–57.

God of shalom. How, exactly, does shalom emerge from worship? Liturgy, Wolterstorff explains, is not the contemplative core of a socially disengaged pietism; nor, alternatively, must social engagement be secular, or should worldly activism be detached from worship and piety. The composite, the symbiosis, of liturgy and action, is a uniquely Christian formulation. Faith without works is dead: liturgy must unfold into morally significant and socially engaged action. In an interview, Wolterstorff explained,

> ... worship and justice are closely connected. The best image I have for expressing the connection is the image of a heartbeat: systolic and diastolic. The church assembles and it disperses. In both its assembling and its dispersing it is living before the face of God, but in two different ways. . . For me, the two belong together. Worship in assemblies is of deep importance, and doing justice and struggling for shalom when dispersed is of equal importance. . . You can't have a heartbeat without having both the systolic and the diastolic phases.[84]

Wolterstorff offers an appreciative summary of the work of Orthodox theologian Alexander Schmemann (1921–83), who spoke of the world itself as religiously significant, indeed as sacrament: "Thus, say[s] Schmemann, the world is a *sacrament* of God."[85] Wolterstorff echoes this thought, and emphasizes, "worship is the response to one's apprehension of the ultimate meaning and nature of *this* world, not of some other world." "It is the response to one's apprehension of *this* world as the epiphany of God. . . . worship has nothing to do with denigration of *this* world and the denial of its worth. It is for one's enjoyment of *this* world that one blesses God."[86]

According to Schmemann, the fall into sin has obscured this theologically rich and religiously significant "ultimate meaning" of nature and the world as sacrament. Secularism is not, fundamentally, a rejection of God; the secularist may even acknowledge God, or gods, or a divine something or other. At its core, secularism is a rejection of the sacramental significance of the world, of its irreducibly religious importance and nature, and indeed

---

84. "An Interview with Nicholas Wolterstorff," in *Hearing the Call*, 417.

85. *Until Justice and Peace Embrace*, 150. Throughout this discussion, Wolterstorff cites Schmemann, *For the Life of the World: Sacraments and Orthodoxy*. Wolterstorff says something similar, reflecting on his own Dutch Reformed tradition: "The affirmation of what is good in creation, society, culture and self was undergirded by a deep sacramental consciousness: the goodness surrounding us is God's favor to us, God's blessing, God's grace. Culture is the result of the Spirit of God brooding over humanity's endeavors" ("The Grace That Shaped my Life," 266–67).

86. *Until Justice and Peace Embrace*, 150.

a rejection of the true nature of human beings as self-reflective features of the sacramental created order. Says Wolterstorff,

> What the secularist sees merely as good things coming his way, the believer sees as gifts from God. What the secularist sees as merely a stupendously intricate world, the believer sees as a glorious work of God. What the secularist sees merely as wrongdoing, the believer sees as sin. So too, what the secularist sees merely as justice, the believer sees as giving God joy. And what the secularist sees merely as injustice, the believer sees as making God suffer. For the believer, justice and injustice are sacramental realities.[87]

Furthermore, one does not respond worshipfully to a right apprehension of the world, as sacramental, simply because one is religiously inclined or aesthetically compelled to do so, but because "it belongs to man's true nature to respond to that apprehension by worship: worship is ontologically grounded."[88] Man is essentially a worshiper; man is innately worshipful. So Wolterstorff leads us back to biblical anthropology, the basic fact of which is the triple mandate of love of God, of neighbor (including also of one's self), and of nature.[89] It is man's 'true nature' to fulfill this mandate through sacramental activity in the world. "Given that human beings mirror the personhood of God in their own personhood," Wolterstorff writes elsewhere, "one cannot with full integrity honor God without honoring those creatures that mirror God, and conversely; the two come together."[90] In this comprehensive sense, the church's worship of God is the seed of Christian ethos.[91]

---

87. "Why Care About Justice," 99.

88. *Until Justice and Peace Embrace*, 151.

89. This formula appears frequently in Wolterstorff's work, and I have argued above (§4.3) that it comes directly from Abraham Kuyper. Representative as well is this: "Deep in the Christian tradition is the conviction that each of us is not to be the center of his own concerns but is rather to love and serve God with all his life, and, in similar fashion, to love his neighbor as himself. One might add to these the conviction that each is also to be a responsible steward of creation within which God has placed us. To love and serve God in all our ways, to love our neighbors as ourselves, and to be responsible stewards of nature—those are clearly proclaimed in the authoritative Scriptures of the Christian community as the fundamental obligations of mankind" (*Reason within the Bounds*, 111).

90. "The Moral Significance of Poverty," 295.

91. There are hints of this same nexus in the work of other neo-Calvinists. For example, Hart writes, "Ethos is incarnation, a community's response to the spirit which guides it, embodiment of its spiritual self. The New Testament expects the church, body of Christ, to be a community whose ethos is embodied in compassion. Such compassion is not a feeling, but a *divine* act of sacrificial love, *God's* self-giving love towards creation in Christ, who on the cross embodied fully what he began in his shepherding,

Notice also that anchoring the inter-relation of worship and action in anthropology brings other, indeed all other, cultural activities into relative religious parity with worship, so that worship, or liturgy, may be viewed as the first among equals of the various activities constitutive of human culture. At least in the sense of fulfilling the love and stewardship injunctions of scripture, worship is not categorically unique: ". . . for the individual who apprehends the world as a sacrament of God, work and worship are fundamentally connected." For this reason Wolterstorff is able to expand the repertoire of actions which are expressive of an appreciation of the sacramental nature of the world beyond worship, to work and to love. "I myself would say that worshiping God is but one manifestation, one expression of that acceptance," that is, of the acceptance of "the world as a sacrament of God." "Another expression is our responsible development of the potentials of the world, and yet another is love of neighbor. Man is indeed *homo adorans*, but he is also *homo laborans* and *homo amans*."[92] The ethos implicit in biblical anthropology, in Wolterstorff's tripartite formulation, is part of the deep structure of shalom. Indeed, it is itself a clear example of created essentialism or of an implicit nomology the discovery of which points us in the direction of shalom.

Human flourishing should be understood as the unfolding or realizing of divine intentional design. Conversely to inhibit human flourishing is to stifle divine authorial intention, as it were, in the crown of God's creative activity, man the *imago Dei*. And indeed Wolterstorff will also speak about human worth as closely linked to the *imago Dei*. In that case, opposition to human flourishing is analogous to opposition to divine vice-regency in the created order. Flourishing is the divinely created intention or plan for human creatures. When flourishing is opposed or impeded, the design and purpose of God are offended. In an essay entitled, "If God is Sovereign, Why Lament?" Wolterstorff lays out the following account of the cultural mandate[93] and its significance for shalom, in terms of a Christian anthropology, indicating both the unique value of human beings and the theological significance of human flourishing:

---

healing, and feeding of sheep-like crowds without a shepherd: harassed, sick and hungry people. But the New Testament also calls Jesus' *followers* to love their neighbor in the *image* of God's love, calls the *body of Christ* to have the *compassion of God* in Christ" ("Creation Order in our Philosophical Tradition: Critique and Refinement," in *An Ethos of Compassion*, 67; emphasis original).

92. *Until Justice and Peace Embrace*, 150–51. Wolterstorff borrows these terms from Schmemann.

93. "And God blessed them. And God said to them, 'Be fruitful and multiply and fill the earth and subdue it, and have dominion over the fish of the sea and over the birds of the heavens and over every living thing that moves upon the earth'" (Gen 1:28).

> May each and every one of you flourish—that is the divine benediction of which you and I are recipients.
>
> *Flourish as animalic persons.* At creation, God performed that strange work, that experiment, as it were, of blending into one being the animalic and the angelic so that we human beings are both persons and animals, both animals and persons—animalic persons, personic animals. God did it intentionally of course. The shalom that God desires for us is shalom within our creaturely condition and circumstance.
>
> *Flourish until full of years.* We human beings have a design plan. According to that plan, we slowly age; then, when full of years at around threescore years and ten, or by virtue of strength, four score years, we die. That is built into our design plan as personic *animals*. God does not desire, and takes no delight in, early death; God desires that we shall live until full of years.[94]

It is clear, Wolterstorff contends, that shalom is both God's cause and the cause of all humankind: "Can the conclusion be avoided that not only is shalom God's cause in the world but that all who believe in Jesus will, along with him, engage in the works of shalom? Shalom is both God's cause in the world and our human calling."[95] In sum, shalom as a vision for the way things were meant to be is itself the charter for the kingdom of God as inaugurated in the Christian narrative. By virtue of its being intrinsic to creation, shalom itself has been present, if implicit and obscured by sin, since the earliest moments of creation. What changes by virtue of the inauguration of the Christ-founded kingdom of shalom is that shalom becomes much more explicit and assumes redemptive garb, necessary for the postfall condition; it becomes the fully revealed, redemptive mandate for the followers of Jesus. Shalom is the cultural mandate republished for a world under the curse of sin

---

94. "If God is Good and Sovereign, Why Lament?," in *Hearing the Call*, 91. The essay was originally published in *Calvin Theological Journal* in 2001. It is interesting that Wolterstorff appears to take death as part of God's original design plan. He concludes the essay saying, "To lament is to risk living with one's deepest questions unanswered. The cry occurs within the context of the *yet* of enduring faith and ongoing praise, for in raising Christ from the dead, we have God's word and deed that God will be victorious in the struggle against all that frustrates God's desire. Thus divine sovereignty is not sacrificed but reconceived. If lament is indeed a legitimate component of Christian life, then divine sovereignty is not to be understood as everything happening just as God wants it to happen—or happening in such a way that God regards what God does not like as an acceptable trade-off for the good thereby achieved. Divine sovereignty consists in God's winning the battle against all that has gone awry with respect to God's will" (ibid., 92).

95. *Until Justice and Peace Embrace*, 71.

THE COMPREHENSIVE ETHIC OF SHALOM

The avertive theo-monism of the Calvinist tradition has been replaced by an ethical kingdom in the here and now, just as the heavenly tabernacle has descended, become incarnate, and dwelt among men; what Wolterstorff calls "avertive" religion is replaced by "world formative" religion, in accordance with the Scriptures and the new covenant. God's cause and God's created design are now man's cause. The human being bears a double responsibility to take up the cause of shalom: it is fundamental to his nature to do so, on a public and social level, and it is fundamentally because of man that shalom has broken down and principally from man that opposition to shalom has always arisen. Both that guilt and that call are embodied climactically on the cross, where through the pangs of birth and the waters of baptism, through the redemptive judgment of God, the shalom mandate is issued anew to the church.

Notice once again, however, that Wolterstorff understands shalom as "our *human* calling." In the very same sentence, shalom is described as "God's cause in the world" for "all who believe in Jesus," and then generically, "our human calling." Is it a Christian calling, a duty or vision incumbent on Christians only, or is shalom the duty and the calling of all humans as such? Is shalom essentially a Christian truth, laying claim and representing epistemic accountability on all people only to the extent that belief in the authority of the Christian scriptures does, and in conjunction with the gospel, such that "pursue shalom" comes hand in hand with "repent and believe the gospel?" Or is it discoverable to the non-Christian person, by, as it is traditionally put, natural reason?

If it were Wolterstorff's intention to argue that shalom is the Christian's duty as a Christian, we could expect the call to be contingent upon a person's being a Christian, for one thing, and we could expect shalom itself to be predicated upon distinctly Christian beliefs. In the preponderance of Wolterstorff's writing on justice and shalom and related issues, he goes to great lengths to draw support for his approach from biblical and theological sources, as we have seen, and he clearly asserts that important aspects of shalom, such as natural human rights and shalom driven activism, cannot be accounted for on purely secular grounds. And yet, shalom as our "human calling," and much else besides, preserves the possibility that shalom, in both theory and praxis, both epistemologically and ethically, is a basic and universal human 'situation,' independent of Christian confession.[96]

The cause of shalom has implications for all of human life. Clearly, if God is the originator and legislator of shalom, there can be no limits to the enforcement and application of what shalom entails. It is perhaps specifically

---

96. This (apparent) ambiguity is resolved in chapter 6.

because of, or at least demonstrative of, the unconditionality of the duty of shalom that Wolterstorff himself has been so prolific in so many different areas (art, education, justice, epistemology and rationality, and so on). He has said as much in a recent interview. Early in his teaching career Wolterstorff found himself chair of a committee tasked with the complete overhaul of Calvin College's curriculum. "You have the sciences, the humanities, and arts, my own passion, justice, and so forth." He found himself asking, "[w]hat holds it all together? Eventually it occurred to me," he explained, "that what can hold it all together is the Old Testament category of shalom."[97]

For this reason I propose turning now to the implications of shalom in the spheres of education and academia, two subjects on which Wolterstorff has written a great deal.[98] Front and center, in addition to *Until Justice and Peace Embrace*, is one of Wolterstorff most acclaimed releases, *Reason within the Bounds of Religion*, and two collections of essays, *Educating for Shalom* and *Educating for Life*.[99] In preparation for bringing our discussion of shalom back toward Wolterstorff's theory of situated rationality, a look at what Wolterstorff has to say about the implications of shalom in terms of theory and praxis is in order.

The present chapter has served to answer a question which was left unanswered at the conclusion of chapter 3 in which we explored doxastic obligation. We found that the moral force of socially conditioned and individually situated doxastic obligations still lacked a clear value theory. This question led us to shalom.

Wolterstorff's conception of shalom is, as we have seen, biblically and theologically grounded. It betrays close kinship with the creation order strand of cultural neo-Calvinism, but turns from the nomological emphasis of that tradition to a semi-eschatological, redemptive ethos of human flourishing. Additionally, Wolterstorff gives careful attention to the organic symbiosis of worship and shalom-driven action. He thus implies that a secular program of shalom-driven action lacks the transcendent grounding that a Christian one enjoys, but it is more than that: shalom is the foremost imperative of the new covenant.

This raises an important question. Wolterstorff opens the preface to *Until Justice and Peace Embrace*, his most extended direct treatment of shalom, with a question: "What should be the Christian's overarching goals with respect to our present social order? . . . How should the Christian insert

---

97. "It's Tied Together by Shalom," in *Hearing the Call*, 423.
98. See also Sloane, *On Being a Christian*.
99. *Reason within the Bounds*; *Educating for Shalom*; and *Educating for Life*.

him or herself into the present social order?"¹⁰⁰ "The answer to this question is," he says, "largely the same as the answer to the question what, from the Christian point of view, *a person's* overarching goals should be with respect to our present social order," because, he explains, "what the Christian should do is essentially, from the Christian point of view, what everyone should do."¹⁰¹

This charter statement raises an important question. What precisely should be the case, from the Christian point of view? Should all people share the same vision for involvement in the present social order given the more fundamental Christian belief that all people 'should' be Christian? Or, from the Christian point of view, should all people share that vision for involvement by virtue of some other commonality—say, by virtue of the vision's being known universally though merely implicitly, or perhaps by virtue of its being clearly revealed in the world and in human nature? In either case, the vision would be essentially Christian but not always recognized as such. If Wolterstorff has something like the former in mind, that from the Christian point of view, all people should be Christian, and that as Christians they would share a particular vision for social involvement, we might expect the subsequent treatise on shalom to take the form of an apologetic for the faith, if an indirect one. And one can indeed discern the lineaments of this approach, especially in the later publication, *Justice: Rights and Wrongs*, in which Wolterstorff argues both that natural human rights are universally assumed and that no secular account has or can be given for this assumption.¹⁰² Elsewhere, Wolterstorff summarizes neo-Calvinism, and echoes Kuyper, saying, "until all God's children are religiously united in the Kingdom of Peace, there is no possibility of unified science."¹⁰³ I should add, however, that it is not clear, not in that particular place or elsewhere, whether Wolterstorff himself endorses this or a similar view of history and science; his wording at that moment is carefully descriptive of historic neo-

---

100. *Until Justice and Peace Embrace*, vii.

101. Ibid.; emphasis original.

102. See chapters 14 and 15. Specifically, Wolterstorff's argument there is that human rights are rooted in human dignity, and it is for human dignity that secularism cannot provide an account. He even argues that the account given for human dignity in the UN Declaration on Human Rights cannot stand on a purely secular foundation and that it in fact requires a religious one. See "Response: The Irony of It All." See also "Can Human Rights Survive Secularization?," parts 1 and 2, where Wolterstorff denies a precedent for natural human rights in the ancient Greeks, claims that no secular account since has been successful, that the Christian and Hebrew Scriptures are the source for our ideas of such rights, and that, consequently, human rights *cannot* survive secularization.

103. *Educating for Shalom*, 64.

Calvinism, though it is clear enough what Kuyper would have meant by those words.[104]

On the other hand, should Wolterstorff intend rather something like the latter, that by virtue of some other commonality, by virtue of something more or less evident in the created order or in human nature, or maybe by virtue of no prior commonality at all, all people should share this, the shalom, vision for social involvement, we would be right to expect shalom to be in some sense pluralistic. And at times this appears to be the view Wolterstorff favors: "'Is one entitled to believe that Jesus was resurrected from the dead?'" he asks. "It all depends."[105] Furthermore, there is no de-culturized and de-personalized science, Wolterstorff contends. Science is and ought to be done according to a person's governing commitments (e.g. religious and religious-like beliefs); but shalom is a universal human calling. Does shalom transcend religious differences? Perhaps. In sum, Wolterstorff will argue for shalom, and craft and proffer his understanding of it on the basis of Christian commitments but toward a pluralistic social vision and praxis.[106]

Wolterstorff's theoretical or scientific pluralism also favors this interpretation. The Christian approach to pluralism in science or academia is not, or ought not to be, to declare independence from the broader world and insist that only on Christian foundations may the true and the good stand (here Wolterstorff demurs to Kuyper). What Christians should do "with the traditions in which we locate ourselves," Wolterstorff says, "is *appropriate* from those traditions what remains of worth as we struggle shoulder to shoulder with other human beings toward a society of justice and peace."[107] The implication is that in a pluralistic world, Christians should not assume that the Christian creed represents the only valid foundation for the practice of science. And yet, this very image of creedal variety is predicated on shalom. A pluralistic view of the practice of science is afforded by a particularistic confession and ethical vision.

---

104. I refer here to Kuyper's thought on there being two sciences, regenerate and unregenerate, and that this duality is a function of the fall. Since the distinction between the two sciences is fundamentally soteriological, a single, unified science would have been only an eschatological hope. See Kuyper's *Principles of Sacred Theology*, 106–82. I do not know to what extent Wolterstorff is sympathetic to Kuyper's regenerate/unregenerate antithesis.

105. "On Being Entitled to Beliefs about God," in *Inquiring about God*, 315. On *what* does it all depend? On the complete deontological concerns of a person's moral situation.

106. See, for example, his discussion of "dialogic pluralism" in *Justice: Rights and Wrongs*, xi–xii; and "Scholarship Grounded in Religion."

107. *Until Justice and Peace Embrace*, ix.

In chapter 5, my focus turns to shalom theorizing and scholarship. I introduce the theory versus praxis debate and then begin an initial investigation into what shalom has to say relative to that question (§5.2). I then analyze in more detail various levels of shalom theorizing (§5.3), revisit questions of shalom and Christian belief (§5.4), and turn once again to the contributions of neo-Calvinism to this discussion (§5.4). The final sections of chapter 5 steer this material back toward situated rationality. There we find that a large part of what we say about scholarship and theorizing applies generally to belief formation and doxastic behavior (§5.5-6). Thus chapter 5 completes our analysis of the relationship between shalom and rationality, between the comprehensive ethic of shalom and the doxastic life.

5

Theory and Praxis
Shalom Theorizing and Scholarship

Following an introductory chapter surveying Wolterstorff's career and background, articulating, and then situating our question, we turned in the second chapter to Wolterstorff's doxastic anthropology. There we witnessed the first steps in Wolterstorff's departure from the canon of epistemological research in the modern west, namely, his replacement of the 'solitary, immobile reactor' with a historically situated, individually conditioned, and ethico-doxastically accountable subject. In the third chapter, we examined the broader moral context within which the doxastic subject always finds himself. As we discovered, Wolterstorff believes that among the significant components of a person's full moral situation are socially constituted practices of belief acquisition or governance: practices of inquiry. After a careful analysis of these practices and the ethico-doxastic situation which they constitute, one important question remained unanswered: whence the 'ought'? Whence moral value? This question drove the fourth chapter, an initial analysis of the comprehensive ethic of shalom, covering a number of biblical, theological, and even ecclesiological topics. What remains now is to articulate precisely how Wolterstorff understands the implications of a shalom ethic on the ethics of belief. Thus, the intention of the present, fifth chapter is to pinpoint the direct bearing shalom has on doxastic concerns, and so to draw with maximal clarity the connection between situated rationality and shalom.

My approach is as follows. Through a brief study of Wolterstorff's many writings on education and the academic life, it will become clear that his thought on these topics, and specifically on theorizing, is basically consistent with the shalom ethic sketched in chapter 4. This consistency allows us to enrich our analysis of shalom by looking at this important demonstration of its practical application. Furthermore, the connection between shalom and academia represents a point directly in between shalom and 'every day' rationality, since it addresses specifically the relevance of shalom in terms of theorizing. Wolterstorff on the one hand examines what it means for an individual scholar or an academic institution to take its shalom duty to heart, and on the other hand he reminds us that theorizing itself, the weighing of theories or hypotheses, is by no means an activity confined to the musty halls of the academy; it is a universal activity. The connection is thus drawn directly from shalom to theorizing to the universal activity of belief formation at the core of our discussion of rationality and entitlement.

I begin the fifth chapter with an introduction to the so-called theory versus praxis debate and what shalom, as a governing ethic for scholarship, has to say about it (§5.2). Through this analysis, we are able to see in broad strokes some initial repercussions of the shalom ethic in scholarly activity. Following that, I introduce more specific questions about the structure of theorizing (§5.3). As Wolterstorff views things, shalom manifests in two levels of theorizing: as a principle guiding what things to study and as representing a plausibility framework for hypotheses. In this discussion, questions emerge in terms of the relationship between the governing ethic of shalom and the role of Christian belief in theorizing. On the one hand, shalom invites Christian belief to play a governing role in theorizing, but only by also submitting it to critique and possible revision. We must ask, therefore, about the relationship between shalom and Christian belief (§5.3). Next, I compare Wolterstorff with neo-Calvinism on this issue, since examining his critique of neo-Calvinism's vision of Christian scholarship will help us view in sharper relief the underpinnings of shalom and its role in the ethics of theorizing (§5.4). The concluding sections (§§5.5–6) turn the discussion back toward 'every-day', situated rationality. I argue that the large part of what we have seen regarding scholarship and theorizing applies, in Wolterstorff's view, more generally to belief formation and doxastic behavior. Thus chapter 5 completes our analysis of the relationship between shalom and rationality, between the comprehensive ethic of shalom and the doxastic affairs of human persons.

5.1 BALANCING PRAXIS AND PURE THEORY IN ACADEMIC SCHOLARSHIP

Wolterstorff wants to remind Christian scholars, perhaps especially fellow Calvinists, of the right orientation of the academic life. He does so by grappling with this basic academic value question, that of the prioritization of theory and praxis and the relationship between them. The theory versus praxis question puts before us two alternatives in terms of the goal of scholarship: the claim that the academic life should be devoted to practical concerns, to, say, public influence for the betterment of society, versus the claim that it is self-contained and self-validating and should devote its energy entirely to the pursuit of knowledge for its own sake. If the former valuation sounds less than scientific, the latter might lean toward "letting society go its own way while they [scholars] lock themselves away in this abiding, socially transcendent stronghold" of higher learning. And so, "as there are scholars who have occupied themselves in that great edifice of culture, so too there have been scholars who have occupied themselves in one or another of these projects of structural reform, making it [structural reform] the governing interest of their theorizing."[1] What does shalom have to say about this?

On the one hand, Christian scholarship should not fall into a tendency toward an academic species of avertive quietism, theory for theory's sake. However, as Wolterstorff affirms, the pursuit of knowledge and higher learning bears in itself shalom value as an aspect of human flourishing. It is a kind of basic human good. Christian scholarship should, therefore, balance theory and praxis, while keeping clear and distinct those practical goals which are shalom-dictated—such shalom non-negotiables as justice and equality.

The scholar faces these issues in very practical terms. Wolterstorff asks the question this way:

> Now suppose a scholar has caught that vision of world-formative Christianity . . . Suppose he or she has seen that obedience to Jesus Christ requires that one not acquiesce in the social world as one finds it, turning away whenever possible toward some supposedly higher world of religious truth or cultural delight, but rather that one must struggle for its reform, doing what one can to introduce justice in shalom. What will such individuals, in their capacity as scholars, then do?[2]

---

1. *Until Justice and Peace Embrace*, 162.
2. Ibid. See also "Christian Political Reflection."

The pursuit of pure theory aims toward the discovery and articulation of a body of knowledge, of "nomological theory," with no determined investment in the utility of its yield. It is study for study's sake, theory for theory's sake, knowledge for the sake of knowing. "Praxis-oriented scholarship," on the other hand, "aims at changing the world."[3] Wolterstorff does not see any reason to prefer, *a priori*, either approach at the expense of the other. So, what is best is a shalom-directed balance of theory and praxis, a balance sensitive to personal and contextual variety: in a word, a situated shalom deontology of scholarship. Wolterstorff makes at least three arguments to this effect. In what follows, I shall analyze each of these arguments and afterward raise the issue of Christian particularism relative to shalom and shalom scholarly duty.

(1) First, shalom endorses both approaches to scholarship (or at least it cannot be presumed in any particular case to disqualify either one), and that dual endorsement is always manifest in a flexible, reciprocal give-and-take between individual and social foci. It is natural that, as an ethical and social vision, shalom invites praxis-minded work. But even practical concerns benefit from a theoretical emphasis. It may even be "too obvious to need arguing . . . that for lifting the burdens of deprivation and oppression and advancing the cause of shalom," which is a purely practical aim, "some theoretical knowledge is useful. It is, in fact, *necessary*."[4] Perhaps that much is obvious. But Wolterstorff goes further. He understands pure theory and higher learning in general as vindicated, even mandated, by the shalom vision for human flourishing. The pursuit of pure theory—of knowledge for its own sake—is among the cardinal virtues of shalom: "To me it seems evident that understanding, comprehension, knowledge, constitutes a fulfillment of our created nature," to the extent that "human fulfillment is less than God meant it to be insofar as there is ignorance in place of understanding, bewilderment in place of comprehension." In sum, "[w]here knowledge is absent, life is withered."[5] Of a devotion to high culture and theory for theory's sake, Wolterstorff says,

> In my view we should not argue that the worth of this lies in making us better persons; often it does not. Neither should we argue that it is indispensable for becoming critical thinkers; there are other ways. Nor need we argue that it is indispensable for certain professions, though it is. All that need be said is that

3. *Until Justice and Peace Embrace*, 164.
4. *Reason within the Bounds*, 125–26.
5. Ibid., 126–27.

science and art enrich our lives. When science opens our eyes to the astonishing pattern of creation, and when music moves us to the depths of our being, then we experience some of the shalom that God intends for us. Art and theory are a gift of God in fulfillment of our humanity. A life devoid of the knowledge that theorizing brings us, and of the images that art sets before us, is a poor and paltry thing, short of what God meant our lives to be.[6]

And yet, can the ethical dubiousness of high culture and ivory tower pursuits, which are by some accounts devoid of practical value, be so easily overcome? What may be viewed as the aloofness of academics, artists, theoretical scientists, and others who appear to produce nothing much for the betterment of society, neither for themselves nor for those in need, may evoke a distinct moral unease. Wolterstorff channels this resentment, saying, "[a]s Rotterdam burns, they study Sanskrit verb forms."[7] But if pure theory enjoys shalom warrant, we should be able to articulate the conditions for putting such concerns, sober as they are, to rest. Can we?

Wolterstorff's defense of high culture and pure theory as embodying cultural flourishing and thus as shalom-enjoined is not intended to vindicate the person who demonstrates little to no practical interest. This is, at least in part, because shalom is never an individualized, subjectivized directive, but it is rather an objective state of affairs which is global in scope; if it is incomplete or unrealized somewhere, it is incomplete or unrealized everywhere. Realized shalom is shalom realized globally and objectively, though not necessarily uniformly. In other words, supposing shalom were fully realized is not to suppose every individual and every social situation embodies identical cultural achievements. We might say, therefore, that shalom requires equal concern for the individual and for the corporate. Thus, subjectively speaking, shalom must inform the theory versus praxis question in terms of both (individualized) situationality but also in terms of the full, objective scope of shalom. In this light, we might say that we welcome the rigorous study of Sanskrit verb forms, so long as there is no fire that the linguist can help to prevent or extinguish.

---

6. "The Mission of the Christian College," in *Educating for Shalom*, 29–30. Here Wolterstorff names "art and theory" together. The implication is that, when he speaks of theoretical knowledge as a shalom good, we can take him to mean this as part of cultural development, or what I call here "high culture," more broadly. As we saw in chapter 4, social or political justice is necessary but not sufficient for shalom. Cultural flourishing is the operative concept, instead of and beyond mere absence of conflict.

7. *Until Justice and Peace Embrace*, 162.

Thus, the picture Wolterstorff presents is of a rich appreciation for knowledge both in terms of its intrinsic and its instrumental values, both valuations gaining a foothold in shalom. "I suggest that if the activities of the scholar are to be justified, that justification must be found ultimately in the contribution of scholarship to the cause of justice-in-shalom. The vocation of the scholar, like the vocation of everyone else, is to serve that end."[8] In practice, the scholar's responsibility is complex and varies from one context to another and from person to person. We may infer this complexity from the fact that Wolterstorff avoids generalizations, and instead encourages scholars to evaluate and re-evaluate, to adjust and re-adjust, for the sake of shalom: "Always," Wolterstorff explains, the scholar "must engage in the difficult and complex task of weighing the one against the other, pure theory against praxis-oriented theory, deciding which holds most promise of contributing most substantially to the cause of justice-in-shalom."[9]

(2) Second, pure theory and praxis-directed theorizing are separated only to their own detriment. Pure theory has much to offer, even if incidentally, the praxis-minded approach, as does the more practical the theoretical purist. Furthermore, it could be argued that neither one actually does nor really could manifest in isolation from the other. Against an exclusive emphasis on pure theory, Wolterstorff warns that nomological theorizing for its own sake is dangerously conducive to the avertive tendencies to which Calvinism has shown itself susceptible. A healthy measure of shalom-directed practical interest might provide the necessary counter-balance. Wolterstorff also points out that interest exclusively in pure theory naturally comes under suspicion: It is argued that even when a scholar sees himself as given over completely to pure theory, this is in fact rarely the case.[10]

But perils equally attend an exclusive emphasis on praxis-oriented theorizing. Praxis, as the sole end of research or theorizing, is, first of all, self-limiting. Fixing one's energy exclusively on the instrumental value of knowledge can stifle creativity and innovation, so a staunch praxis-driven approach might narrow the scope of potential advances and thus may not be maximally productive even toward its own end. In fact, from a purely practical point of view then, a focused pursuit of pure theory may be praxis's strongest ally.

More importantly, many would argue that explicitly application-oriented theorizing is inherently distracted by a singular focus on a particular,

---

8. *Reason within the Bounds*, 116.
9. Ibid., 133–34.
10. See ibid., 128–35.

given application. Influenced and guided as study is by a chosen end, it is often difficult to avoid bias. In other words, not only might one's focus be narrowed by the emphasis on praxis, it may also be corrupted. Given these weaknesses, pure theory is thought to stand as a corrective, since its only concern, we suppose, is the disinterested pursuit of increased knowledge and better understanding. So, even if the distinction between theory and praxis rarely works out to be as stark as I am portraying it here, an overall balance appears to be, so far as we can speak generically, both ideal and inevitable.

(3) Third and last, Wolterstorff reminds us that if we are thinking in terms of shalom *obligations*, we should remember that deontology is always situational. No attempt at generalizing doxastic obligations can apply, as is, universally; no generalized theory/praxis directive will make sense for all people in all socio-historical situations. But given this situationality, there are ways in which we can think about the role of commitments, even world-formative commitments like shalom, in all theorizing.

So the relative valuations of theory and praxis will always prove to be a function of person and context, and thus always subject to change: "If the scholar is to act responsibly, he cannot evade the difficult task of ascertaining priorities in his concrete situation."[11] Individual and, we should add, fluid situationality are best viewed in reference to and as ultimately responsible to shalom, and so a self-conscious shalom scholar understands his situation as at all times to be fundamentally a shalom situation: "a responsible decision by the scholar . . . requires that he become 'self-conscious.'" And how does one foster this self-consciousness? One does so by returning to the source of our knowledge of shalom and by seeking out where we most acutely have fallen short of it. Wolterstorff writes, "as to the path to self-consciousness, there is none better than that of listening attentively to the message of the Bible, that great unmasker of deceit, while at the same time listening to the cries of those who make the claim of deprivation and oppression . . ."[12]

All this is not to suggest that there is nothing of substance to be said about the shalom duties of the scholarly life, but it does indicate that little can be said in abstraction. We have noted that a scholar's approach to the theory versus praxis question is effectively a shalom issue; it is a question of a person's shalom obligations. Recalling what we have said earlier about situated rationality, obligations are trimmed and tailored according to numerous personal, social, and historical factors. And given Wolterstorff's

11. Ibid., 134.
12. Ibid., 145.

Reid-inspired insights in terms of doxastic anthropology, we can distinguish between actions found within the realm of genuine responsibility and actions which are not within the volitional reach of the subject and so also beyond the sphere of obligation. This complex structure offers a way to speak about situated obligations and about situationally given responsibilities and freedoms. Within that structure, shalom does indeed inform scholarly theorizing in concrete ways. As we shall see in section §5.3, Wolterstorff says that shalom informs theorizing in precisely two ways.

5.2 TWO LEVELS OF SHALOM THEORIZING

So far in this chapter, we have discussed the role of shalom in directing a scholar's activity. As we have seen, Wolterstorff's view is that the scholar's most basic value question must be answered in terms of situated shalom deontology. Moving forward, we now focus more precisely on the weighing of theories and ask a related but more narrow question: how exactly should shalom affect the activity of theorizing? To put it another way, if a scholar is truly and self-consciously a shalom scholar, how should this impact the weighing of theories? In this section, we will see that Wolterstorff's view with regard to this question is divided into two component questions: a more basic question of what to study, and an applied question of what to affirm regarding that subject matter. Shalom informs theorizing on these two levels.

Wolterstorff's principle answer to this question is that Christian belief, or Christian "commitment," we may call it, not only may but should assume a governing role in the pursuit of knowledge.[13] He makes this claim against the modern approach which holds that reason must establish religious be-

---

13. I should mention that, strictly speaking, there is some ambiguity here, since the question targets the relationship between *shalom* and theorizing, but I offer an answer, at least at this point, in terms of *Christian belief* and theorizing. As we will see shortly, where we speak of the role of Christian belief in theorizing, Wolterstorff utilizes generic terms such as "control-belief," "choice-principle," and "authentic" and "actual commitment." So it is not necessary to speak specifically of Christian belief playing these roles, since Wolterstorff's approach would allow other beliefs to fill those categories as well, but it is not erroneous either. Additionally, shalom is a Christian ethic that comes to bear on theoretical activity. Thus, shalom, as an ethic that is largely if not particularly Christian, comes to bear on the theoretical significance of Christian beliefs. There is a kind of methodological humility enjoined by shalom itself that makes this possible. That epistemic humility is a distinctive feature of Wolterstorff's theory of rationality, which is why I wish to draw attention to it. I mention it below just briefly, in terms of the revisability of one's actual (Christian) commitment, but I address it more directly in chapter 6.

lief as, we might say, 'reasonable' (rational, justified, warranted, supported by sufficient evidence, whatever it might be) before (if ever) affording it operative significance in thinking, theorizing, or decision making. Wolterstorff argues instead that religious believers ought to, and are fully entitled to, reason directly *from* their religious convictions rather than always having to reason *to* them in order to satisfy a purportedly non-religious standard of rationality.[14]

And how, exactly, should that be done? Opening a discussion of theory and praxis in *Reason within the Bounds of Religion*, Wolterstorff announces, "[t]wo fundamental sorts of decisions face every scholar. He must decide which matters to investigate. And on the matters under investigation, he must decide which views to hold."[15]

Level Two: Control-Beliefs and Which Views to Hold. Part I of *Reason within the Bounds of Religion*, the entirety of the first edition, is a sustained argument for allowing religious beliefs—in his case Christian ones—to determine or guide in some way "which views to hold."[16] Wolterstorff's posi-

---

14. The central claim of Wolterstorff's essay, "Can Religious Belief be Rational If It Has No Foundations?," in *Practices of Belief*, is that religious beliefs are not *prima facie* irrational even if they fail to meet the criteria of classical modern foundationalism. Wolterstorff goes further in other publications, particularly in *Reason within the Bounds* as we shall see throughout the remainder of this chapter, arguing that one may self-consciously take the truth of one's religious beliefs for granted in theorizing. Another piece on this question specifically in light of modern theology is "Is It Possible and Desirable for Theologians to Recover from Kant?," republished in *Inquiring about God*. See also, "The Role of Religion in Decision and Discussion of Political Issues," in *Religion in the Public Square*, 75, where Wolterstorff discusses the "religious-reason restraint" often enforced in public political discourse, if particularly in the United States.

15. *Reason within the Bounds*, 111.

16. In fact, the first edition of *Reason within the Bounds* offered no such distinction. The first edition was published in 1976. In the second edition, published in 1984, the entirety of the text of the first edition, "unchanged," Wolterstorff says, became Part I, and a Part II was added, along with a new preface (9). Wolterstorff articulates this distinction between "which matters to investigate" and "which views to hold" in the new preface (ibid.) and on the first page of Part II (ibid., 111). In both places, he goes on to explain that the original 1976 text (the entirety of Part I) treated exclusively this second matter, "which views to hold." He also points out that Part II is devoted to the former, "which matters to investigate." (Part II was first published in *Christian Scholars Review* in 1980.) In other words, Wolterstorff's own thinking moved, over the course of several years, from a more focused, narrow treatment of the place of Christian belief in the epistemology of theorizing to the broader issue of the value of scholarly work. In this chapter, I have reversed this order for two reasons: (1) in order to highlight the connection between shalom, treated in the previous chapter, and the structure of theorizing, and (2) because shalom itself is presupposed in Part I. So in my view, the material in Part II is theoretically prior to the material in Part I, but this is clear enough

tion is that a Christian scholar's Christian beliefs should help him determine what views to hold. In this way, Christian beliefs assume the role of what Wolterstorff calls *control-beliefs*.

"Everyone who weighs a theory has certain beliefs as to what constitutes an acceptable *sort* of theory in the matter under consideration," he writes. "We can call these *control-beliefs*."[17] Control-beliefs "include beliefs about the requisite logical or aesthetic structure of a theory, beliefs about the entities to whose existence a theory may correctly commit us, and the like."[18] Control-beliefs, in other words, provide an *a priori* plausibility structure for hypotheses.

Control-beliefs play a variety of roles, which Wolterstorff categorizes into two, positive and negative. He says, "[c]ontrol-beliefs function in two ways. Because we hold them we are led to *reject* certain sorts of theories."[19] "Negatively," he says, "the Christian scholar ought to reject certain theories on the ground that they conflict or not comport well with the belief-content of his authentic commitment."[20] Theories which do not meet the plausibility constraints of control-beliefs do not receive consideration. On the positive side, "control-beliefs also lead us to *devise* theories. We want theories that are consistent with our control-beliefs. . . we want theories that comport as well as possible with those beliefs."[21] Wolterstorff adds in a note, "sometimes the situation is not so much that we *search for* a theory consistent or comportible with some control-belief of ours. Rather, our control-belief *suggests* such a theory to us."[22]

Additional complexity attends Wolterstorff's discussion at this point in terms of "authentic" and "actual" Christian commitment. For Wolterstorff, "authentic" commitment is the whole of a person's Christian identity, including membership in a community with a tradition and sacred scriptures, an ethical framework, and a set of beliefs. The scope here is broad; authentic commitment must not be reduced to doctrines, confessions, or creeds, though these may be part of it. "[T]hough authentic Christian commitment is not to be identified with believing certain things, it does in fact

---

from the two issues treated (and the order in which Wolterstorff himself lists them): which matters to investigate and which views to hold.

17. Ibid., 67.
18. Ibid., 67–68.
19. Ibid., 68.
20. Ibid., 76. I explain the notion of authentic commitment and its counterpart, actual commitment, below. Both concepts reappear in section §5.5.
21. Ibid., 68.
22. Ibid., 153n31.

have a belief-content."²³ More precisely, authentic commitment is the ideal of Christian faith, though a person affirming that ideal may fall short of it: "the complex of action and belief that its realization *ought* in fact to assume, for any given person, is what I shall call his *authentic* commitment."²⁴ Actual commitment, conversely, is whatever a person in fact believes and practices. "Anyone who is fundamentally committed to being a Christ-follower will in consequence do and believe certain things . . . We can, when referring to a specific person, call the complex of action and belief in which his fundamental commitment is *in fact* realized his *actual* Christian commitment."²⁵

Although one may be tempted to construe "authentic" and "actual" commitment along the lines of "objective" and "subjective," this would be mistaken. The distinguishing feature of Wolterstorff's categories is that both are largely, if not entirely, situational. This is rather more obvious for actual commitment, though perhaps less intuitive for authentic commitment. And yet of the latter, Wolterstorff says,

> "[a]uthentic Christian commitment, as I have explained it, is relative to persons and to times. For authentic Christian commitment is how one's Christ-following *ought* to be actualized. And that varies not only from person to person but also from time to time within a given person's life. What I ought to be doing today by way of following Christ differs from what you ought to be doing, and from what I ought to have been doing when I was younger. Likewise what I am obliged to believe as a follower of Christ differs from what someone else is obliged to believe, and differs from what I as a child was obliged to believe. So authentic Christian commitment as a whole, but also the belief-content thereof, is relative to persons and times. One might insist that there are certain propositions which belong to the belief-content of all authentic Christian commitment whatever. Probably so. But certainly they will be few and simple."²⁶

With these categories in mind, note Wolterstorff's claim that "[t]he Christian scholar ought to allow the belief-content of his authentic Christian commitment to function as control within his devising and weighing of

---

23. Ibid., 74.

24. Ibid., 72. He adds, "Notice that on this view authentic Christian commitment is not to be identified with subscription to dogmas. Indeed, it is not to be identified with the believing of propositions, dogmatic or otherwise. But notice also that it does *incorporate* this in several ways" (ibid., 73).

25. Ibid.

26. Ibid., 74–75.

theories. For he like everyone else ought to seek consistency, wholeness, and integrity in the body of his beliefs and commitments."²⁷

One might wonder why Wolterstorff prefers authentic commitment to actual commitment for this controlling role in theorizing. It might be more intuitive to say that what one actually believes would influence one's theoretical activity. The answer is not explicit, but from what he says, we may venture a guess. Wolterstorff writes,

> Rare will be the Christian scholar all of whose control beliefs are contained within his actual commitment. This is justifiably the case. . . . In general, no one is *just* a Christian. He is also, say, an American, a Caucasian, a member of the middle class, of somewhat paranoid personality. All of these appellations suggest characteristic sets of beliefs which, in the appropriate circumstances, may function as control within his theory-devising and theory weighing.²⁸

Here Wolterstorff appears to be saying that to engage in theorizing *as a Christian* means to self-consciously prioritize, at the methodological level, the beliefs and actions distinctive of one's Christian identity. Each designation, each identification, he says, represents a distinct set of beliefs. If one is both a Christian and an American, one's actual commitment represents some mixture of authentic Christian and authentic American beliefs and practices. If that is the case, then when Wolterstorff advocates Christian scholarship in terms exclusively of authentic Christian commitment, he probably has in mind a kind of perpetual self-review on the part of the scholar, in terms of the relation between his or her actual and authentic Christian commitment, so that a good part of scholarship is revisiting, time and again, the basic question of consistency mentioned above. In this sense, theorizing is, among other things, a process of self-analysis, critique, and revision.

A second point confirms this interpretation. Wolterstorff considers the possibility that in the course of theorizing as a Christian, under the control of one's authentic Christian commitment, one encounters either an apparent inconsistency internal to one's authentic Christian commitment, or an apparent conflict between the product of theorizing and some aspect of one's authentic Christian commitment. He asks, "[w]hat happens when a person becomes convinced that, within the body of his belief, incompatibility has emerged . . . ?" And he also asks, "[w]hat happens when incompatibility

27. Ibid., 76.
28. Ibid., 82–83.

emerges for the Christian scholar between the results of science and what he regards as the belief-content of his authentic commitment?"[29]

In Wolterstorff's view, the Christian scholar ought to be ready to "allow scientific developments to induce revisions in *what he views as* his authentic Christian commitment." "So far," he says, "I have been pressing the point that the Christian . . . ought to let the belief-content of his authentic commitment function as control over his theory-weighing." Yet, he says, "[m]y emphasis *here* is almost the opposite."[30] By self-consciously engaging in scholarship as a Christian, the Christian scholar, in a sense, exposes the belief-content of his authentic commitment—the distinct propositional claims of the faith—to critique and possibly even to correction.[31] Wolterstorff's description of this vulnerability is reminiscent of his Reid-inspired doxastic anthropology:

> The scholar never fully knows in advance where his line of thought will take him. For the Christian to undertake scholarship is to undertake a course of action that may lead him into the painful process of revising his actual Christian commitment, sorting through beliefs, and discarding some from a position where they can any longer function as control. It may, indeed, even lead him to a point where his authentic commitment has undergone change. We are all profoundly *historical* creatures.[32]

The activity which Wolterstorff has in view here is the weighing of theories, not conclusive adjudication. Control-beliefs, in other words, inform specifically which sorts of theories may be considered, which hypotheses are legitimate. Wolterstorff is not proposing that all the results of theorizing be deduced or deducible from subjectively determined control-beliefs, nor that theorizing is merely the task of drawing out the implications of one's control beliefs.[33] His claim is not so strong; rather, it is only that one's control-beliefs open a particular field of scientific inquiry by giving some indication of a distinction between coherent and generally incoherent possibilities in terms of the *a priori* plausibility of hypotheses. One example might be the

29. Ibid., 92.

30. Ibid., 94; emphasis added.

31. "Can it be that scientific developments change how one's following of Christ *ought* to be actualized—change what one *ought* to be doing and believing? This, I suppose, is the ultimately alarming possibility. But I think the answer must be ye" (*Reason within the Bounds*, 96).

32. Ibid., 96–97.

33. "The belief-content of the Christian scholar's authentic commitment will not, by and large, actually contain his theories. The theories are not already there in the belief-content, just waiting to be extracted" (*Reason within the Bounds*, 77).

belief that Jesus of Nazareth was the Son of God come in the flesh. Naturally, this belief would form a solid part of Christian control-beliefs, and it would require that, *a priori*, hypotheses such as *God does not exist, God has no son*, and *Jesus had only one nature*, would be marked off as unacceptable. If belief in the orthodox doctrine of the incarnation serves as a control-belief, the particular content of that belief—two natures in one person—outlines for us a plausibility field for theoretical hypotheses. Science thus carried out will emerge 'within the bounds' of given control-beliefs, or within the bounds of religion. Rather than viewing "science as a consensus enterprise" in which religious convictions play no role, Wolterstorff concludes that "[w]e must instead see science as the articulation of a person's view of life, in interaction, of course, with the world and with one's fellows."[34]

The qualification that science is the articulation of a person's control-beliefs in interaction with the world and with one's fellows is significant. It prevents once again a Christian, or anyone else, from simply accepting or rejecting only those theories which comport with what he already believes. Rather, Wolterstorff suggests that Christian theorists take account of their Christian beliefs when going about the task of weighing theories to the extent that theorizing is done both scientifically and in accord with the Christian faith. If this is done properly, we may expect mutually formative interaction between the scientific expression of Christian beliefs and the scientific expressions of other control-belief sets, particularly those which compose a person's "world" and which are represented by a person's "fellows."[35]

In sum, Wolterstorff explains, "[m]y contention . . . is that the religious beliefs of the Christian scholar ought to function as *control-beliefs* within his devising and weighing of theories. This is not the only way they ought to function. . . But their functioning as control-beliefs is absolutely central to the work of the Christian scholar."[36] So in terms of "which views to hold," Christian beliefs may assume the role of control-beliefs.

Level One: Choice-Principles and Which Matters to Investigate. As Wolterstorff became aware at a later stage, however, another question is more fundamental than the question of control-beliefs and what to believe, the question of *which matters to investigate*. And one's answer to that question,

---

34. "The Integration of Faith and Learning," in *Educating for Shalom*, 45.

35. For what Wolterstorff calls "dialogic pluralism," see *Justice: Rights and Wrongs*, ix–xi, 360–61. Cf. "Scholarship Grounded in Religion"; and "Epilogue," in *Religion, Scholarship, and Higher Education*, esp. 14–15; and "The Travail of Theology in the Modern Academy," esp. 45–46. See section §6.3 below.

36. *Reason within the Bounds*, 70.

whether explicit and conscious or implicit and uncritical, represents a methodological stance of some significance. So, how does a scholar decide "which matters to investigate?"

The Christian academic should employ the vision of shalom as a "choice-principle," such that his academic life as a whole serves the advancement of the kingdom of peace specifically by guiding his first and most basic decision, what topics or disciplines to concern himself with.[37] "I suggest," Wolterstorff says, "that if the activities of the scholar are to be justified, that justification must be found ultimately in the contribution of scholarship to the cause of justice-in-shalom. The vocation of the scholar, like the vocation of everyone else, is to serve that end."[38] Choice-principles should be viewed by the Christian scholar as "a strategic point of entry" into the "battle taking place in history between the forces that advance and the forces that retard the coming of shalom."[39]

When Wolterstorff applies the same principle to institutions, specifically to educational institutions, it becomes clear that he understands the issue to be an ontological one: Christian scholars should be what might be called *shalom scholars*, Christian schools *shalom colleges* and *shalom grade schools* which produce *shalom-minded graduates*. "The graduate who prays and struggles for the incursion of justice and shalom into our glorious but fallen world, celebrating its presence and mourning its absence—that is the graduate the Christian college must seek to produce."[40] So in terms of both individuals and institutions, shalom serves as a kind of key mission statement. "Always," the Christian scholar "must engage in the difficult and complex task of weighing the one against the other, pure against praxis-oriented theory, deciding which holds most promise of contributing most substantially to the cause of justice-in-shalom."[41]

So, the ontology of educational institutions no less than that of individual scholars is shalom-determined. One illustration of this in terms of the balance of the shalom values of pure theory and of praxis-directed theorizing on the institutional level is Wolterstorff's proposal for a curriculum for higher education based on shalom. What should be taught—the

---

37. See "Choice-Principles for the Scholar," chapter 20 of *Reason within the Bounds*. See also *Until Justice and Peace Embrace*, 165–76.

38. *Reason within the Bounds*, 116.

39. Ibid., 142. Notice here that shalom, not Christian belief or authentic commitment, serves as a choice-principle. The significance of this distinction depends upon whether shalom is essentially or necessarily Christian. In the way that Wolterstorff describes shalom, I believe that it likely is, but Wolterstorff does not say so directly.

40. "Teaching for Shalom," in *Educating for Shalom*, 26.

41. *Reason within the Bounds*, 133–34.

choice-principle question in the educational context—should be couched in terms of shalom conducivity, and what should emerge, he affirms, are shalom minded graduates. Schools should embrace an intensely shalom-driven curriculum based on scripture and based upon careful attention to the state of shalom on a global scale. And quite overtly, a school's goal should be to inculcate shalom-mindedness in its graduates.[42] "What I mean," he adds, "is not just that we must teach *about* justice—though we must; I mean that we must teach *for* justice. The graduate whom we seek to produce must be one who *practices* justice."[43]

The following excerpts from an essay entitled "The Project of a Christian University in a Postmodern Culture," illustrate Wolterstorff's shalom ethic of scholarship:

> A visitor came one day to the Free University of Amsterdam and stopped at the information desk. "Where can I change some money?" he asked. "Right here behind me, to your right." "And where can I get something to eat?" "Down this hall and then take a left. You'll see the cafeteria almost right away." "And do you have a chapel somewhere?" asked the visitor. "A chapel?" said the officer. "Oh yes, I think we do; let me ask a minute." "Yes, I'm told it's on the sixteenth floor. Take the elevator over there, all the way up to the fifteenth floor; you will then see a small stairway going up to the chapel."
>
> The visitor stood in line to change his money. He pushed his way through the crowd to get some lunch—a bowl of soup, and two currant buns. Then he took the long ride up to the fifteenth floor, got out, and climbed the stairway to the chapel. He turned

---

42. He writes, "I submit that the curriculum of the Christian college must open itself up to humanity's wounds . . . It is a call for a more comprehensive model . . . that incorporates the arts, the sciences, the professions, and yes, the worship and piety of humanity, along with humanity's wounds, and brings them together into one coherent whole . . . What might such a model be? What should be the overall goal of Christian collegiate education? There is in the Bible a vision of what it is that God wants for God's human creatures—a vision of what constitutes human flourishing and of our appointed destiny. The vision is not that of disembodied individual contemplation of God; thus it is not the vision of heaven, if that is what one takes heaven to be. It is the vision of *shalom* . . . it is *as a school* that the lure of shalom will direct and energize it. But given that understanding, the curricular model that I propose for Christian collegiate education is what I shall call the *shalom* model. The goal for which Christian educators are to teach is that our students be agents and celebrators of shalom, petitioners and mourners" ("Teaching for Shalom," in *Educating for Shalom*, 23–24).

43. "Teaching for Shalom," in *Educating for Shalom*, 24.

the handle; but the door was locked. After looking around and seeing no one, he descended to the madding crowd.[44]

The parable Wolterstorff offers here is a subtle rebuke of the avertive Christian academic.[45] The visitor appears to have wanted only to pass through the crowd of busy worldly figures, to push his way past the bustling *hoi polloi*, staying only as long as necessary. One gets the distinct feeling that he sat alone to eat his lunch, his only goal being to satisfy his appetite before ascending to the deserted sixteenth floor in order to devote himself to private acts of piety. But heaven was *closed* to his avertive religion. In a sad twist of irony, the visitor, having found the chapel door locked, and after slipping past the crowds aloof and indifferent, looked around for help. Upon finding no one around to help him escape the company of other people, the visitor turns back—turned back even by heaven itself—to join in the business of life in this world. It is a caustic portrayal of the avertive academic.

In the same essay, Wolterstorff conveys the alternative:

> . . . there are certain realities immensely important to the Christian which the Christian university, so I suggest, should do what it can to keep before its staff and students. . .
>
> It must keep before them the faces and voices of suffering from around our world. Critical ethical discussions conducted in the academies of the well-to-do in the West lose touch with human reality. To compensate, a Christian university must do what it can to confront its members with the suffering of the world—partly to let us learn from the wisdom so often present in the voices of suffering, partly to evoke in us the empathy which is the deepest spring of ethical action, partly to remind us that an ethic that does not echo humanity's lament does not merit humanity's attention.[46]

This section presents a proper shalom academic ethic. Why must the Christian college or the Christian school bear the responsibility of keeping before its staff and students the suffering of the world and humanity's lament? Why must perpetual interest in the "faces and voices of suffering" be a constant part of the self-identity of a Christian educational institution?

---

44. "The Project of a Christian University in a Postmodern Culture," in *Educating for Shalom*, 133–34. Wolterstorff is slightly mistaken: the chapel in the main building of the Free University of Amsterdam is on the fifteenth floor, with the elevators going only up to the fourteenth.

45. The parable could also be read as a rebuke of all or any non-shalom-directed, ivory-tower self-absorption, though it is rather more likely that Wolterstorff has a particular case in mind.

46. "The Project of a Christian University," in *Educating for Shalom*, 133.

Simply because a Christian person or institution is primarily a shalom institution. Now shalom, Wolterstorff writes, is not realized if anywhere, to any person, it is denied. If flourishing is stifled or justice is absent or threatened, shalom itself represents the responsibility *of all people* to the extent that their situation allows to advance shalom where ever it is opposed. If a person can materially contribute nothing to the aid of people suffering, it is no less his genuine duty to share in solemn lament and sympathy. Indeed for Wolterstorff himself, face to face encounters with lives touched by suffering, and his own personal trials, worked deep-structure changes in the way he handled and applied himself as a scholar.[47]

These two excerpts summarize on the one hand the shalom duty of institutions, while commending a methodology for pursuing shalom and for preserving an active shalom self-consciousness. On the other hand, they serve as a poignant reminder of the shalom duty of individual scholars. It must be noted as well, if it risks over-reading, that in Wolterstorff's parable, heaven itself is shut—or withheld, for a time—to the avertive-minded academic.

5.3 SHALOM AND CHRISTIANITY

We have seen, first, that the Christian academic should account for his Christian commitments in a way that constitutes his professional activity self-consciously as Christian. This claim has been worked out on two levels, in terms of control-beliefs and choice-principles. But Christian beliefs cannot boast exclusive rights to function as control-beliefs and choice-principles. These categories are open to other commitment sets as well—a different religion altogether, atheism or agnosticism, or beliefs more political or social in nature. It will not be a surprise then when the attendant theory of rationality levels accordingly the theoretical field and provides for the operative significance not only of Christian but, at least initially, any other shalom-conducive control-beliefs.[48] So, Wolterstorff's proposal for the theoretical

---

47. See the sections entitled "Cries of the Oppressed" and "Lament for a Son" in "The Grace the Shaped My Life," in *Hearing the Call*, 12–15; Afterword to *Educating for Shalom*, 295–99; and *Lament for a Son*.

48. As noted in section §5.2, Wolterstorff welcomes this pluralism: "I think that as we struggle to form a new image of science, we shall have to give up the vision of science as a consensus enterprise other than in some ultimate eschatological sense. We shall have to give up the notion that one must limit oneself to saying what every rational person would agree on. We must instead see science as the articulation of a person's view of life, in interaction, of course, with the world and with one's fellows . . . the responsible pursuit of science does not yield consensus but pluralism; we human

significance of Christian convictions is in two parts: (1) choice-principles which guide, on the ontological level, the self-constitutive choices of the Christian scholar or Christian educational institution—what to study, how and what to teach, and so on; and (2) control-beliefs which imply a field of plausibility. This two part structure, notice, is transferable and not organically bound to Christianity, though it ought to be bound to shalom. How shall we understand this, given that shalom is a biblical concept?

Recall from section §3.2 what Wolterstorff has said about the assumptions operative in the social status of practices of inquiry. Such practices "acquire their point and plausibility, and their results become intelligible, within a context of ontological and epistemological conviction. Outside that context, employing them makes no sense and their results remain mute. To employ them is to presuppose that frame of conviction."[49] Now we see that, according to Wolterstorff's proposal, shalom is, or ought to be, that frame of conviction. Wolterstorff draws a single line of demarcation, a line between the forces that advance and the forces that encumber the realization of shalom, rendering the call particularly acute for the follower of Christ or for the Christian institution to have clear just how and how effectively one's principle undertaking aids the advancement of shalom; but that call is not exclusively Christian. More precisely, that obligation is not contingent upon assent to Christian claims.

Wolterstorff conceives the theoretical significance of Christian belief in the academic life as an answer to the pure theory versus praxis-oriented theory question in terms of shalom: shalom is makes Christian-shalom-guided and Christian-shalom-governed science possible. Shalom is Christian global-mindedness. But is shalom-mindedness necessarily Christian?

In section §5.2 above, we noted Wolterstorff's threefold response to the theory versus praxis question. First, theory and praxis both bear intrinsic shalom value, and, second, theory and praxis are interdependent. Third, by the transcendent vision of shalom we are bound to ask about the shalom obligations of every situated individual and institution, shalom being *the most basic*, and possibly the only such universal and basic deontological category. It is precisely *that* individualized shalom-accountability which Wolterstorff has put in terms of control-beliefs and choice-principles.

Thus, while it certainly seems that Christians and readers of the Christian Bible may lay unique claim to shalom, it is clear that shalom is also kind of 'natural law' universally available to the natural mind apart

---

beings *see* things differently, without that fact itself being the sign of irrationality on anyone's part. The central beliefs with which we each unavoidably operate do not enjoy consensus" ("The Integration of Faith and Learning," 45).

49. "Entitlement to Believe and Practices of Inquiry," in *Practices of Inquiry*, 97–8.

from scripture or regeneration. And if so, the world-formative teleology of theorizing would not be incumbent upon Christian scholars particularly (or exclusively) but upon all scholars universally. Indeed, as Wolterstorff says, "Calvinists did not deny—indeed they insisted—that the capacity for apprehending the will of God for our lives belongs to all human beings simply by virtue of our created nature."[50] So at the very least a *capacity* to recognize shalom obligations is given in God-createdness, an ontological status more basic than fallenness or regeneration. Even given sin, says Wolterstorff, ". . . no matter what the extent of a person's perversity, that capacity is never lost . . ." And he goes further: ". . . indeed, the *workings* of that capacity are never fully *suppressed:* God's will is communicated in natural law."[51] Wolterstorff then warns, ". . . let us not suppose that the coming of God's Kingdom of shalom depends solely on what church people do."[52]

If we grant that these creational ought-to-bes are knowable apart from scripture or regeneration or the teaching of the church, all we are affirming, he seems to say, is that such ought-to-bes are observable aspects of the world. It may be the case that the best account for these creational intentions is uniquely the propriety of the Christian faith, the "message of the Bible," as Wolterstorff says; but they, creational intentions, are no more the exclusive epistemic property of Christian people—or "church people"—than mathematics, physics, or logic.[53]

In terms of the church's role, then, Wolterstorff defends the uniqueness of the Christian church as the "sacrament" of the world, serving as a steady indicator toward a better day, and even despite its own shortcomings, pointing the world toward the fulfillment of its creational potential in terms of shalom as revealed in the Bible: "But through all the dark days of its existence, there is one way in which the church has remained the sacrament of, the effective pointer to, a new day: down through the ages it has been the bearer of the Bible . . ."[54]

Where is the specific and distinctive content of Christianity? It is in the simple fact that shalom is a biblical concept. And yet this may amount merely to the fact of a biblical announcement of ought-to-bes which are inherent

---

50. *Until Justice and Peace Embrace*, 18.

51. Ibid.

52. Ibid., 145.

53. Some Reformed Christian thinkers in the Kuyperian tradition argue that not even these basic areas constitute common ground between Christian and non-Christian thought. Examples of application include Poythress, *Redeeming Science*; and Poythress, *Logic*. For an explanation of the methodology of this approach, see Oliphint, *Covenantal Apologetics*.

54. *Until Justice and Peace Embrace*, 145.

in creation itself, and evident in nature, there for all to see. If readers of the Christian Bible enjoy a privileged vantage point on shalom, they cannot boast of exclusive epistemic rights to it. Shalom is universally knowable—even universally known. We can see this, first, because it is inherent and evident both in creation and in human nature itself, and, second, because *were it not* universally evident, it could not bear universal deontological weight, as it surely does, from Wolterstorff's point of view.[55] Shalom is not the sole property of Christian belief. Shalom is the governing or central principle of Christianity—of Christian views of creation, salvation, and history; but the particularly confessional propositions which constitute the Christian faith need not be the governing principle of shalom.[56] More attention is devoted to this connection in chapter 6.

In Wolterstorff's case, the sources for shalom are not a handful of propositions hinting vaguely at a mere Christianity, but a number of distinctively Dutch Reformed biblical and theological themes.

---

55. Certainly there are echoes here of the classical Reformed position on the creature's knowledge of God. In sum, this has been that the knowledge of God is not only amply available to the creature, but irresistibly so, both around him and within him as *imago Dei*. The Apostle Paul states clearly in Rom 1:18ff that all men know God and are thus without excuse. He says there that all men know God and yet refuse acknowledge him as God. Thus the knowledge of the one true God is objectively clear but subjectively and culpably obscured due to sin. As will become clear shortly, the redemptive illumination of the mind, if we may phrase it that way, which answers the subjective obscuration due to sin, is echoed in the role Wolterstorff sees for two things: listening to the voices of the oppressed and listening to Christian Scripture.

56. We might note in this regard the following summary statement near the conclusion of "A Theistic Grounding of Human Rights," chapter 16 of *Justice: Rights and Wrongs*: "My argument has been hypothetical. I have articulated a theistic grounding of human rights, arguing that if God loves, in the mode of attachment, each and every human being equally and permanently, then natural human rights are grounded in that love . . . I have not argued that God does in fact so love every creature who bears the *imago Dei*. I have argued that a grounding of natural human rights is available to the person who holds the theistic convictions indicated. I have not argued for those theistic convictions themselves. The reader will have discerned, however, that I do in fact hold those convictions" (360). The strategy Wolterstorff describes here is as follows: he affirms the universality of natural human rights and offers a possible account for natural human rights along the lines of a particular and rather minimal Christian confession, the creation of humankind in the image of God. He thus affirms a connection between a widely affirmed moral and political principle and Christian thought grounded in the Bible. He seems therefore to hold that belief in human rights follows necessarily from the belief that all human beings are created in the image of God; but he does not affirm that belief in human rights follows *only* or *exclusively* from that belief.

5.4 WHAT ABOUT NEO-CALVINISM?

In sections §4.3 and §4.4, we reflected on Kuyperian neo-Calvinism, comparing it to Wolterstorff's notion of shalom. We found that Wolterstorff had developed shalom with the Kuyperian tradition in mind, benefiting from it here and there, distancing himself from it elsewhere. Wolterstorff has also devoted careful thought to the Protestant and specifically the neo-Calvinist approach to the theory versus praxis question. His principal claim is that neo-Calvinist academic work is guilty of broad neglect of the praxis value of scholarship and the practical obligations bearing on scholarly activity. He offers two closely related reasons for this oversight: (1) an isolationist tendency implicit in the Kuyperian notion of sphere sovereignty, and (2) a truncation of the biblical view of history that effectively relegates the Christian scholar to a pre-lapsarian approach to his vocation. Examining Wolterstorff's critique along these lines will help us to clarify exactly how, in his view, shalom informs the theory versus praxis discussion.[57]

(1) In Wolterstorff's estimation, neo-Calvinism has displayed intense concern for the cooperation of Christian commitment and worldly engagement, particularly in terms of academia and scholarly theorizing. But neo-Calvinist thinkers have, he argues, generally failed to appreciate, in a consistently biblical way, the relationship between theory and practice. Too frequently, neo-Calvinist scholarship is characterized by disinterest in the world: "In the neo-Calvinist concept, the goal of scholarly endeavor . . . is, for the non-philosophical sciences, to develop a body of nomological theory—a body of laws, abstract, general, and integrated—rather than a body of theory useful for the struggle to reform society . . ."[58]

As we will see, there is some indication that Wolterstorff attributes this tendency, at least in part, to Kuyper's emphasis on sphere sovereignty and Dooyeweerd's emphasis on differentiation.[59] If academia is a perfectly sovereign sphere, academic theorizing governed by and expressing Christian

---

57. The parable with which we concluded section §5.2 reflects upon the very same criticisms we will unfold in this section.

58. *Until Justice and Peace Embrace*, 165. Note the strong language in this excerpt: "Turning from liberation theology to neo-Calvinism as expressed in Herman Dooyeweerd, one is struck first by the differences. Here the cries of the wretched of the earth are not given voice. Here there is little talk of oppression, and consequently little of liberation from oppression; the talk is more of 'authority structures'" (ibid., 53).

59. See Dooyeweerd, *A General Theory of the Modal Spheres*. For a contemporary study connecting sphere sovereignty and responsibility, see Baus, "Dooyeweerd's Societal Sphere Sovereignty."

commitments is an end in itself. No pressing need to direct academic work toward the distinct and separate social or political spheres presents itself.

To be sure, the integrity of the spheres is important for shalom cultural flourishing:

> As a direct corollary to this [the "normative nature" of the "particular type, or structure" of an institution], we should see to it that the institutions belonging to one sphere do not dominate those belonging to another, because when one sphere is dominated by another, life in the former is distorted and cannot flower in its own unique normed manner. We are to work for the *sovereignty of the spheres* . . .[60]

But Wolterstorff recognizes, on the other hand, that the sovereignty of the spheres is liable to over-emphasis and, consequently, might tend toward isolationism:

> Kuyper never tired of insisting that just as the Christian politician ought to work for the reform of social structures with the support of Christian people generally, so in a similar way the Christian scholar ought to work for the reform of scholarship with the support of Christian people generally. Thus, it was *parallelism* of scholarly and social reform that Kuyper stressed, rather than scholarship *in the service of* social reform.[61]

Indeed, "Many of the critics of the neo-Calvinist project of Christian scholarship have castigated the scholarship that has emerged as hopelessly abstract, so far divorced from the real issues of life as to be useless to them." And, "I think," Wolterstorff adds, "there is some merit to that criticism."[62]

The sovereignty of the spheres, in a worst case scenario, instead of encouraging flourishing, tends toward a cold, unbending isolationism, undercutting what should be the scholar's accountability to the full, objective realization of justice-in-shalom. By virtue of this stark integrity of the academic sphere, the scholar is invited and encouraged, in the name of the doctrine of creation, to pursue scholarly interests without concern for injustice and suffering. Consequently, the danger is that, on this view, the plight of the oppressed is confined within the social and political spheres. The most the scholar may be obligated to do is peer down from the ivory tower in sympathy and, perhaps, supply his politically and socially engaged peers with nomological reflection on the issues they face or with data-laden

---

60. *Until Justice and Peace Embrace*, 58.
61. Ibid., 165.
62. Ibid. Wolterstorff mentions no one in particular.

sociological studies. He can write about it. If the integrity of the academic sphere is too inflexible, it might never occur to the scholar to direct his work toward practical, non-academic ends relative to the brokenness of the world.[63] He has the means and motive to address only scholarly brokenness.

Neo-Calvinist scholarship, Wolterstorff observes, surveys soberly the Kuyperian conflict with the forces of non-Christian thought at the level of control-beliefs: "If one carefully scrutinizes what goes on in scholarship, says the neo-Calvinist, one sees that often the root of what leads scholars to reject a certain theoretical claim is that they more or less consciously perceive that claim to be out of accord with their religious commitment."[64] Neo-Calvinist scholarship also maintains the distinctively Kuyperian recognition that this conflict is inevitable, precisely because *all* thinking is religious, in the formal sense of always taking something as ultimate: "This is a dynamic operative in all scholars," Wolterstorff explains, "since everyone has a religion (that is to say, everyone absolutizes something, everyone fixes on something as giving unifying coherence to his endeavors). The thing that makes a body of theorizing *Christian* in character, then, is that the Christian religion is allowed to control the theory acceptance of the scholar."[65]

The neo-Calvinist has understood Christian commitments as founding, and in this way controlling, the yield of the Christian scholar's theorizing. With these precepts, these Christian non-negotiables, scholarly output must maintain consistency; no product of Christian scholarship may emerge which is in conflict with the Christian confession. Again, Kuyper's two sciences and the integrity of Christian science entail that Christian scholars work toward a body of theory which complements the Christian faith.[66]

We may recall from the foregoing discussion that theory acceptance and control-beliefs are downstream from the core questions of the self-definition of a scholar. Choice-principles are more basic. Wolterstorff conceives of the more basic question of what a scholar should focus on, what sort of scholar he should be, in terms of choice-principles, and he is concerned that some scholars are self-consciously Christian only at the level of theory

---

63. This is not to say that "scholarly action" is impractical or shalom-impotent. Wolterstorff's own research, writing, and speaking perhaps serve as an example of activity that is both scholarly and potentially fruitful from a practical point of view.

64. Ibid., 166.

65. Ibid.

66. Kuyper's claim is that there are fundamentally two sciences, the science of the regenerate (Christian) and the unregenerate (non-Christian). See his *Encyclopedia of Sacred Theology*, esp. division II, chapter 3, "The Twofold Development of Science," 103–28. For a brief contemporary analysis, see van Woudenberg, "Abraham Kuyper on Faith and Science."

acceptance, and that they thus neglect the more fundamental question of choice-principles.

The avertive neo-Calvinist scholar may steadfastly affirm Christian conviction in terms of control-beliefs and theory acceptance, but neglect Christian influence at the more basic level of choice-principles. To put it pointedly, the result of this truncated Christian self-understanding is that the ontological question—the opportunity for shalom-directed self-definition—is overlooked and the Christian scholar, though able to talk like a Christian academic, is not in any basic way oriented toward being an agent of shalom or toward bearing the fruit of Christian service.[67]

(2) In what sense, then, is this, the worst of avertive Christian scholarship, Christian?[68] It is Christian only in a truncated sense: it is *creational*.

---

67. An illustration of Wolterstorff's interest in correcting this oversight is the addition of Part II to *Reason within the Bounds*. The whole of Part I focused on control-beliefs: "Two fundamental sorts of decisions face every scholar. He must decide which matters to investigate. And on the matters under investigation, he must decide which views to hold. *In the first part of this book I addressed myself to the bearing of the Christian faith on the latter of these two sorts of issues*." In Part II, Wolterstorff addresses the former question, that of choice-principles: "Here," in the second part, "I address myself to the bearing of the Christian faith on the former, paying particular attention to the pure-versus-praxis-oriented-theory debate" (*Reason within the Bounds*, 111). "God is enjoining us to participate in his own cause of human fulfillment—to be his agents in the world." But sadly, "there is within the Christian tradition a strange reluctance—even a refusal—thus to link what God sets as human responsibility and what he sets as the goal toward which he is working in history." Note that the evidence Wolterstorff offers for this claim is drawn from a Reformed confessional document, *The Westminster Shorter Catechism* Q. 1: "For example, the Westminster divines would not disagree with what I have said concerning the fundamental character of human responsibility. Yet in the catechism they composed they said that the end of man is to know God and enjoy him forever" (ibid., 111). On the other hand, Wolterstorff chides liberation theology for its underdeveloped vision: "[I]t leaves unanswered the question, 'After liberation, then what?'" (ibid., 113). He responds thus: "I suggest that immediately at hand in the Christian Scriptures is a better concept for describing God's goal for human existence . . . The concept I have in mind is the concept of *peace*—in Hebrew, *shalom*, in Greek, *eirenē*" (ibid., 113-14).

68. The wording of the answer I offer to this question here in this paragraph is my own, but I believe it to be the sum of Wolterstorff's cautionary word regarding the implicit dangers of the sovereignty of the academic sphere. Wolterstorff certainly does express his concerns in theological and biblical language, arguing directly from Scripture in many places, but he does not emphasize the redemptive-historical language I use here. My use of this language is intended to unpack Wolterstorff's third "point of unease" with the creation-order tradition, the conspicuous absence of Christology/soteriology (discussed in section §4.4), and Wolterstorff's claim that the cultural mandate is insufficient as a charter for self-consciously Christian scholarship. See "Points of Unease with the Creation Order Tradition," in *An Ethos of Compassion*. More on this below.

But, neglecting the fall and thus the subsequent, supervening Lordship of the crucified and risen savior, it is never, properly speaking, *redemptive*. Creational neo-Calvinist scholarship is thus functionally pre-lapsarian.

Wolterstorff is arguing, in other words, that the standard framework of the neo-Calvinist scholar has penetrated only deep enough into the structure of theorizing to make cosmetic changes, and not yet to the foundation of the scientific enterprise in order to make even the ontological constitution of scientists and institutions distinctly Christian. To put it in biblical and theological terms, this tendency toward superficiality, which induces the sort of scholarly isolation Wolterstorff decries, may be diagnosed as an over emphasis on the first and second chapters of Genesis—that is, on God's work in creation and the cultural mandate—and a failure to account for the fall and the redemptive promise in chapter 3.

Neo-Calvinism works with a template of a 'way things ought to be,' a positive and in some sense re-formative program which Dooyeweerd and others articulate in terms of the historical differentiation of the spheres, a differentiation which sharpens the sphere parallelism mentioned above.[69] Among Wolterstorff's "points of unease" regarding this focus on creation structures is his claim that it recasts the directive for Christian living in purely legalistic ("nomological") language.[70] So this approach emphasizes implicit, creational laws and structures, and tends to anchor its redemptive categories in original design structures prior to and apart from the soteriological thrust not only of the New Testament but of all of Scripture beginning in Genesis chapter 3. Ultimately, Wolterstorff argues, the legislative interest of neo-Calvinist thinking which follows this pattern befogs, at the methodological level, the fall into sin and brokenness. For that reason it fails to recognize the teleological (or eschatological), shalom-directed, shalom-driven, redemptive and eschatological charge of the Old Testament prophets, Jesus himself, and the New Testament. It short-circuits the biblical narrative so that we move directly from creation to restoration, without a sober reckoning with the effects of the fall. The Protestant scholar, Wolterstorff explains, acts as though "cultural fulfillment could be attained without

---

69. Wolterstorff discusses Dooyeweerd and cultural differentiation in *Until Justice and Peace Embrace*, 55–59. He says in summary, "In short, what constitutes genuine progress in history as opposed to nonprogressive alteration? The beginning of Dooyeweerd's answer is that *differentiation* is the norm for history. Cultural activity, and thereby history itself, ought to move in the direction of increasing differentiation. Insofar as cultural activity does not do so, it is regressive and thereby disobedient, for differentiation is at the heart of the realization of creation's potentials" (ibid., 55–56).

70. See Wolterstorff, "Points of Unease with the Creation Order Tradition," in *An Ethos of Compassion*, ed. Walsh, Hart, and Vander Vennen. This material is addressed in section §4.4.

intermingling the struggle for fulfillment with the struggle for lifting the bonds of deprivation and oppression."[71]

Surely neo-Calvinism is not without a 'mission': It has laid heavy emphasis upon the cultural mandate in its interest in world re-formation. The cultural mandate, found in Genesis 1:28, makes explicit man's status as vice-regent and keeper, or steward, of the garden, and so it represents the creator's emphasis on the creature's duty. But since it is a pre-lapsarian mandate, it does not account for the basic creation-fall-redemption-consummation narrative of the Christian story, and it therefore falls short of the gospel. To put it another way, Wolterstorff suggests that the cultural mandate is a poor stand-in for the great commission: "The cultural mandate is insufficient as a grounding for the practice of scholarship," Wolterstorff contends. "One needs as well the mandate to work for shalom."[72] For ". . . a scholar's inquiries," he argues,

> must take their course in the light of the fallen condition of our actual society. Intellectual culture is never to be severed from the deprivations and oppressions to be found in our actual social conditions. One cannot proceed as if we lived within a society which is pristine and unfallen, whose only deficiency is that it is not yet fully developed.[73]

This oversight has cost the neo-Calvinist an important advantage in the struggle to advance shalom. The methodological feature to which the concept of choice-principles calls our attention Wolterstorff calls a potential "strategic point of entry" in the cultural battle in which Christians are called to serve on behalf of the kingdom of peace.

"[T]here is a curious abstractness, a curious ahistorical quality, to the Protestant view. There is no sense of the seesaw battle taking place in history between forces that advance and forces that retard the coming of shalom,

---

71. *Reason within the Bounds*, 142. And he says, "Characteristically, they [neo-Calvinists] see this pursuit as grounded in the so-called 'cultural-mandate'—which they interpret as the mandate given by God to mankind to work toward the differentiation of the various social spheres, and then toward developing the potentials within each. That is why they are inclined to resist praxis-oriented theory and favor the pursuit of pure nomological theory: for them it represents letting scholarship 'come to its own.'" He responds, "But to speak only of the cultural mandate is to give scholars no principle for determining the direction of their scholarship . . . One needs as well the mandate to work for shalom" (*Until Justice and Peace Embrace*, 172).

72. *Until Justice and Peace Embrace*, 172.

73. Ibid., 142.

with the consequent necessity for the scholar to choose his strategic point of entry."[74] Thus the avertivism Wolterstorff wishes to redress.

"[I]n the position which I have developed," Wolterstorff writes, "scholarship is placed directly in the service of mankind."[75] And he insists, " only if scholars consider the particular ways in which their society falls short of justice and shalom can they responsibly direct their scholarship."[76] The Christian's scholarly activity is entirely enclosed in shalom—founded upon it, controlled by it, motivated by it, and accountable to it. Shalom is the motive, means, and end, of Christian theorizing *as* Christian. Shalom does not abrogate created design or created ontological structures. Rather, shalom grows out of a soteriological interest in created entities *as fallen*. Shalom is *redemptive*, and thus—for that reason particularly—properly restorative of creation, and in the fullest sense *Christian*.

The choice, whether a scholar pursues praxis or pure theory, depends on a prerequisite assessment of worldly affairs. Scholars must weigh the relative needs for work or theory, "[a]nd always they will have to do this weighing," Wolterstorff explains, "in the light of their total, concrete situation. In particular, they will have to do it in the light of the deprivations and oppressions to be found in the social order as it stands. They cannot act as if they were above history."[77]

Not only are other spheres permitted to set the scholarly agenda, Wolterstorff insists that the Christian scholar is ultimately accountable to the oppressed and to the brokenness of the world: "one of the factors they will have to consider is the social consequences of *not* pursuing praxis-oriented theory. . . if instead they choose to pursue pure theory—then of course they will be responsible for allowing those dynamics [of injustice] to take their course . . . Social responsibility is inescapable for the scholar."[78] Wolterstorff's emphasis on fallenness as the salient feature of our present redemptive-historical context is unmistakable.

In the end, shalom appears to be a heavily praxis-oriented directive for the Christian scholar. Even the intrinsic value of knowledge and learning which Wolterstorff has defended (see §5.2) is predicated on the shalom value of cultural and human flourishing; it is not, at the end of the day, an

---

74. Ibid.
75. Ibid., 140.
76. *Until Justice and Peace Embrace*, 172.
77. Ibid.
78. Ibid.

end in itself.[79] In our own terms: the sovereignty of the spheres is checked by the sovereignty of the crucified and risen savior.

In sum, Wolterstorff diagnoses the errors of avertive neo-Calvinist scholarship, for all the good it has achieved, in terms of an over-emphasis on sphere sovereignty and a truncated view of the biblical narrative. Missing, he says, is the ultimate shalom-accountability of all spheres and shalom self-consciousness, at the ontological level, of Christian scholars and institutions. In my view, Wolterstorff's 'shalom neo-Calvinism' is in this sense a 're-formation' of neo-Calvinist scholarship, with reference to the biblical structure of creation, fall, redemption and consummation.[80]

We turn now to the final section of this chapter in which all that we have said about scholarly theorizing is applied to the doxastic life and to rationality at the popular level. Scholars are not the only theorists, merely the only professional ones. Nor is shalom self-consciousness in theorizing exclusively a scholarly matter; but it pertains to rationality itself.

5.5 CONNECTING ACADEMIC THEORIZING AND POPULAR RATIONALITY

In this section, we will observe the categories by which Wolterstorff translates to the popular level in terms of theorizing in general, belief formation, and rationality, what we have seen regarding scholarly theorizing. Two concepts already mentioned help to make this connection: authentic

---

79. Wolterstorff might appear to disagree: "Man's shalom . . . Does it also include theoretical knowledge—the understanding of man, the universe, and God that scholarship can give us? I find it impossible to answer no to this question. To me it seems evident that understanding, comprehension, knowledge, constitutes a fulfillment of our created nature. To me it seems evident that human fulfillment is less than God meant it to be insofar as there is ignorance in place of understanding, bewilderment in place of comprehension . . . Knowledge—*some* knowledge, anyway—is of inherent worth" (*Reason within the Bounds*, 126–27). And yet, that "worth" is without a doubt *shalom* worth. So we call the worth of theoretical knowledge in some cases "inherent," but it is not an abstract and perfectly self-justifying worth: it is still a derivative worth.

80. Dennison describes neo-Calvinism as having gone in "at least two directions" in the twentieth century, referring to creation-order thought and Wolterstorff's idea of shalom ("Dutch Neo-Calvinism and the Roots for Transformation," 279). I would suggest that shalom is better thought of as a corrective to creation-order thought than an alternative. Perhaps this is simply because I find it more compelling, but perhaps also because it appears to have developed in Wolterstorff's own thinking not as a different reading of Kuyper but as a reformative reading of Kuyper and the founding principles of neo-Calvinist interest in culture.

commitment and actual commitment.[81] Wolterstorff uses these terms to explain the function of Christian belief in theorizing at the popular level.

We have been discussing a shalom ethic for theorizing. If the relevance of this discussion to an analysis of Wolterstorff's theory of situated rationality is to be clear, it must be pointed out that the theorizing activity in question here is not exclusively academic. The academic setting merely brings into focus the deliberative weighing of hypotheses, but such is by no means confined to its intensified instantiations in universities and laboratories or scholarly tomes and academic journals. Theorizing is something everyone does; it is basic for human life.

"I shall not assume," Wolterstorff says, "that theories are propounded or entertained only in the pursuit of some *Wissenschaft*," in the pursuit of some specialized science or nomological theory of this or that. "The fisherman who suggests that fish will not bite after a heavy rain seems to me to be propounding a theory. In other words scientific activity is not to be differentiated from other human activities on the ground that it deals with theories, nor even on the ground that it deals with theories of a special kind—*scientific* theories."[82] And he says, "[s]cience and ordinary life can be viewed as on a continuum with respect to the presence of theories and with respect to the actions performed on those theories."[83] In Wolterstorff's view, there is no irreducible distinction between academic theorizing and the theorizing undertaken by the layperson in daily activities. While it may be incumbent especially on the scholar to concern himself with the confluence of beliefs and principles in the methodology of theorizing, it is part and parcel of the life of every person to have before the mind's eye an authentic commitment which he may manage, at various times, to actualize only in part.

Between authentic commitment and actualization lies an additional pair of descriptive categories which aid in considering this popularized modulation of shalom theorizing: acceptance governance and direction governance, analogous to control-beliefs and choice-principles respectively.[84] Acceptance and direction governance represent two important ways in which a subject exercises control over his knowing and believing, ways in which the will may play a role in the doxastic life.

---

81. Explanation of authentic and actual commitment appears in section §5.2 above. As we will see here, there are close parallels between these terms and the notions of theory and praxis.

82. *Reason within the Bounds*, 64.

83. Ibid., 65.

84. *Until Justice and Peace Embrace*, 168–72.

Wolterstorff rejects hard doxastic voluntarism.[85] Nonetheless, he says, "the will does have a role: we *are* able in various ways to *govern* the workings of our belief dispositions."[86] First, *acceptance governance* indicates the fact that there may be situations in which the option to withhold assent is a real one. "We can govern our belief dispositions in such a way that when in situations in which a certain disposition would normally have been activated, we can resist such activation and avoid automatic acceptance of the proposition in question."[87] *Direction governance* means that a person can decide where to focus his doxastic activity and thereby determine the topics about which he will reason: "Without in any way revising my reasoning disposition . . . I can govern what sorts of things I will do my reasoning about."[88]

It is clear that acceptance governance and direction governance are corollaries of control-beliefs and choice-principles, and that they are directly analogous the role of the will in belief formation which we explored in chapters 2 and 3. Acceptance and direction governance represent the fact that doxastic governance is a part of daily life in ways parallel to the control and choice determinations which every professional theorizer faces. Thus, says Wolterstorff, "scholarship does and should reflect social reality. It is an illusion to suppose otherwise."[89] And likewise, "it is with respect to our capacities for the governance of our beliefs," that there are, for every person thus able to govern his believing, "norms, obligations, responsibilities."[90] "The merit of rationality in our beliefs," he says elsewhere, "is grounded in the proper governance of our assent."[91]

The categories of control-beliefs and choice-principles pin down the precise ways in which Christian or any religious commitments should impinge upon the pursuit of scientific knowledge. Theorizing is no different for the general public, however, and Wolterstorff employs the categories of authentic and actual commitment in terms of acceptance governance and direction governance in order to apply what he has said about professional or scientific theorizing at the public level. Therefore we may understand the

---

85. "It does seem to me that philosophers have often exaggerated the role of the will in belief formation, suggesting things that would imply that by an act of will you could, for instance, simply decide to give up the belief that you are presently holding a book in your hands—whereas surely you cannot do so" (*Until Justice and Peace Embrace*, 168).

86. Ibid., 168.

87. Ibid., 168–69.

88. Ibid., 169. For example, "I can decide whether to spend the next year reasoning about aesthetics or about social theory" (ibid.).

89. Ibid., 172.

90. Ibid., 169.

91. "Can Belief in God Be Rational," in *Practices of Belief*, 228.

entire discussion about theorizing in terms of its highly refined instantiations in the academy as reflective of the public activity of weighing options and hypotheses, assuming a particular field of possibility, and so on. Ultimately, Wolterstorff's analysis of theorizing is built upon his Reidian doxastic anthropology, which maps the territory of volition and accountability in the epistemic life. Whether his account is focused on academic theorizing and couched in terms of control-beliefs and choice-principles, or whether it is focused on the general practice of weighing options and comes to us in categories such as acceptance governance and direction governance, the substance is essentially the same: shalom-directed rationality.

5.6 CONCLUSION

Wolterstorff has offered a detailed account of precisely how the scholar, if specifically the Christian scholar, should go about embracing shalom as the governing vision for his work, and it begins with understanding shalom itself. Wolterstorff's emphasis on listening to the voices of oppressed peoples is part of the process of shedding self-delusion and naiveté, but Scripture, he affirms, is *the* "great unmasker of deceit."[92] The Christian scholar, in other words, should turn his mind toward the shalom vision of how the world ought to be and allow that vision to speak normatively into his world and his situation of moral accountability. Thus two voices should speak in concert to the scholar: the voice of shalom and the voice of the oppressed. When the two meet, the harsh deficiencies and injustices of our present world are brought into sharp relief, and the scholar may then discern what role he may best assume in the struggle for renewal and the advancement of shalom.[93]

The scholar, as we have seen, is responsible to shalom on two levels which Wolterstorff specifies in terms of choice-principles and control-beliefs. First, the scholar can direct his intellectual activity toward a potential body of theory which, in the light of shalom, he understands as shalom

---

92. *Reason within the Bounds*, 145.

93. In the following quotation, Wolterstorff reflects specifically on the project of *Until Justice and Peace Embrace*, and the very same approach is evident. What he says offers a glimpse into his own sense of purpose and shalom calling: "I have explored normative questions concerning the social order by taking a certain vision of what the social order ought to be like—namely, the shalom vision—drawing out some of the implications of that vision, and setting it within the larger interpretative and legitimating context of the Christian gospel; and I have held up our modern social order against the normative structure to see where it falls short. I have picked out some of those shortfalls, explored the dynamics that have produced them, and asked, what, if anything, can be done to alter those dynamics" (163).

warranted, at least, or better, shalom-promoting, in terms of either praxis or nomological theory. Second, the scholar weighs hypotheses in light of shalom, allowing shalom to serve as a kind of deductive first premise laying out a plausibility framework for hypotheses.

This amounts to a plea, even a charge, for the scholar to take careful measure of his freedom and to bear the tasks of self-determination and theoretical investigation with the transcendent vision of shalom foremost in his mind. "[M]y plea," he says, "is for the *integration* of social commitment and theorizing—or, more specifically, for the integration of Christian commitment and theorizing, by way of the commitment becoming the *governing interest* of the theorizing."[94]

And beyond the strictly academic activity of the professional scholar, choice-principles and control-beliefs represent spheres of volitional activity or of epistemic self-governance. So the significance of the activity of the scholar in both of these ways is that it rests on the subject's capacity for self-determination. This allows the pattern—the two-level structure of shalom theorizing—to be mirrored on the public level in ways reflective of Wolterstorff's Reidian doxastic anthropology and his situated approach to rationality.

In light of the discussion of shalom over the course of chapters 4 and 5, we may now say that where in chapters 2 and 3 we found room for doxastic volitional action and thus for doxastic deontology, what we had really located was room for 'shalom doxastic deontology'; we had begun to illuminate a narrow refraction of the reign of shalom in the lives of human beings in terms specifically of the life of the mind. Wolterstorff's concept of shalom thus provides the ethical framework which our analysis of situated rationality in chapters 2 and 3 awaited.[95]

The Christian scholar in particular, if not every Christian individual, should be clear on what shalom requires and on the immanent implications of the reign of Christ; but all scholars, indeed all people, have only but to open the ears of their hearts, we may say, to the voices of the oppressed, the forgotten, the downtrodden, the should-not-bes that surround us. From the strained souls of fellow men come the righteous, corrective cries of injustice, neglect, and exploitation, and by such cries we are reminded that there is a way things ought to be, and that in so many ways, our world falls short.

---

94. Ibid., 163–64.

95. It is perhaps also worth noting that shalom elucidates how different strands in Wolterstorff's work, such as the more theoretical strands (not only on epistemology, but also e.g., on aesthetics) and the more socially self-conscious ones, coherently hang together.

Shalom rationality represents theoretical reflection on the epistemology of this grand commission.

In closing, consider the following excerpt from an article in which Wolterstorff interacts with Gary Gutting on the topic of social evidentialism.[96] Wolterstorff concludes his comments with a nod toward shalom. We see here, as elsewhere, Wolterstorff's claim that the notion of an exclusively epistemic ethic is an abstraction which, in effect, pretends to uproot the epistemic life from the soil of human relations: from social structures, practices, and obligations, socially and historically situated subjectivity, and ultimately from the provenance of all moral value, God's creation as such—in other words, from shalom. He writes,

> It would be a profound mistake, however, to assume that the significance of rationality in our lives is exhausted by its relation to epistemic responsibility; it would even be a mistake to suppose that the significance of the more limited phenomenon of offering reasons to each other is exhausted by its relation to that. We offer each other reasons so as to advance a dialogue, to engage in mutual inquiry, to move toward consensus, to correct what we regard as mistakes, etc. And a clue to the significance of the occurrence of reasons in these kinds of situations is the fact that it is natural to contrast giving reasons to each other with coercing each other, rather than with believing something unjustifiedly.
>
> . . . it is not so much epistemic as moral reasons that oblige us to engage in dialogue with those who disagree with us, offering reasons for, reasons against, and so forth—and then to listen to each other, hoping to learn. Engaging in reason-based listening, dialogue, is an important component in what it is for

---

96. "Once Again, Evidentialism—This Time, Social," is found in *Practices of Belief*. "The rough idea" of social evidentialism, Wolterstorff explains, "is that social situations of religious diversity place on believers a requirement that does not hold for them in situations of consensus—the requirement, namely, that they produce justifying arguments for their theistic beliefs or for their being entitled to hold those beliefs" (266). See also Wolterstorff's analysis of Gutting's position (271–77). After offering some critical remarks, Wolterstorff expresses sympathy with the general thrust of Gutting's concerns. He says, "The main 'truth' in the region of Gutting's discussion is that someone who is my religious other may alter my situation with respect to entitlement by pointing to some actual or purported defect in my belief of which I was previously non-culpably ignorant. His pointing to that defect may be the decisive thing which places me under obligation to employ some practice of inquiry to get rid of that defect—or to employ some practice of inquiry to determine whether it really is a defect. In that way, the dissenting other may indeed alter my situation with regard to entitlement" (ibid., 286).

each community to treat the others with dignity. It is essential to friendship across boundaries. It is essential to authentic flourishing.[97]

With all that we have seen thus far, what Wolterstorff has in mind here can hardly be missed. He draws clearly the connection we have been working toward throughout our study: rationality is itself a shalom-constituted thing for the simple reason that rationality is a part of normal human life and social interaction: "not so much epistemic but moral reasons" is to say that "noetic rationality is grounded in practical rationality," and thus that the conduct of the mind, like all of life, is accountable to shalom.[98] It is beyond question that Wolterstorff views rationality thoroughly and intrinsically in terms of shalom. In the following concluding chapter, I marshal evidence from the present and each of the preceding chapters in order clarify and defend the claim that Wolterstorff's theory of rationality is a shalom doxastic ethic.

---

97. Ibid., 287–88.
98. "Can Belief in God Be Rational," in *Practices of Belief*, 228.

6

A Shalom Doxastic Ethic and the Status of Christian Belief

The purpose of this study is to present an interpretation of Wolterstorff's theory of rationality as a shalom doxastic ethic. As noted in chapter 1, a theologically self-conscious study of situated rationality presents itself, first, in terms of an appreciation of Wolterstorff's work as the work of a Christian philosopher, which, it would seem, includes no forthright defense of the truth of Christian belief.[1] Wolterstorff never says, to my knowledge, that he writes in defense of the Christian faith—at least not directly, and he rarely points out that he writes as a Christian or from a Christian point of view. Certainly relative to our topic—rationality and the ethics of belief—there are precious few overt indications that this work is motivated by Christian belief and commitments. Wolterstorff's widely influential responses to classical foundationalist and evidentialist challenges to the rationality of Christian belief, and those offered by Plantinga, are either internal critiques of these traditional, modern positions, or purely philosophical (epistemological) arguments, and neither strategy is overtly or directly Christian or theological.[2] In what sense, or to what extent, then,

---

1. In fact, Wolterstorff's most influential theological works are critiques of traditional theological doctrines (including eternity, immutability, impassibility, and simplicity). And yet, he very often argues against the traditional doctrines on biblical grounds. See section §4.2, n43.

2. Wolterstorff has indicated that a reluctance to offer evidence for Christian belief or for theism, even a "revulsion" to doing so, is characteristic of the continental Reformed tradition, and that Reformed Epistemology is Reformed precisely by aligning itself with this methodological feature of historic Calvinist thought. See Wolterstorff's

is Wolterstorff's work Christian? Wolterstorff's self-description as "one who was bequeathed the Reformed tradition of Christianity," as much as any account he offers of his intellectual development, draws particular attention to this question.[3]

Of more direct significance here is the potential this material has in terms of an integrative account of Wolterstorff's work. Insight into the relationship between Wolterstorff's theological background and his approach to rationality might help his readers bring together apparently distinct and differentiated bodies of writing. Wolterstorff has made significant contributions in several distinct fields, but rarely are connections drawn between them either in secondary literature or by Wolterstorff himself.[4] I suggest that the best way of integrating Wolterstorff's work—on historical philosophy, say, or his writings against classical foundationalism, on the arts, ethics, culture, political theory, and Christian education—is to seek a unifying foundation in his Christian belief and Christian self-understanding, which is precisely what I attempt here. Christian belief will indeed serve as a fruitful interpretive avenue if Wolterstorff is writing as a Christian, if his Christian belief serves as a governing or motivating commitment—and I believe that it does.

The value of this study is, therefore, impressed upon us both in terms of an account of Wolterstorff's work as Christian and in terms of a unifying principle for his numerous interests. In sum, if Wolterstorff is a consistently and self-consciously Christian thinker, and I think he is, his view of the ethics of belief will be an informative explanatory key to his thought.

In this final chapter, I argue that Wolterstorff's theory of situated rationality takes for granted a Christian view of history and ethics and that, therefore, situated rationality is in effect a Christian view of the ethics of belief. And if it is, situated rationality amounts to a robust if implicit Christian apologetic. In this way, an inquiry focused narrowly on epistemic merit according to Wolterstorff leads to a significant discovery regarding the nature of Wolterstorff's interest in rationality as basically shalom-driven.

We begin with a survey of the findings of each of the previous chapters (§6.1). The goal here is to present a succinct and coherent narrative which unifies our research up to this point around the thesis, which is this:

---

introduction to *Faith and Rationality*, esp. 7–8, and see section §1.2 of the present study, esp. n31 where I suggest that Wolterstorff's description of the Reformed tradition in this regard requires qualification.

3. "If you ask who I am, I reply: I am one who was bequeathed the Reformed tradition of Christianity." "The Grace That Shaped My Life," in *Hearing the Call*, 19.

4. The best candidate for a unifying concept is, as noted, shalom. See "It's Tied Together by Shalom," in *Hearing the Call*, 423–29, and section §4.5 of the present study.

Wolterstorff's Christian value system is essential to his theory of rationality. Shalom is the *sine qua non* of situated rationality.

As I have noted at several points, this raises the question of the epistemic status of Christian belief, since it appears to live a double life in Wolterstorff's thought: it is the essential grounding for his theory of rationality, and according to his theory of rationality it is situationally rational. If this duality appears to undermine the defensibility of situated rationality, I submit that in fact it does not. In the third section of this chapter, I address this question of the epistemic status of Christian belief (§6.2).

On the one hand, Wolterstorff's own Christian belief, with shalom at its center, functions as a control-belief in his theorizing about rationality; for it to do this, it must be actually entitled.[5] On the other hand, situated rationality tells us that Christian belief is situationally rational. Since the relationship between shalom and the situationality constitutive of Wolterstorff's theory of rationality is central to my interpretative hypothesis, I address it in detail in this section. I first answer a potential objection to the coherence between them, and then I propose a 'Wolterstorffian' theology of situationality which solidifies the connection upon which my thesis depends. I then answer two possible objections to the interpretation I am proposing (§6.3), and then, in closing, I offer brief evaluative comments and raise a few questions specifically in terms of the theological status of Wolterstorff's notion of situationality (§6.4).

6.1 SHALOM DOXASTIC ETHICS: A BRIEF SYNOPSIS

In this section, I offer a synopsis of the preceding chapters, focusing on the evidence I have produced up to this point for my description of Wolterstorff's theory of rationality as a shalom doxastic ethic. I can now state my thesis more fully, as follows. In his approach to rationality, Wolterstorff takes for granted a Christian view of history and ethics, and these are essential to his theory of situated rationality, and that, consequently, situated rationality is in effect a Christian view of the ethics of believing.

---

5. We may note at this point that this study does not include an exposition of the content of Wolterstorff's personal Christian belief, his actual Christian commitment— his doctrine of God, his particular soteriological emphases, or anything of the sort. Although Wolterstorff speaks often of the Reformed tradition and of the thought of Abraham Kuyper, his interaction with Reformed and Kuyperian literature is complex. Even where there might be an easy answer to "What is the Reformed or Kuyperian view of X?" we cannot assume that Wolterstorff fits the mold. These details are not, however, necessary for my thesis. The relevant concept is shalom.

Much of what we learned from the opening biographical material vindicated Wolterstorff's self-description as "one who was bequeathed the Reformed tradition of Christianity."[6] This reception, we learned, came by way of the concentrated piety and biblical devotion of rural, Dutch-American life, and, more self-consciously, through undergraduate studies at Calvin College. At Calvin Wolterstorff encountered firsthand the writings of the intellectual forebears of the culture and worldview he had absorbed in his youth, Abraham Kuyper being the towering figure among them.

Kuyper championed the idea of Calvinism as the fullest expression of a Christian world and life view.[7] Kuyper's Calvinist worldview emphasized a present-age distinction between Christians, or the regenerate, and non-Christians, the unregenerate.[8] Kuyper therefore viewed Christian culture, understood in terms of a Calvinist worldview, as locked in an antithetical confrontation with the cultural forces of secularism. Thus in the neo-Calvinist tradition, it was every Christian's duty to win new ground for Christ through self-consciously Christian cultural activity: Christian education, Christian political involvement, a Christian presence in the fine arts, and so on.[9] Wolterstorff recalls his philosophy professor William Harry Jellema emphasizing precisely this point: "'There are two cities,' said one of our teachers, Henry Jellema, with gripping charisma . . . 'the *civitas Dei* and the *civitas mundi*. Your calling is to build the *civitas Dei*.'"[10]

As we anticipated in light of this biographical background, the Dutch-Calvinist tradition has turned out to be a significant influence on Wolterstorff's approach to the ethics of belief.[11] Many of Wolterstorff's earliest and

---

6. "The Grace That Shaped My Life," in *Hearing the Call*, 9.

7. See especially Kuyper's *Lectures on Calvinism*.

8. See section §5.4 n66.

9. The precise nature of Kuyper's own views on the question of culture remains unclear. This is perhaps due to the fact that some version of a Kuyperian view of Christ and culture took hold in Dutch-American Reformed culture, while the greater part of Kuyper's writing on common grace and related issues remained untranslated, as did the *Reformed Dogmatics* of Herman Bavinck, until relatively recently (published in English in 2003–2008). A recent publication of some importance in this discussion is Bolt, "The Imitation of Christ as Illumination for the Two Kingdoms Debate." Bolt contends, "When Kuyper's followers appeal to him for support in using expressions such as 'building the kingdom on earth,' or 'advancing the kingdom on earth,' they do so without justification" (15), and that "[o]ne cannot appeal to Abraham Kuyper in defense of the proposition that the eschatological kingdom of Christ should in some way provide content for the concrete life of peoples, communities, and nations" (ibid., 18).

10. "The Grace That Shaped My Life," in *Hearing the Call*, 10. Wolterstorff discusses dual citizenship in the *civitas mundi* and the *civitas Dei* in "Christian Political Reflection: Diognetian or Augustinian."

11. In chapter 1, for example, we noted the plainly non-foundationalist character of Christian belief in Wolterstorff's native, Dutch-Calvinist context.

most significant influences had inherited from Kuyper a worldview-sized Calvinism, including the irreducible plurality of ultimate (religious) commitments and an expansive Christian approach to culture and world-involvement.[12] Somewhere in the distant background, then, we might say that Kuyper's Calvinism serves as a unifying purpose and singular *telos* for Wolterstorff's work; or, in some way, a distinctly Christian worldview is operative. Stated differently, indeed perhaps to understate it, in his approach to rationality (as much as to anything else), Wolterstorff takes for granted the truth of Christian belief and intends to develop a Christian perspective on the issue.[13]

Wolterstorffian approaches to situationality, rationality, and Reidian belief-forming dispositions are best approached beginning from Wolterstorff's departure from epistemological tradition via his critique of the platonic epistemological self, what he calls the "solitary, immobile reactor." In his view, a number of theoretical problems attend the traditional approach. Contrary to the traditional super-situational construction, Wolterstorff claims that believing is always *human* believing—the believing of particular, situated individuals, and never just 'believing' in the abstract. Wolterstorff replaces the traditional construction, which lay at the core of modern epistemology, with a mobile, socially engaged, and morally situated and accountable epistemological subject.

Subsequently, Wolterstorff develops his notion of situationality—not only individualized situationality, but a dynamic and personalized, historically formed, doxastic anthropology. Out-Reiding Plantinga and even Reid himself, Wolterstorff 'historicizes the belief-forming self.'[14] This rich doxas-

---

12. See also sections §4.1 and §4.3–4.

13. Although, again, without going so far as to offer direct argumentation for Christian theism. See n2 above. I should clarify here the notion that Wolterstorff is developing a "Christian perspective." I simply mean that Wolterstorff is a Christian, he believes that his Christian belief is true, and he does not self-consciously set his Christian belief aside as he thinks about rationality and the ethics of belief (per his critique of modern, platonic epistemology and views of science). So in a plain but unavoidable sense, his perspective is a Christian perspective. In this chapter, I am attempting to show that there is more theology involved in his theory of rationality than there appears to be. But I am not arguing that Wolterstorff's theory of rationality is simply Christian belief in epistemological garb, thus rendering it easily dismissible as not serious philosophy by anyone looking for a reason to do so. It should be clear from chapters 2 and 3 of the present study, and from scores of Wolterstorff's own publications, that his view of rationality, independent of Christian theology, is intelligible and defensible, and applicable to anyone, Christian or not. This entire study presupposes that it is. In section §5.2 above, I discuss in detail Wolterstorff's view of what it means to theorize from a Christian point of view.

14. See "Historicizing the Belief-Forming Self," in *Practices of Belief*, 118–43.

tic anthropology incorporates the full personal, professional, historical, and cultural richness of a person's moral situationality, and seals decisively the uniqueness of the particular doxastic accountability of individuals.

Accordingly, in terms of belief entitlement, Wolterstorff maintains the priority of the situational availability of beliefs over doxastic obligation. He argues that (situational) availability precedes the deontological weight of beliefs and doxastically significant actions. This means that even reasons (propositional evidence), while important, must also be subordinated to the complexities of situationality, and so cannot be the sole measure of sound or permissible or rational believing.

In all of this Wolterstorff benefits a great deal from Thomas Reid, specifically in terms of the mechanics of belief-forming dispositions.[15] By historicizing doxastic agency, Wolterstorff's Reidian account of belief-forming dispositions as historically and experientially conditioned is refined yet further. The formation of a disposition to draw inductive inferences is one example: such dispositions—some innate, some acquired—are formed and refined through individual experience.[16] Thus the distinction sharpens between the solitary, immobile reactor of philosophical tradition and Wolterstorff's socially engaged doxastic subject. In terms of the ethics of belief, the old guard is done away with. Wolterstorff's situationality decisively undercuts generic, universal, doxastic normativity, confirming this conclusion: *all rationality is situated rationality.*

Wolterstorff adopts what I have called "Reidian doxastic optimism," the idea that the normal, undisturbed operations of the belief-forming faculties are aimed at truth and generally successful at finding it, and that these faculties respond effectively (truth-conducively) to individualized conditioning and experience. Reidian optimism contrasts sharply with John Locke's dismal take on the situationality and progressive (regressive,

---

15. Wolterstorff also benefits a great deal from Reid's common sense response to classical modern foundationalism, as noted in sections §2.5 and §2.6. Wolterstorff has written a great deal on rationality and epistemology in Thomas Reid. For a Reidian response to foundationalism and modern skepticism, see the following essays in *Practices of Belief*: "Can Belief in God Be Rational," esp. the section entitled, "Belief-Forming Dispositions" (231–39), and pgs. 246–48; "Reformed Epistemology"; "Reid on Common Sense"; and "What Sort of Epistemological Realist was Thomas Reid?" See also "Is It Possible and Desirable for Theologians to Recover from Kant?," in *Inquiring about God*; "Thomas Reid on Rationality"; and "Reid's Way with the Skeptic," chapter 8 of *Thomas Reid and the Story of Epistemology*, and the section entitled "The Dependence of Philosophy on Common Sense" (246–49). Wolterstorff says that Reid has "almost disappeared from the canon" in part because philosophical tradition "misunderstood him by failing to see the radicality of his rejection of the prior tradition of modern philosophy" (*Thomas Reid*, ix).

16. See section §2.3.

for Locke) conditioning of the same faculties as detrimental to the truth-conducivity of doxastic habits. Upon this Reidian optimism rests, at least in part, Wolterstorff's 'innocent until proven guilty' approach to rationality. Thus appears the principle that we are culpable or praiseworthy for our believings if and only if we can govern them, and only to the extent that we are able to do so. Wolterstorff maintains this principle against Plantinga's notion of proper function, which, Wolterstorff argues, is too narrow to account for the volitional aspect of doxastic conduct, and thus, in light of this principle, fails to provide for the moral accountability essential to doxastic ethics.

In terms then of situationality, rationality, and Reidian belief-forming dispositions (and doxastic optimism), Wolterstorff lays the groundwork for a radically re-configured approach to the doxastic life. The distinctiveness of his contribution here is best captured in the claim *that rationality is always individually and historically situated*. Although Wolterstorff does not always make the connection explicit, I will argue below that the situated integrity of the doxastic subject—the integrity of doxastic situations, protecting the subject from the tyranny of platonic doxastic norms—is itself motivated by the biblical ethic of shalom.

The next step hinges on Wolterstorff's notion of practices of belief and doxastic self-governance: *doxastic rationality is always practical rationality*. That is, the rationality of what one believes is reducible to the rationality of what one does. This implicit ethic of practical rationality anticipates the direct dependence of situated rationality on Christian belief and on shalom in particular.

Essential here is the situational availability of beliefs and the role of agency and intention in accounting for (doxastic) responsibility. The situational availability of a belief is a necessary condition of that belief's bearing moral weight. This is because volition—genuine moral agency—is necessary for accountability: ought implies can, as can is necessary for ought. And one can do nothing about a belief that is not situationally available to one.

What Wolterstorff calls "practices of inquiry" are the socially esteemed actions a person may (or may not) and sometimes ought (or ought not) to take in terms of managing his doxastic affairs in light of social and moral accountability. Examples are searching on the internet, reading the news, consulting an expert, enrolling in a course, and so on. Practices of inquiry are the actual means available for taking doxastic action. In other words, doxastic rationality is always practical rationality and appears in the form of doxastically directed practices, practices which are distinctive to and even constitutive of a socio-historical 'location' and one's participation in it or one's belonging to it.

Speaking now in terms of ethics, we may distinguish between good and right, or between practical rationality and moral value. In fact we may prioritize the practical suitability of a means to a given end over the moral valuation of either or both means and end. Thus, a pronouncement on the moral value of an action (a means) is distinct from and logically subsequent to the question of practical rationality or expediency.[17] So, for example, it may be in a narrow and strictly practical sense "rational" to steal what would otherwise require considerable sacrifice to pay for or lie beyond the scope of financial possibility, particularly if that thing were an obvious good (a healthy meal, for example). But of course theft raises moral questions such as principles of human interaction, and questions of justice, private property, social responsibility, citizenship and legal obligation, among other things. So an action may be rational (in an a-moral, practical sense) while raising complex moral issues. With this distinction in mind, we can see that, as far as we have come in terms of accounting for the permissibility, obligation, praiseworthiness and blameworthiness which permeate the doxastic life, an essential element is missing: a theory of moral value.

For Wolterstorff, furthermore, truth is not a categorical end. From the 'de-platonizing' and the historicizing of the doxastic self it should be clear enough that one can no longer think exclusively in terms of alethic rationality, or of subjecting the whole of complex situationality to impersonal, super-situational, factual truth and reasons.

Wolterstorff makes it clear that truth cannot be our categorical doxastic end. He does so, among other places, in his interaction with Roderick Chisholm,[18] and he expresses appreciation for John Locke's defense of the instrumental value of rightly conducting one's doxastic activities toward (religious) truth, not as an end in itself, but for the sake of corporate, social well-being. Wolterstorff writes, "[m]ore than well-being is involved: honoring the dignity of oneself and of the other is also involved." And he adds, "[1] f Locke's comment, thus modified, is correct, then discovering the truth on matters of morality and religion is not a fundamental categorical duty but an instrumental duty."[19] So a categorical end or duty governing the norma-

17. This would be evident in any ethical theory with a teleological emphasis, such as Aristotle's. An action must first be good for a human being, according to the nature of a human being, before it can bear positive moral value.

18. See the following essays in *Practices of Belief*: "Ought to Believe—Two Concepts"; "Can Belief in God be Rational"; and "Entitlement to Believe" (esp. 103–5).

19. "Entitlement to Believe," in *Practices of Belief*, 110. Wolterstorff says elsewhere, "I hope that our theologians will join the conversation, *qua* Christian theologians . . . And I *very much* hope that they will assist in the cultivation of the virtues needed for true dialogue among people who genuinely disagree about God and the good. If we do not cultivate and exhibit those virtues, Bosnia is everybody's future" ("The Travail of Theology in the Modern Academy," 46).

tivity of believing, supposing there is one, remains unidentified. If truth is not a categorical end in the matter of doxastic conduct, what is?

The structure and mechanics of doxastic situationality, situational entitlement, and socially constituted doxastic practices, considered alone, lack a theory of moral value, without which it would fail to bear specifically on rationality as the ethics of belief. In other words, doxastic situationality, a Reidian doxastic anthropology, the situational availability of beliefs, the role of doxastic volition, and (the situational availability of) practices of inquiry are informative *epistemological* categories, but apart from an infusion of moral value, no normativity enters our analysis, and evaluative judgments remain groundless. Wolterstorff's discussion of these issues is consistently deontological; but no account of normativity has yet been given. The cumulative effect of an analysis of Wolterstorff's situated rationality that ends at this point is a rather conspicuous emphasis on the outstanding question of moral value.

Thus the significance of shalom, a vision of peace and justice global in scope. It is taught in the Bible and appears as the 'ought-to-be' of all things as created by God. Essential to shalom is the enjoyment by every human being of justice and the fulfillment and protection of his or her rights.[20] Shalom is justice *plus* enjoyment in one's relationships (with one's self, with others, and with God).

In Wolterstorff's view, shalom is the substance of biblical teaching both in terms of the history of redemption in Christ and in terms of the cosmic scope of redemptive eschatology. Shalom is the Bible's vision of the movement of all things from creation, through the fall, to the inauguration of the kingdom of restoration in the resurrection of Christ, toward its (that is, shalom's) full, eschatological realization. In Wolterstorff's view, shalom, as a global vision of how things 'ought-to-be,' is not merely taught in Scripture, it encapsulates the apex of Christian history and redemption: "The Christian gospel, at bottom, is an answer to the question, how can we human beings flourish?"[21] "Shalom," in his view, is the name given in scripture to the fulfillment of Christian hope.

Wolterstorff tracks an avertive strain in Christian thought which conflicts with ethical emphases of shalom. The historic beatific vision teleology of a Roman Catholic view of the Christian life, the Reformed confessions which similarly point man heavenward, and the myopic religiosity of much of American Evangelicalism (if especially Calvinism) all risk a graceless

---

20. I discuss shalom rights and obligations in section §4.1, though the discussion there is relatively brief. See especially Wolsterstorff, "A Theistic Grounding of Human Rights," in *Justice: Rights and Wrongs*, 342–61.

21. "It's Tied Together by Shalom," in *Hearing the Call*, 424.

disinterest in justice in the world in the here and now. Elaborating somewhat, we might be able to express Wolterstorff's chief concern this way:[22] we often find in Reformed theology and ethics a heavy, even exclusive, concern for the eternal and the heavenly. In effect, theological interest in the Christian life often begins at the point of the fall, neglecting the original glory of creation. This is so much the case that salvation is often understood, if implicitly, as salvation *from* the world, rather than *of* the world. We should rather appreciate the Bible's concern for creation, where the Logos of God figures most gloriously (John 1:1–3; Col 1:16–17), and heed with more seriousness the glory of man as image of God and all that this status demands of man *in this life*, in the here and now. "Earth is a temporary stopping point," writes Wolterstorff. "But from that it does not follow that Christ's jurisdiction does not extend to this temporary stopping point . . ."[23]

One particular feature of Wolterstorff's interaction with neo-Calvinist creation order thought deserves attention here.[24] Wolterstorff claims that shalom ought to precede the ontology of social spheres and institutions. The creation order tradition holds that these structures manifest the divine establishment of social spheres as such and institutions as such, so that the Christian's duty in fulfilling the cultural mandate, renewed by Christ in a fallen world, is specifically to realize or restore these creational essences.[25] Wolterstorff laments the legalistic tone of this charter for Christian action, noting that, on this model, Christ himself as crucified and resurrected savior plays no substantive role in a Christian's understanding of his basic ethical outlook. Wolterstorff responds with the claim that shalom, the eschatological kingdom of which Christ is the inaugurator and over which he is king, should supersede the ontology of social spheres and institutions. He suggests that, instead of fixing a Christian ethic on abstract, a-moral essences nomologically conceived, we ought instead to prioritize Christ's kingdom of peace and utilize and establish such entities as will protect, preserve, and advance shalom. For Wolterstorff, our approach to creation and our activity in it should be first according to Christ as redemptive king, as prince of

---

22. I owe many of these insights to helpful conversations with James Skillen, former director of the Center for Public Justice in Washington, D.C. Skillen's bibliography is vast. See for example his *The Good of Politics*.

23. "Christian Political Reflection," 155.

24. See sections §4.3 and §4.4.

25. Wolters says, for example, "Redemption, then, is the recovery of creational goodness through the annulment of sin and the effort toward the progressive removal of its effects everywhere. We return to creation through the cross, because only the atonement deals with sin and evil effectively at their root. Mark's version of the great commission bids us 'preach the good news to all *creation*' (Mark 16:15) because there is need of liberation from sin everywhere" (*Creation Regained*, 83).

restorative shalom. To put it differently, Wolterstorff's concern is that the creation order tradition is too much law and too little gospel. By contrast, he emphasizes, the central role of the reconciling work of Christ in the ethos and substance of shalom.

Wolterstorff says that God's historical redemption reaches its apex, and a kind of partial fulfillment, in the resurrection of Christ from the dead. The resurrection of Jesus Christ is the essence of shalom: it is the fulfillment of the Old Testament prophetic vision, and it provides the reflexivity of rights and obligations essential to shalom as an objective, ought-to-be state of affairs.[26] Without the self-giving of Christ on the cross, there would be no grounds on which to affirm the coordination of rights and duties upon which shalom as a universal human obligation rests. Without a doubt, the basic ethos of situated rationality is not even theistic, for Wolterstorff, but specifically Christian.[27] Wolterstorff's ethic is uniquely Christian, and the moral substance of (situated) doxastic rationality is then essentially Christ-centered.

Wolterstorff understands shalom in terms of an explicitly Christian ethos, one reflected not only in the Old Testament's trajectory toward the New in terms of peace and reconciliation, but also in terms of the selfless love embodied on the cross borne by Christ, the "prince of shalom" (Isaiah 9:6). Wolterstorff's shalom ethic is Christ-centered, and shalom is the basis and the principle motivation for Wolterstorff's approach to the ethics of belief.

It is important then to make explicit the deontological implications of shalom relative to practices of inquiry and the doxastic life. Making explicit the connection between shalom and the ethics of belief drops a keystone into my rational reconstruction. One way to bridge the gap is via Wolterstorff's shalom-driven discussion of the theory versus praxis question.

According to Wolterstorff, both theory and praxis are vindicated by the ethic of shalom, but, not surprisingly, a generic and universally enforceable formula is beyond reach. Wolterstorff provides several categories for conceptualizing various "levels of shalom theorizing," I have called them, or the concrete ways in which shalom should influence theorizing and scholarly work, particularly for the shalom-conscious scholar, i.e. the Christian

---

26. See section §4.1.

27. See section §4.5. Furthermore, as observed in section §4.5, Wolterstorff gives careful attention to the organic symbiosis of worship and shalom-driven action. He thus implies that a secular program of shalom-driven action, such as a non-religious program for social justice which seeks to amend apparent brokenness among human relationships and in the social and political orders, lacks the transcendent grounding of a Christian one.

scholar. The closing link we require is this: Wolterstorff's reminder that whatever applies at the scholarly level in terms of theorizing is merely a highly self-conscious version of belief-formation at the popular level. Since all people theorize, the same structure for shalom deontology in theorizing may be translated into a general theory of doxastic ethics. In sum, in Wolterstorff's view, shalom and its multifaceted ought-to-be of the world fills and governs the space of volitional possibility, both at the practical level and more narrowly in terms of scholarly conduct. And as I argue below, this means that Wolterstorff's notion of situationality itself has theological genes.

6.2 THE EPISTEMIC STATUS OF CHRISTIAN BELIEF

As mentioned above, the question of the epistemic status of Christian belief in Wolterstorff's theorizing about rationality is complex. In this section I attempt to clarify the issue by distinguishing between the role of Wolterstorff's Christian belief as control-belief in his theorizing about rationality, which implies Wolterstorff's taking his own Christian belief as actually entitled, and the status of Christian belief as situationally rational, according to Wolterstorff's shalom doxastic ethic. The connection between the actual entitlement and functional significance of Wolterstorff's Christian belief, on the one hand, and on the other the theory of situated rationality which confers on Christian belief a rationality dependent upon situations deserves careful attention, but more speculation is required at this point than elsewhere. In that regard, I submit that Wolterstorff's neo-Calvinist control-beliefs provide the necessary historico-ethical framework within which his notion of situationality takes shape, so that the actual entitlement of Wolterstorff's theological control-beliefs (shalom in particular) is the necessary precondition for Wolterstorffian situationality.

In what follows, I draw attention first to the role of actually entitled Christian belief in Wolterstorff's approach to doxastic ethics and second to the consequent situated rationality of Christian belief itself. Third, in order to clarify the relationship between actually entitled Christian belief as control-belief and the situational rationality Christian belief, I raise and then answer one possible source of inconsistency between them and then propose a theology of situationality which brings them together.

1. *Entitled Christian Belief as Control-Belief.* In chapter 1, we found ample biographical reason to expect that Wolterstorff would allow Christian belief to play the roles both of choice-principle and control-belief, that he

would take his Christian belief as entitled and consequently as a starting point and governing commitment in his thinking. This expectation is met with clear confirmation in several autobiographical sources. There can be no doubt that Wolterstorff's Christian belief guides his thinking; on numerous occasions, he tells us so himself.[28]

The brief autobiographical sketch found in "The Grace that Shaped my Life" hangs on the theme of a developing understanding of the biblically focused Calvinism at the heart of Dutch-American culture. "The piety in which I was reared," he says, "was centered in the Bible . . . not on experience, and not on the liturgy, but on the Bible . . ." and "[t]he center from which all lines of interpretation radiated outward was Jesus—Jesus Christ."[29] Wolterstorff offers a delightful account of the signals of this devotion that characterized his childhood.[30] He was led by this influence to Calvin College, to where, he recounts, "I came with the conviction that I was called to make my thoughts captive to Jesus Christ."[31] He was challenged to do even "more than that," to "embody Christ in culture."[32]

Of his time at Calvin College, Wolterstorff writes, "[f]or our purposes, what was important was Kuyper's model of theory-construction." And Kuyper's model stood boldly against inherited tradition: "Since Aristotle, everybody in the West had regarded proper theorizing as a generically human activity. To enter the chambers of theory one must lay aside all one's particularities and enter purely as a human being." But Kuyper, says Wolterstorff, "didn't believe it—didn't believe it was possible." Kuyper "especially insisted that one could not shed one's religion. A person's religion, on Kuyper's view, was not an inference or a hypothesis but a fundamental determinant of that person's hermeneutic of reality. . . Thus Kuyper thought that the goal

---

28. Here I focus on Wolterstorff's Christian belief in its controlling role; I do not explore the role of Christian belief as choice-principle, which would be to answer this question: what shalom value, theoretical or practical, does extended study of the ethics of belief offer? Although I do not answer this question directly, we may assume that if on a practical level the ethos of doxastic conduct is, or ought to be, peace in one's relationships and cultural flourishing, Wolterstorff's work on entitlement and situated rationality provides the theoretical background necessary for understanding how exactly such a shalom doxastic ethic would function. It represents his effort as a scholar to promote and advance shalom.

29. "The Grace that Shaped my Life," in *Hearing the Call*, 5.

30. "We 'dressed up' on the Lord's Day, dressed up *for* the Lord's Day, and entered church well in advance of the beginning of the service to collect ourselves in silence, silence so intense it could be touched . . . But what remains in my ear are the psalms we sang" ("The Grace that Shaped my Life," in *Hearing the Call*, 2).

31. Ibid., 9.

32. Ibid.

of constructing a generally human philosophy was vain." Says Wolterstorff, "I believed this when I first learned of it in college days; I believe it still."[33]

In the same essay, Wolterstorff recounts his attendance in 1978 at a conference on Palestinian rights. His account of this experience and the subsequent change in his life bear openly a continuing and indeed intensifying sense of Christian service as the central theme of his work:

> I felt cornered, confronted—confronted by the word of the Lord telling me that I must defend the cause of this suffering people. My tradition yielded me the category: it was a call. Not to answer the call would be desecrating disobedience.
>
> I have not changed my profession. But I have gone to the Middle East several times. I have bought and read yards of books. I subscribe to out-of-the-way journals. I became chair of the board of the Palestine Human Rights Campaign. I have written; I have spoken. It hasn't always been pleasant . . . But it is a sacred call.[34]

Neither less sacred nor less fervent was Wolterstorff's interest in apartheid, which began with a trip to South Africa in 1975.[35] Reflecting both the shalom demand for a self-conscious balancing of theory versus praxis[36] and his own distaste for the avertive-prone essentialism of neo-Calvinism,[37] he says of that experience, "I came late to thinking about justice, late and fortuitously, or perhaps providentially. It was injustice that impelled me to think about justice, not the imperatives of some theoretical scheme or the duties of some academic position."[38] Wolterstorff's response confirms that the biblically grounded Calvinism of his upbringing was still, in the late 1970s, the governing category of this thought and work. And its continuing influence is confirmed in this introductory statement from *Justice: Rights and Wrongs*, published in 2008: "The account of primary justice that I develop is a the-

---

33. Ibid., 11.

34. Ibid., 12–13. Of the volume in which this essay appears, *Hearing the Call*, Wolterstorff says, "Those who read around in these essays will soon discern that the author is a member of the Reformed tradition of Christianity. They are an example of living within a religious tradition in the modern world, interpreting, supporting, criticizing" (*Hearing the Call*, x).

35. In "The Grace that Shaped my Life," in *Hearing the Call*, he says that the conference in South Africa took place in 1975 (13). In *Justice: Rights and Wrongs*, he says that it took place in September of 1976 (vii).

36. See section §5.1.

37. See section §5.5. See also "How my Mind has Changed: The Way to Justice," in *Hearing the Call*, 430–38.

38. *Justice: Rights and Wrongs*, vii.

istic account, specifically, a *Christian* theistic account; for I am a Christian believer who holds that God and justice are intimately intertwined."[39]

All of this detail is of more than biographical interest. We see demonstrated throughout it a mainstay of Reformed Epistemology: the rejection of the claim that Christians are under an obligation to offer arguments for their Christian belief in order to be entitled to it or before accepting it as true:

> I see no reason to suppose that people who hold as one of their immediate beliefs that God exists always have adequate reason to surrender that belief—or ought to believe that they do. I see no reason to suppose that holding the belief that God exists as one of one's immediate beliefs always represents some failure on one's part to govern one's assent as well as one ought.[40]

In other words, the Reformed epistemological notion of immediate or "properly basic" beliefs counters the evidentialist challenge and defends the *prima facie* entitlement (rationality) of believing in God. Wolterstorff's distinctive take on this question should come as no surprise at this point. He says that "those abstract and highly general theses of evidentialism no longer look very interesting, once we regard them in the light of the criterion offered... issues of rationality are always situation-specific."[41]

In addition to direct biographical evidence, the function of entitled Christian belief as control-belief is at the center of a subtle argumentative strategy employed by Wolterstorff in at least a few different contexts. He often argues following this pattern: a belief *B* is taken for granted by our culture generally—by Christians, non-Christians, and even many of Christianity's detractors. He then adds a second thesis, something like *B* is historically a Christian claim, or no convincing, non-Christian account for *B* is on offer, or, even stronger, that no non-Christian account for *B* is plausible or even possible. This indirect argumentative strategy displays in practice the Kuyperian notion of religious commitments working themselves out in apparently non-religious spheres, and it even indulges in a bit of positive apologetics. It also demonstrates entitled belief in (theoretical) action.

An argument along these lines appears in *Justice: Rights and Wrongs*. In that text, Wolterstorff offers a detailed account of natural human rights. Shalom does not figure prominently in the text. It is not even listed in the

---

39. Ibid., x. See also *Until Justice and Peace Embrace*, particularly the preface and chapter 1, "World Formative Christianity."
40. "Can Belief in God be Rational," in *Practices of Belief*, 262.
41. Ibid.

index.⁴² But the goals of the volume are to demonstrate, first, that natural human rights are assumed in the moral conscience of our culture; second, that natural human rights are grounded not in Enlightenment individualism but in the Christian Scriptures; and third, that no secular account for the natural human rights assumed in our moral thought has been given or even can be given. Though it is not described as such by Wolterstorff, the text therefore amounts to an indirect argument for the universality of a Christian shalom deontology and moral teleology of human life. It is an indirect apologetic for Christian belief.

How this material and the 'innocent until proved guilty' emphasis of situated rationality are parallel would be a worthwhile research question: the imposition of universal, generic doxastic norms may in fact be described as a (doxastic) violation of natural human rights and the integrity of the individual. We cannot enter into such questions here, though a similar idea will emerge below, in theological terms. Notice, however, that the entirety of Wolterstorff's discussion of natural human rights functions as an implicit argument for the truth of Christian belief, and that argument depends in part on an extended demonstration of the theoretical yield of entitled Christian belief.⁴³

---

42. A brief section entitled "The Moral Vision of Scripture: Eirenéism," includes this statement: "The flourishing life, thus understood, was called *shalom* by the Hebrew writers of the Old Testament, "*shalom*" being translated with the Greek "*eirenē*" in the Septuagint; the New Testament writers followed in the steps of the Septuagint translators. So if we need a name for this moral vision . . . best to call it *eirenéism*" (*Justice: Rights and Wrongs*, 226).

43. Wolterstorff appears reluctant to put it in precisely these terms, as noted. Nonetheless he appears to vindicate my interpretation when, toward the close of the sixteenth chapter, in a section entitled "What Has Not Been Argued," he says this: "My argument has been hypothetical. I have articulated a theistic grounding of human rights, arguing that if God loves, in the mode of attachment, each and every human being equally and permanently, then natural human rights are grounded in that love . . . I have not argued that God does in fact so love every creature who bears the *imago Dei*. I have argued that a grounding of natural human rights is available to the person who holds the theistic convictions indicated. I have not argued for those theistic convictions themselves. The reader will have discerned, however, that I do in fact hold those convictions" (*Justice: Rights and Wrongs*, 360). What proves this concession to be somewhat understated is this: at the close of chapter 15, he says, "An option that is not available is holding that there are natural rights inherent to a worth possessed by all human beings, but that this worth has no ground, no properties or relationships on which it supervenes. That makes no sense. Worth cannot just float free." And then he says, "In the next chapter I offer a theistic grounding of natural inherent human rights . . . For I know of no other argument for this position than one that employs those very theistic premises that I will use in my grounding proposal" (ibid., 341). Perhaps Wolterstorff has not argued for "those theistic convictions" *directly*, but it seems to me that he has certainly argued for them *indirectly*. He has argued, in effect, that so long as someone affirms inherent

The argument from *Justice: Rights and Wrongs* exemplifies the indirect structure described above, and, to tip my hand, the same strategy has been employed here in our discussion of situated rationality. Following Wolterstorff, we undertook a descriptive study of the practical and ethical substance of the doxastic life, finding the platonic abstractions of the tradition untenable. We found that doxastic rationality is dependent upon practical rationality and thus is infused throughout with the moral substance of human interaction, of personal and social relationships, of social roles and reciprocal responsibilities, and so on. We then, following Wolterstorff, and Paul at the Areopagus, gave a name to that anonymous normativity: what is assumed in our general moral conscience we called the shalom of the God of the Bible. Chapter 4 demonstrated that Wolterstorff's account of the basic moral substance of practical rationality is not even generically theistic, but distinctively Christian, and flows from the redemptive self-giving of Jesus Christ on the cross and his resurrection from the dead. We find then that the shalom of God in Christ fills the space of volitional possibility with the self-evident call of divinely authored natural teleology and the pointed deontology of Christian obedience. Wolterstorff's doxastic ethic functions within a moral situationality permeated by shalom. In theoretical terms, the theory of situated rationality is shaped by a control-belief centered around shalom.

Finally, I propose below a direct correlation between Christian belief—Kuyperian Calvinism in particular—and the situational integrity of doxastic subjects. By restricting doxastic accountability to the redemptive-historical here and now, and by thus barring the hasty and unwarranted intrusion of revealed categories (elect and non-elect, and so on) into a genuinely

---

human worth, the Christian account for inherent human worth is his only option (until he produces an alternative, which Wolterstorff says is unlikely). Indeed, Wolterstorff himself says, "if one believes that there are natural inherent human rights, then the fact that the secularist cannot account for those rights, whereas the theist who holds the convictions about God's love that I have delineated can do so, is an argument for theism (of that sort). Not a foundationalist argument, but an argument nonetheless" (ibid., 361). Still, I should qualify my claim: I take Wolterstorff's argument to imply that, so long as we hold to the idea of rights or inherent human worth, we are, by his argument, compelled to look favorably on Christianity; but that argumentation does not include a claim to the *uniqueness* of the Christian account of inherent worth; it argues simply that *we all agree* on inherent human worth (even if some claim not to, our actions affirm it), and Christianity provides a rich account for such worth. This argument may imply an argument for the truth of Christianity, but not necessarily so. Wolterstorff says, "That same moral vision of Scripture in which inherent natural human rights first gained recognition can now be used as a resource for articulating a grounding of such rights. The resources of other religions can be employed as well, those of Judaism, obviously, perhaps those of Islam. But it seems unlikely that any secular attempt at grounding will be successful" (ibid.).

historicized ethico-doxastic situation, we are led to a denial of abstract, universal doxastic norms (such as evidential ones—the rational supremacy of reasons) in general and for Christian beliefs in particular (religious ones). And this posture is based on Christian belief itself. Thus, the best account for a denial of the universality of abstract doxastic norms, a central feature of situated rationality, and even of Christian doxastic norms in particular, is the controlling, theoretical function of entitled Christian belief.

2. *The Situated Rationality of Christian Belief.* Our study of Wolterstorff's theory of rationality began with his 'common sense' critique of the platonic abstractions of traditional epistemology. The solitary, immobile reactor proved time and again to invite untenable, impractical doxastic obligations. We found it explanatorily unhelpful and, even worse, largely unrelated to reality. Belief is always and everywhere *someone's* belief; it is always the believing of a unique, individually situated, socially embedded, morally responsible, and historically constituted, doxastic subject. Chapter 2 clarified Wolterstorff's iconoclastic claim that all rationality is situated rationality, or, more specifically, that rationality is always individually and historically situated rationality.

In the third chapter we found that availability was a necessary precondition for morally significant accountability. This ethical principle applies to doxastic actions just as it does to any others. We found that, since beliefs are situationally available (or entitled) by virtue of historically and socially constituted practices of inquiry, doxastic rationality must be incorporated into a broader picture of practical rationality which is understood in terms of the subject's full moral situationality: doxastic rationality is always practical rationality situationally embodied. Chapters 2 and 3 confirm the undiscriminating thesis that there are no specifically doxastic norms, and that practical norms are irreducibly situational. And since all doxastic subjects are situated beings, no doxastic obligations are exempt from situational constraints and the moral prerequisite of situational entitlement.

Clearly, Wolterstorff believes that Christian belief is situationally rational. He says so specifically: "'Is one entitled to believe that Jesus was resurrected from the dead?' It all depends."[44] This statement is principally about the rational status of belief, of Christian belief in particular, in light of a general theory of rationality that all rationality is situated rationality. It is therefore *not* a statement about Christianity *per se*—at least not directly. It expresses the claims that no belief can be any more or anything other than situationally rational, and that this also applies to Christian belief.

---

44. "On Being Entitled to Beliefs about God," in *Practices of Belief*, 315. More on this quotation below.

We now have clearly before us actually entitled Christian belief as control belief, and Christian belief as situationally entitled. But I believe we can go further in terms of clarifying the connection between them. It is possible, in my view, to say concretely how entitled Christian belief yields the ethical situationality essential to Wolterstorff's doxastic ethic. But before drawing this profound point of consistency in Wolterstorff's theory of situated rationality, one candidate for at least a *prima facie* inconsistency between Christian belief and the situated epistemic credentials of Christian belief ought to be addressed.

Christian Truth and Situated Rationality. Can Christian belief be true but not reasonable?[45] Situated rationality appears to imply that there are situations in which Christian belief is not rational, less then rational, or even irrational, or that there are situations in which rejecting Christian belief, or perhaps holding no position on the matter at all, is in some situations more rational than accepting Christian belief as true, which is counter-intuitive from the point of view of a Christian theology of revelation. A handful of oft-quoted biblical passages appear to lend strength to this concern.

Psalm 19 says that the "heavens declare the glory of God, and the sky above proclaims his handiwork." Though metaphor plays a role here, the imparting of knowledge is clearly taught: "Day to day pours out speech, and night to night reveals knowledge." The psalmist emphasizes, furthermore, the unqualified effectiveness of this communication: "There is no speech, nor are there words, whose voice is not heard. Their measuring line goes out through all the earth, and their words to the end of the world."[46] Addressing a similar theme, the apostle Paul writes in Rom 1 that "what can be known about God is plain to them,[47] because God has shown it to them." Paul says that God's "invisible attributes, his eternal power and divine nature, have been clearly perceived, ever since the creation of the world."[48] And as Paul explains to Timothy, the apostolic teaching is "deserving of full acceptance."[49]

---

45. The suggestion that a belief might be true but unreasonable is in one sense not cause for alarm. Heliocentrism, though true, would have been unreasonably held even after the claims of poor Aristarchus of Samos were neglected and at least until Copernicus in the sixteenth century. As I argue in this section and in section §1.3, the concern I raise here in relation to the tension between truth and rationality or reasonability carries more weight when viewed from a biblical or theological point of view.

46. Ps 19:1–4

47. The referent of "them" appears in the preceding verse: "men, who by their unrighteousness suppress the truth."

48. Rom 1:18–32

49. 1 Tim 1:15; 4:9

Such passages appear to leave little room for an epistemic situation in which the knowledge of God is not sufficiently clear to render indefensible agnosticism or unbelief. "They are without excuse," Paul says. Indeed, if through Jesus Christ the Son of God "all things were made," and if "in him was the life, and the life was the light of men," and if he is "the Alpha and the Omega, the first and the last, the beginning and the end," one might ask: how could Christian belief, in any situation, attain to less than the highest standard of rationality?[50]

There are two available responses to this concern. First, one must not exaggerate the theological significance of what Wolterstorff means by "rationality." The concern appears to view rationality as largely, if not exclusively, soteriologically defined, and, consequently, it mistakes situated rationality for an epistemology of biblical soteriology in which (Christian) belief and unbelief are the principal operative categories. Second, if we remember that situated rationality is the doxastic refraction of a practical and situated moral context, we may to take into account a distinction between the unrestricted, unqualified reality of shalom deontology and the situational presence of the gospel with the church as its historically situated herald: the reign of Christ is cosmic, but he appears to play by the rules of creation and history. As the apostle Paul writes, "how are they to believe in him of

---

50. John 1:3–4, Rev 1:8; 22:13. Oliphint argues that "unbelief"—by which he means non-assent to Christian claims—"is at root the quintessential sin," and that unbelief is, "therefore, necessarily, quintessentially irrational." "The Irrationality of Unbelief," *Revelation and Reason*, 60. He says, "It should be first of all noted that in the history of thought, to the present day, no consensus exists on just how the notions of 'rational' and 'irrational' should be defined." He then says, "however the concept is defined and defended, it must have as its foundational concern the way in which a person (or group of people) relates to the world." So, Oliphint proposes to draw from biblical revelation in order to clarify the concept: "[A]ccording to Paul, it is sin's irrationality that lies at the root of the thinking, and the behavior, of unbelief" (ibid., 60). His argument is not that "rationality is traditionally this or that" or that it is "best defined thus," and then that "unbelief satisfies the definition." Rather, his contention is that unbelief, as a central concept in the biblical notion of sin, is irrationality itself. From the biblical point of view, he might say, "unbelief" and "irrationality" are more or less interchangeable terms. Reflecting the same methodology, Lane Tipton argues with specific reference to Acts 17:30–31 that the apostle Paul's notion of "proof" is redemptive-historically and biblically constituted: "Paul's conception of the resurrection as proof of final judgment in Acts 17:31b depends on revealed categories derived from redemptive history." "Resurrection, Proof, and Presuppositionalism: Acts 17:30–31," in *Revelation and Reason*, 41. See also Van Til, "Nature and Scripture." Van Til argues that general or natural revelation (revelation in nature) should be understood as necessary, authoritative, sufficient, and perspicuous. These attributes are more typically associated with special revelation, or scripture specifically. Van Til's thesis is largely a development of the notion that the revelation of God in nature is sufficiently clear to render "men" "without excuse," as Paul says in Rom 1:20. See also Calvin, *Institutes* I.1–5.

whom they have never heard? And how are they to hear without someone preaching?"[51]

A key statement for understanding Wolterstorff's position on the situated rationality of Christian belief is this, quoted once already: "'Is one entitled to believe Jesus was resurrected from the dead?' It all depends." "It all depends," he says, "on what sort of person and what sort of situation."[52] In light of biblical passages such as those quoted above, the sentence may appear provocative—but only if mistaken for a claim about belief in the resurrection in the abstract or about the alethic merit of such a belief. Certainly Wolterstorff himself grants it high alethic merit: that Jesus was resurrected from the dead is, in his view, true, and his belief that it is true is (again, in his view) entitled. But this statement is not intended by Wolterstorff to say anything about the abstract believability of the claim that Jesus rose from the dead, nor about the historicity of the resurrection; Wolterstorff is not here (directly) concerned with the *truth-value* of Christian claims. What he has in mind is entitlement in terms of situational availability and situationally available doxastic practices. Wolterstorff might allow us to rephrase it thus: one is entitled to believe in the resurrection only if the belief that Christ was raised from the dead appears within one's situational horizon in a way that is accessible to one by means of presently acceptable practices of inquiry. If it does not so appear, not only is one not entitled to that belief, one would even invite charges of irrationality, or non-rationality, perhaps—at least non-entitlement—were one to somehow, some way, end up affirming it.

Suppose a person is raised in a non-religious home and educated in secular grade schools, and then educated in a secular institution of higher learning in, say, the natural sciences, studying under only confidently naturalistic (anti-supernaturalistic) faculty and researchers. If this person's "context of ontological and epistemological conviction," as Wolterstorff says,[53] were thoroughly naturalistic, Wolterstorff could say that belief in the redemptive-historical fact and significance of the resurrection of Jesus Christ from the dead is highly unlikely to be situationally available to him; thus, barring a change in his context, he is not entitled to belief in the resurrection.

But something might change in his context. Someone may offer a defense or an articulation of Christian belief which he finds compelling, or which challenges his naturalism. Given that his naturalistic belief system is rather well reinforced, this may be difficult, but opportunities present

---

51. Rom 10:14
52. "On Being Entitled to Beliefs about God," in *Practices of Belief*, 314–15.
53. "Entitlement to Believe," in *Practices of Inquiry*, 97.

themselves when Christian belief enters his situation in morally or socially charged ways. A close friend may become a Christian, perhaps he reads *Justice: Rights and Wrongs* and finds himself moved by the theological richness of the notion of the *imago Dei*, perhaps he senses the moral profundity of religiously motivated social action. If it becomes a shalom issue, in other words, for our naturalist, to lend an ear to his colleague's or his friend's Christian belief, then an important change has taken place in terms of the situational availability of Christian belief. Until and unless such a change occurs, he is within his epistemic rights to remain an anti-supernaturalist.[54]

Clearly, this argument from Christian belief against situated rationality is answerable. Having eliminated a potential wrinkle in the coherence between entitled Christian belief and Christian belief as situationally rational, in what follows, I bring the content of Christian belief to bear directly on situationality in terms of a theology of situationality. The goal here is to make explicit the connection between entitled Christian belief as control-belief in theorizing about rationality and the situated rationality of Christian belief itself.

3. *Theology of Situationality.* Against the avertive tendency of Calvinist thought which, redemptive-historically speaking, effectively begins at the fall, Wolterstorff argues for a more creationally minded approach to ethics and Christian action. A self-conscious appreciation for the glory of creation in our view of the Christian life, particularly of man as the image of God, enhances (rather than depreciates, as some might fear) our view of the gravity of sin: we are not merely fallen or generally morally fallible, but rather, we are image-bearing vice-regents of the creator God who have turned away from God in sin and rebellion. Furthermore, an emphasis not only on

---

54. This is, I think, a consistently Wolterstorffian scenario. (For an example of someone situationally entitled to religious belief, see Wolterstorff's analysis of events in the life of Virginia, in *Divine Discourse*, 273–80.) A possible rejoinder from a Christian point of view is as follows. We may allow a degree of suspicion regarding the objective coherence of this person's naturalism, particularly if Christian belief is true. If Christian belief is true, or at least if we believe that it is, particular lines of critical examination of a naturalistic worldview should present themselves. We may expect, in other words, that if Christian belief is true, naturalism cannot also be true, and that in that case, a large part of commending and defending Christian belief will be pointing out the internal inconsistencies (what Dooyeweerd would call the "antinomies") of naturalism. More importantly, and conversely, a healthy portion of the naturalist's resources would have to be devoted to wishing these inconsistencies away. Instead of resting comfortably beyond the reach of Christian witness in doxastic-situational bliss, we might say, we may expect that the unbelieving naturalist would be much busier than he appears to be, tirelessly suppressing the truth about God and his law that is evident everywhere around him and within him as God's image (see Rom 1:18–32).

the goodness of creation but on the redemptive-historical already-not-yet (or here and now) precludes lording over 'historicized' people categories to which creatures have, to put it one way, no concrete epistemic access: regenerate and unregenerate, perhaps elect and non-elect in particular. We might call this restraint *redemptive-historical epistemic humility*.

The creation, in other words, is the field both of humanity's original glory and its subsequent fall and moral decay. It is where humanity's flourishing and communion with the creator were intended to unfold, and where all of its god-like capacities were meant to develop unto the glory of his creator, but where the sinful self-worship and autonomy of a race in rebellion now feature in a world crippled by sin and brokenness.

The work of salvation and restoration inaugurated in the resurrection of Jesus Christ is decisive, but it is not complete, or better, not yet consummated. So the proper structural basis for a view of the Christian life is not *fall→eschatological redemption* but rather *creation→fall→(present) semi-realized redemption→fully-realized redemption (yet-to-come)*.

On the latter, salvation is accomplished but not yet brought fully to fruition. Creation here and now, even in its brokenness, is the context for the inauguration of God's kingdom of peace. Right where Moses stood, God instructed him to remove his sandals, for, the Lord said, "the place where you are standing is holy ground" (Ex 3:5). This is, I think, a Wolterstorffian theology of situationality.[55]

Within this context of presently though partially realized redemption, fully realized categories of "elect" and "non-elect" play only a subtle, perhaps implicit, role in a Christian approach to ethics, if any at all; though such categories are distinctive aspects of a Reformed and Calvinist soteriology

---

55. Likewise, *Justice: Rights and Wrongs* appears to be a self-consciously redemptive-historical study of rights and justice. So, for example, summing up his discussion of the inherent worth of human beings as a ground for inherent natural rights, Wolterstorff says, "Our Judaic and Christian heritage neither denies nor overlooks the flaws of human kind; some strands in the heritage appear even to revel in them. But in the face of all the empirical evidence, it nonetheless declares that all of us have great and equal worth: the worth of being *made in the image of God* and of being *loved redemptively by God*." Notice that Wolterstorff alludes to a tendency to fixate on the fall and fallenness. Some strands of Christian thought "revel" in sinful misery; that is, this point in the Christian story receives undue attention, even impiously so. Coordinately, redemption and Christian living might tend to divert our attention from our present redemptive-historical situation. Against those avertive strands in Christian thought which tend to begin at the fall and point toward other-worldly deliverance, Wolterstorff's grounding for inherent human worth begins at creation in the image of God, and it then focuses on the present redemptive-historical context without indulging in over-realized soteriological and eschatological categories. Additionally, the claim that "all of us," meaning all human beings, are "redemptively loved by God" might be particularly effective in a Calvinist context at preventing the hasty intrusion of categories such as elect and non-elect into our ethical thinking.

and views of history and eschatology, in the not-yet of redemptive history, they are neither fully realized nor evident to the human eye.[56] Redemptive-historical epistemic humility presents itself when soteriology (redemption) stands within what Wolterstorff suggests is its proper relationship to situationality (history). When it does, there can be no universal, categorical doxastic requirement to believe the Christian gospel, such that, without regard to situation or personal history, it is rational to believe the gospel and irrational not to.

To put it another way, Wolterstorff believes that shalom is the very essence of the world in terms of divinely given intention and hope for the flourishing of the natural world and human culture, and that shalom is therefore the inescapable teleology of humanity and its environment. This means that a shalom ethic permeates not only our world but even our very beings as humans. This ethic is most universally evident as teleological, and it is given particular deontological force in the Christian scriptures, "that great unmasker of deceit."[57] Principally because shalom is *creational*, but also because it is *universally knowable*, there is no limit to its ethical force, whether understood teleologically or deontologically.[58] But even though shalom is *creational* and *universally knowable*, what I have called redemptive-historical epistemic humility comes into play as a component of a biblically constituted, redemptive-historical situationality. The biblical notion of "creation" is not only ontological but eschatological and historical as well: Creation is not merely the object of divine creative activity, it is the theater of the creator's ongoing relationship with the creature, principally with humankind. The historical movement from creation to fall to redemption to consummation is intrinsic to the natural order.[59] Therefore, not only

---

56. We might say that what I have described as "redemptive-historical epistemic humility" represents a restored Kuyperianism. In section §5.5 we discussed the avertive tendencies specifically of Kuyperian and Dooyeweerdian thought. Although Wolterstorff benefits a great deal from this tradition, it would appear that he offers a significant corrective in this regard.

57. *Reason within the Bounds*, 145.

58. I mention both possibilities simply because it appears to me more precise to speak in terms of a Christian-shalom deontology and a universal shalom teleology. The reason for this distinction is that it might plausibly be argued that the force of Christian deontology is provided by divine authorship; by thinking of shalom in terms of teleology then, the Christian believer can sympathize more with a non-Christian or even non-theistic appreciation of a shalom ethic. None of this is essential for my thesis, however.

59. For example, Rom 8:20–22: "For the creation was subjected to futility, not willingly, but because of him who subjected it, in hope that the creation itself will be set free from its bondage to decay and obtain the freedom of the glory of the children of God. For we know that the whole creation has been groaning together in the pains of childbirth until now."

does shalom fill the spaces of situated deontology because it is a universal ethic, in light of a clear demarcation of redemptive-historical episodes shalom forthrightly denies the universalizability of Christian-doxastic norms, short of the consummation of redemptive history. Or, we might say, the biblical view of history itself demands that it cannot be everywhere rational to believe that Christ was raised from that dead, nor everywhere irrational to deny it.

This is the implication of Wolterstorff's claim that situational entitlement or availability must precede doxastic accountability.[60] Wolterstorff appears to deny, even on the basis of Christian views of creation, history, and historical redemption, the validity of super-situational doxastic normativity. A self-conscious appreciation of creation in our view of the Christian life—as the erstwhile glorious proclamation of God (natural or general revelation) and creational potential unto the creator's glory, then the field of sinful rebellion, then as the scene of the inauguration of redemption in Christ—precludes avertive religion and the ethical oddities such avertiveness invites. "It all depends."[61]

The same creational emphasis can be turned against the avertive yearnings of philosophical tradition as well. We might say that, as avertive Christianity turns too eagerly toward the eschaton, so the philosophical tradition turns presumptuously toward the platonic heavens.[62]

Putting it this way allows us to suggest that Wolterstorff's insights in terms of the peculiar and platonic tendencies of traditional epistemology benefit from the same Christian-creational emphases, enabling us to offer a theological account for the manner of Wolterstorff's wrestling with philosophical tradition. In the same way that the avertive proclivities of Reformed theology are indicative of inadequate notions of creation and redemptive history, the avertive, platonic propensities of philosophical tradition are attributable to a neglect of both the God-createdness and derivative glory of the world, and the course of redemptive history set in motion by the fall.[63] Thus we may detect a grappling with the godliness of man (as image of God) in the avertive tendencies of epistemological tradition, but perhaps an aversion to his creatureliness (as *not* God, as finite and fallen).

I believe that something like this theology of situationality is the best account of the available evidence for the situationality distinctive of

---

60. See section §3.2.

61. "On Being Entitled to Beliefs about God," in *Practices of Belief*, 315.

62. See chapter 2.

63. As *Justice: Rights and Wrongs* proposes a theistic grounding of natural human worth, we can imagine a parallel defense of a Christian-theistic grounding for a properly grounded approach to epistemology and rationality.

Wolterstorff's approach to rationality, though there is not, I should add, sufficient evidence to conclude with conviction that this is in every detail Wolterstorff's self-understanding. Wolterstorff does not mention redemptive-historical epistemic humility or a redemptive-historical background to situationality. So while there is no direct, primary evidence making these connections, it seems to me that this is a most plausible reconstruction of the underlying coherence in Wolterstorff's thought in terms of entitled Christian belief yielding a situationality which supervenes on doxastic ethics.

6.3 ANSWERING POSSIBLE OBJECTIONS

Two possible objections merit attention. One is an alternative and apparently more intuitive interpretation than the one I propose in terms of a theology of situationality. A second objection might be the claim that situated rationality bears no natural or necessary connection to shalom, and that the association is arbitrary. In what follows, I explain these objections and offer responses to each.

Objection 1. An alternative interpretation of the relationship between Christian belief and situated rationality is as follows: Wolterstorff understands rationality as situated purely by virtue of lucid, inductive observation. If so, resorting to a theology of situationality to explain situated rationality begins to look unnecessarily elaborate. Akin to a Reidian common sense approach, this is perhaps more attractive, as it claims to be a less inventive hypothesis, and because it appears to require less creativity in associating apparently unrelated bodies of Wolterstorff's work. In fact, this alternative thesis fails to account for the preponderance of the evidence, particularly the evidence from chapters 1 and 4. To affirm that situated rationality comes about in complete detachment from theological and biblical commitments is to under-appreciate Wolterstorff's statement, "I am one who has received the Calvinian tradition," to assume that he quickly forgets what he writes about shalom when he turns to other subjects, or, quite simply, to read Wolterstorff selectively. If we take Wolterstorff at his word, we are compelled to seek connections within his diverse body of work in terms of Kuyperianism or Calvinism or Christianity or specifically, perhaps, shalom.

Suppose shalom is a categorical end for practical reason. Shalom, as a categorical end, would imply a number of hypothetical ends as a personal, historical, situation presents them; whatever promotes and protects shalom in a person's situation will serve as a hypothetical end for practical reason. Theoretical knowledge, economic and social justice, the absence of war and the full, objective realization of peace, health, love, friendship, cultural flourishing of all kinds, are obvious examples. A philosopher seeking ultimately to advance shalom would see lucidity and integrity in inductive observation, a sober account of actual doxastic practices, the actual historicized and situated integrity of doxastic subjects, etc., as hypothetical ends given his vocation, principled choice, governed self-direction, and so on. This seems to be consistent both with Wolterstorff's understanding of shalom and with his own work. Conversely, as noted, two complementary traditions, Calvinism and modern epistemology, have demonstrated in different ways an aversion to the here and now and deficient concern for praxis and practical implications. Wolterstorff's situated rationality manifests both practical motivation and theoretical avidity; shalom serves, we might say, as the motive, means, and end for Wolterstorff's approach to the ethics of belief. Situated rationality, in his thinking, is deeply rooted in Christian belief.

Objection 2. The second potential difficulty appears at the end of chapter 3, in conjunction with the fact that historicized, individualized situationality—the material from chapters 2 and 3—lacks a theory of moral value. This incompleteness led us to shalom in chapter 4—but it indicates only that situated rationality lacks moral value, not that it requires shalom in particular. The objector asks, why introduce shalom into a discussion of rationality and doxastic ethics? What compels this association? Why even suppose the two topics have anything to do with one another? Perhaps shalom fits the bill nicely, but if the connection between situated rationality and shalom is not necessary, then my thesis—that Wolterstorff's approach to rationality constitutes a shalom doxastic ethic—may be an interesting creative suggestion, but it is not an accurate descriptive hypothesis. In what follows, I offer a two-part response to this objection, consisting first of Wolterstorff's many statements to the effect that Christian shalom is not one moral option among many but the universal source for human ethics; and second, my own semi-creative response to it as a conjecture along Wolterstorffian lines.

It should simply be recognized that Wolterstorff never speaks of shalom as merely that which Christians *believe* to be humanity's goal in terms both of *telos* and calling.[64] In many instances, Wolterstorff addresses a large-

---

64. He does, however, make hypothetical claims of the form, *if one believed X (Christianity, Christian theism), then one might argue thus.* See *Justice: Rights and Wrongs*, 360–61. Does an argument of this form challenge my claim that Wolterstorff does not take shalom obligation to be contingent upon belief that Christianity is true, but rather that he takes it to be a universal, human obligation? Of course not, since holding that shalom obligations are contingent upon Christian belief is incoherent: Christianity would be true only as long as one believed it to be true, and only for the one who so believed. We would not say that any such belief is a true belief, and anyway, such notions are foreign to Wolterstorff's thinking. These hypotheticals—"*if* one were a Christian,"

ly Christian readership, and for such an audience this qualification—that the shalom of scripture is not a private, Christian matter, but is significant for all image-bearing creatures—would have been superfluous to the point of strange, though we might have reason to expect it when he is addressing a broader audience. And in fact, Wolterstorff explicitly affirms in many places that shalom is our *human* obligation. It is not a hypothetical obligation *in the case that* we take Christian belief as true: it is intrinsic to human nature and to the whole natural order.

To put it another way, if Wolterstorff finds shalom in the Christian scriptures and then affirms it as true for all people everywhere, and even to a large extent universally evident as the testimony of nature, he is making a rather strong if indirect assertion of the truth of Christian belief.[65] For clearly, it is *from the Christian scriptures* that we learn to identify the teleology of human nature as traceable to the creative activity of God the Father, Son, and Holy Spirit. So it would appear that in Wolterstorff's thought we can detect sufficient evidence that he takes Christian belief not only to be true but to wield a forthrightly particularistic claim on the nature of the world and humanity. We may say, therefore, that we are going beyond the clear contours of Wolterstorff's thought by entertaining the possibility that a value system other than Christianity may fit the bill. The move from chapter 3 to chapter 4 was the correct one.

It should also be noted that at the end of chapter 3, we recognized not that the historicized situationality of the doxastic self lacked moral value or moral significance; on the contrary, the purpose of the analyses of chapters 2 and 3 was to objectify practices of inquiry and a person's (moral) location within a (morally charged) situationality, in order to analyze the deontology already implicit in the doxastic aspects of daily, practical rationality. We embarked on an inductive study of the practical rationality of situationality not because situationality lacked moral value; we undertook that study precisely in order to understand the moral substance we always and already find there. What we found missing at the close of chapter 3 was an account for the moral substance of actual situationality.[66] It was there; it just did not yet have a name.

---

or "*if* one in fact held these theistic beliefs"—are gracious and theoretically prudent but perhaps to some extent merely rhetorical, since Wolterstorff is clearly a Christian.

65. Whether this is also an argument for the *exclusive* truth of Christianity is a somewhat different question, since this procedure nowhere requires, strictly speaking, that the Christian scriptures are the *only* revelation of shalom.

66. This displays, once again, a kind of apologetic methodology. Wolterstorff builds general agreement on the contours of practical rationality in such a way that the question of accounting for moral value is left open. The apologetic task is then to ask, what

Perhaps the matter is not so easily settled, however. We also noted, in section §5.3, that choice-principles and control-beliefs (and direction and acceptance governance) are merely formal markers not tied intrinsically to the content of Christian belief. We recognized therefore that such categories give us *a priori* no information about which beliefs may serve as choice-principles or control-beliefs, and therefore no grounds to deny wholesale non-Christian beliefs (other religious beliefs or beliefs of a social or political nature) the right to assume these roles. And indeed, Wolterstorff endorses what he calls "dialogic pluralism."[67] This would appear to present a problem for my thesis: if Wolterstorff sees shalom as teaching an ethic of inter-faith dialogue and the occasional rationality of a plurality of religious beliefs on the basis of the idea that religious truth itself is pluralistic (or situational), it is no longer so clear that situationality is necessarily related to a Christian, shalom ethic.

I submit that this problem should not actually arise for our thesis, for at least the following two reasons. First, to take *dialogic* pluralism as affirming an *ultimate* pluralism of religious truth is to introduce or even favor a hypothesis of obvious incoherence on Wolterstorff's part, over a hypothesis of coherence and consistency. If it is true that various religious beliefs are in conflict with each other, then to say that they are equally true is also to say that they are equally false.[68] But more importantly, interpreting dialogic pluralism in this way is to say that Wolterstorff argues, on the unique mer-

---

is the necessary condition for the historicized situationality (and morality) we find in chapters 2 and 3? Can secularism account for it? Can another religion account for it? Or is Christianity the best explanation available? Wolterstorff's distinctively Christian account for it is rich, and it therefore demonstrates a kind of indirect argument for Christian belief or for a Christian worldview. This is precisely the procedure in *Justice: Rights and Wrongs* (see 360–61), as we have noted.

67. Wolterstorff uses the term in *Justice: Rights and Wrongs*, ix–xi, 360–61, though the concept surfaces in numerous other places. Wolterstorff's "Scholarship Grounded in Religion" and "Epilogue," in *Religion, Scholarship, and Higher Education*, though the term "dialogic pluralism" does not appear there, are helpful for understanding what he has in mind (see esp. 14–15). A passage which bears openly the here and now shalom-demand for justice, redemptive-historical epistemic humility, and dialogic pluralism appears in "The Travail of Theology in the Modern Academy." There Wolterstorff says, "As we are all walking the road to that new university which lies still over the hill, we must be in conversation on two fundamental issues: How can the perspectival pluralization of academia, which justice demands, be secured without sacrificing peace and coherence of purpose? And what would an epistemology that gives up on foundationalism without sinking into relativism look like?" These are, essentially, the questions motivating dialogic pluralism, a diverse dialogue in which "what appear to be substantive disagreements are nothing more than equally valid responses to Mystery" (45–46).

68. Or it is to deny that they are in genuine conflict, which I think is more often the intention.

its of Christian belief, against the uniqueness of any religious belief. This is obvious incoherence. But certainly we have sufficient reason to expect consistency between dialogic pluralism and shalom: they are presented to us by one and the same author. And certainly the more charitable hermeneutic ought to be favored.

Another reason this problem does not arise for our thesis is this. To take dialogic pluralism as a difficulty in this way, as an affirmation of religious relativism (or John Hick's version of pluralism, for example), would be to ascribe to Wolterstorff a species of avertive epistemological pride. Dialogic pluralism enjoys the creational emphases and concerns of the Kuyperian tradition and a shalom ethic which emphasizes the situational integrity of doxastic subjects. Relativism does not. We might put it this way: it is undeniable that there are many religions in today's connected world, and that we labor side by side with followers of religions different from and even contrary to our own. From a vantage point purportedly enjoying epistemic superiority, the relativist thesis assumes that the privileged observer may adjudicate on the truth-value of all religious beliefs. Dialogic pluralism, on the other hand, is an epistemological take on the presence of religious diversity which emphasizes the irreproachable ethical good of humble dialogue between persons and peoples. Given the present reality of religious diversity, Wolterstorff can say, "'is one entitled to believe that Jesus was resurrected from the dead?' It all depends," it depends "on what sort of person and what sort of situation."[69] And it clearly does so depend, given Wolterstorff's notion of entitlement.

Finally, the claim that the end of chapter 3 offers no compelling reason to proceed to chapter 4, mistakes the approach of the present study for the architecture of Wolterstorff's own belief system. It is not the case that Wolterstorff reasons his way to Christian belief by moving from Western philosophical heritage, to a situated doxastic anthropology with the help of Thomas Reid, to practical doxastic rationality, and then to a position of favoring a Christian account for these discoveries. On the contrary, Wolterstorff reasons from his Christian belief, but he does so in a way that does not force him to enter a pluralistic, redemptive-historically conditioned dialogue with the full force of realized eschatology.[70] Shalom, with all its

---

69. "On Being Entitled to Beliefs about God," in *Practices of Belief*, 314–15.

70. It is worth noting that *Until Justice and Peace Embrace*, in which shalom figures prominently, was released in the same year as *Faith and Rationality* (1983), which contains Wolterstorff's seminal essay, "Can Belief in God Be Rational If It Has No Foundations?" That is, his most extended argument for a universal calling in the form of shalom was published in the same year as this influential essay critiquing the evidentialist challenge to belief in God.

theological substance, is not inferred from situated rationality; it is rather the reverse, that situated rationality is inferred from shalom and a Christian view of creation and history.

I conclude this section with a quotation from Wolterstorff. Notice here that the controlling function of entitled Christian belief, the situational rationality of beliefs (even Christian beliefs in particular), and the necessary connection between them are all affirmed in this excerpt.

> ... my view is by no means that the work of Christ, the biblical meaning of Creation, etc., are somehow subject 'to the ongoing immanent process of shifting historical conditions.' Those things, and the rest of the biblical *kerygma*, all remain fixed no matter what transpires in history. My question is only, what is it that we are obliged to do and believe by way of actualizing our faith? And my emphasis fell on what seems to me the obvious but often overlooked truth that the specific texture of such obligation varies from person to person. From this it of course does not follow that everything varies, that *nothing* remains constant. In fact it seems to me obligatory for every Christian to acknowledge that he is responsible to God, to believe that Jesus Christ came into the world to save sinners, to believe that it is God's will that we should love him above all and our neighbor as ourselves. Nonetheless, I remain convinced that it is vastly less important for us to try to determine what is absolutely universal in that which God holds human beings responsible for believing by way of actualizing their faith, and more important for each of us to determine what it is that God holds *him* responsible for believing by way of actualizing his faith. The former is an "academic" question, the latter, existential... What I in my situation am held responsible by God for doing and believing is not determined by what I and others *believe* on the matter; it is determined simply by what God does in fact hold me responsible for.[71]

6.4 QUESTIONS ABOUT WOLTERSTORFF'S NOTION OF SITUATIONALITY

Linking Wolterstorff's work on rationality and epistemology to Reformed, Kuyperian Christianity and to Wolterstorff's notion of shalom has produced

---

71. "On Avoiding Historicism," 184. The fact that the article containing this passage was published in 1980 demonstrates remarkable consistency in Wolterstorff's approach to these issues over the course of many years.

a distinctly Wolterstorffian theory of rationality, a 'shalom doxastic deontology,' I have called it, that represents a forceful though indirect argument for biblically informed Christian belief as a worldview and ethic. Doing so has also opened several avenues for Wolterstorff studies and for Calvinist thought on related issues. So, in closing, I shall mention a handful of theological questions that, I think, might rank high on the agenda of anyone interested in issues raised by Wolterstorff's shalom-based approach to the ethics of belief. These questions focus on Wolterstorff's notion of situationality.

As noted in section §6.2, Wolterstorff lays hold of a notion of situationality that resists the eschatological anxiety of some Calvinistic thought on ethics and culture. More specifically, Wolterstorff's notion of situationality capitalizes on a renewed redemptive-historical sensitivity which grants a greater appreciation for the goodness of creation in terms of the redemptive-historical not-yet. This meant that soteriological categories of regenerate and unregenerate and of elect and non-elect were epistemically inaccessible, and that their role in the ethics of belief must be attenuated accordingly. Methodological observance of this inaccessibility, a distinctive feature of Wolterstorffian situationality, we dubbed "redemptive-historical epistemic humility," and on account of it, such soteriological categories are rendered irrelevant to doxastic ethics situationally understood. And we pointed out, furthermore, that this Kuyperian, creational emphasis offered both philosophical and theological yield. Having said all that, one issue deserves attention here: specifically, the biblical and theological credentials of the non-soteric character of Wolterstorffian situationality.

Jesus says, "I have not come to bring peace, but a sword."[72] And according to Luke, Paul proclaimed that the resurrection of Christ from the dead was proof of coming judgment,[73] perhaps just the sort of reckoning envisioned in Matt 25:31–46. Certainly Wolterstorff's shalom situated ethic reflects the redemptive purposes of God in Christ, but a covenantal antithesis between regenerate and unregenerate or Christian and non-Christian, so heavily emphasized by Kuyper and in these and other biblical passages, seems to play little role. So one might ask: Does situationality represent a disproportionately rosy view of biblical religion by, perhaps, suspending the ethics of belief in a redemptive-historical holding pattern? One might raise theological concern, in other words, in terms of what appears to be the purely and brutely phenomenal nature of situationality.[74]

72. Matt 10:34
73. Acts 17:31
74. Sloane says "empirical" where I say "phenomenal," though he does not register

This possibility catches one's theological attention because, following scripture, Reformed theology traditionally holds that knowledge of the one true God is not merely available in nature, but inescapable. As discussed above in section §6.2, Ps 19 says that "the heavens declare the glory of God," and that "day to day pours out speech," speech which "goes out through all the earth." This would appear to mean that all situations are confronted inescapably, and perceptibly, with Christian content. In Rom 1, Paul writes that "what can be known about God is plain to them, because God has shown it to them," and that "his eternal power and divine nature, have been clearly perceived . . . [s]o that they are without excuse." And he adds, "[t]hey know God's decree that those who practice such things deserve to die . . ."[75] For Paul, then, more than a few non-specific features of a bare theism are involved in the knowledge that is inescapably and universally given (not to say that bare theism is the implication of Psalm 19); even the moral requirements of God and the high price for sin are known—by all.

In other words, it might appear from such passages that at least a few theological realities, namely, the holy nature of God and the attendant ethico-religious demand of perfect righteousness, permeate the phenomenal realm. And if that is the case, situations are not strictly or merely phenomenal. Brute, non-theistic, phenomenalism would represent something of a failure to take into account this revelation and the richly and overtly theological essence of creation, traditionally called *general* or *natural revelation*.[76] Wolterstorff's notion of situationality appears to under-appreciate

---

any theological concerns. He says that "a main feature" of Wolterstorff's theory of rationality is "its being integrally related to empirical observation of the nature of human believings" (*On Being a Christian*, 97; see ibid., 97–102). The issue in view in this section is the possible conflict between Wolterstorff's notion of situationality, as one in which no immediate theological claim is made on the doxastic subject, with the doctrine of general revelation and a few biblical passages, which teach that theological knowledge is objectively clear and subjectively apprehended, everywhere. In order to emphasize this potential discrepency, I prefer the reminder of Kantian anti-revelational phenomenalism over Sloane's "empirical."

75. The referent of these third person plural pronouns (them, they, etc.) is the "men" of verse 18: "For the wrath of God is revealed from heaven against all ungodliness and unrighteousness of men, who by their unrighteousness suppress the truth." "Men," of course, is gender inclusive.

76. Wolterstorff quotes Ps 19:2–4 in the opening paragraph of *Hearing the Call*, but he omits verse 1 and reproduces only verses 2–4, which mention the daily pouring forth of speech, the nightly declaration of knowledge, and then the extension of this communication to the ends of the earth. As a result, the excerpt Wolterstorff offers proclaims the propagation and abundance of speech and knowledge, but makes no mention of its content. When verses 2–4 are read out of context (without verse 1), they sound vague and esoteric. But verses 2–4 are not given entirely without context. Wolterstorff introduces the quotation as follows: "We are called, one and all, called by

the non-verbal but clear and content-specific revelation of God in creation and even within human consciousness itself.

The same line of questioning may be translated into historical categories. According to traditional Calvinist thought, as *The Westminster Confession of Faith* has it, God, "from all eternity, did . . . freely, and unchangeably ordain whatsoever comes to pass." "[N]or," the Confession adds, "is the liberty or contingency of second causes taken away, but rather established."[77] In terms then of a Reidian, historical individualization of the doxastic subject, a mainstay of Wolterstorffian situationality, again, the assumption that this process is exhaustively non-covenantal, non-religious, or non-theistic—brutely phenomenal, in other words—appears to be in tension with the view of history spelled out in the Reformed tradition as determined in every detail by the Triune God. This Reformed view of history and the phenomenalism of Reidian situationality are somewhat at odds, offering distinct views of historical facts and events. Reidian situationality appears to assume that phenomena, what the Confession calls "second causes," are explanatorily exhaustive and sufficiently informative for ethics: in order to know what there is and how we ought to act, phenomena are sufficient. By contrast, the Confession so emphasizes the primacy of divine activity that its authors felt the need to assure the reader that the divine primary cause is not all there is. Can these two simply meet in the middle? That remains to be seen.

Specifically in terms of rationality, then, if there are no situations which are in any sense non-theological or non-theistic or wholly beyond the scope of general or natural revelation, as these passages appear to teach, then there are no situations in which we have no awareness of God and the good. If so, then beliefs in the existence and something of the nature

---

the goodness of what there is, called by the goodness of what there is not but could be. Sometimes the call comes in words; sometimes the call is wordless" (*Hearing the Call*, ix). By thus replacing verse 1, Wolterstorff has effectively made verses 2–4 about non-verbal cries from creatures about brokenness, instead of non-verbal proclamations from (non-human) creatures ("the heavens" and "the sky above") regarding the glory of God and his handiwork. In other words, a less than charitable read of this passage could easily find Wolterstorff exchanging the theocentric situationality of all the world, we might say, as scripture presents it, for a world-centered ("secular") religion, and using the Bible itself to do so.

77. *The Westminster Confession of Faith* 3.1. See also WCF chapter 5 on the doctrine of providence, which begins, "God, the great Creator of all things, doth uphold, direct dispose, and govern all creatures, actions, and things, from the greatest even to the least, by his most wise and holy providence, according to his infallible foreknowledge, and the free and immutable counsel of his own will, to the praise of the glory of his wisdom, power, justice, goodness, and mercy" (WCF 5.1). See also the *Belgic Confession*, article 13.

of the one, true God; in the moral requirement of perfection; and in the specific wages of sin are permanent features of any self-conscious person's moral, doxastic situation. On this basis, it might never be rational to deny the existence of God, claim moral ignorance, or follow a contrived religion, regardless of the particulars of an individualized situation.[78] Rather, denying what is "plain" within and all around one, and what one on some level knows,[79] would constitute a cut and dry case of irrationality.

And yet, in a passage already cited, Paul writes, "faith comes from hearing, and hearing through the word of Christ."[80] Wolterstorff's insistence on the opportunity to believe something—in this case the gospel—through various features of situational availability—in this case through hearing it preached or taught—as a necessary condition for culpable rejection of that belief appears to enjoy biblical support as well. Indeed, as much as the Reformed tradition has developed its doctrine of general or natural revelation along the lines of passages such as Ps 19 and Rom 1:18ff, it has been wary of a theology constructed exclusively with 'natural' materials, and it has consistently denied that the grace of God in Christ unto salvation is thus revealed, that is, non-verbally in nature.[81] So, while he ordains created means for his redemptive purposes, only God knows "the hearts of all the children of mankind" (1 Kgs 8:39). God alone 'sees' trans-historical realities such as the vital covenant, the regenerating work of the Holy Spirit, and the distinction between elect and non-elect.

In sum, Reformed theology has sought to strike a balance, according to scripture, between those theological truths which are given in nature, those which are given in scripture only, and those which are unavailable to man in the redemptive-historical already-not-yet. Wolterstorff's theory of situated rationality attempts to strike that balance as well.

---

78. For examples of the view I am outlining here, see Gaffin, "Epistemological Reflections on 1 Corinthians 2:6–16," in *Revelation and Reason*, 13–40; Oliphint, "The Irrationality of Unbelief"; and Oliphint, "Primal and Simple Knowledge," in *A Theological Guide to Calvin's Institutes*, 16–43.

79. Rom 1:21.

80. Rom 10:17.

81. See, for example, Berkouwer, *General Revelation*, 285–332; and Berkhof, *Systematic Theology*, 128–33.

Bibliography

Alston, William P. *Epistemic Justification: Essays in the Theory of Knowledge.* Ithaca: Cornell University Press, 1989.
———. *Perceiving God: The Epistemology of Religious Experience.* Ithaca: Cornell University Press, 1991.
———. *A Realist Conception of Truth.* Ithaca: Cornell University Press, 1996.
———. *The Reliability of Sense Perception.* Ithaca: Cornell University Press, 1996.
Anderson, Owen J. *Benjamin B. Warfield and Right Reason: The Clarity of General Revelation and Function of Apologetics.* Lanham, MD: University Press of America, 2005.
———. *Reason and Worldviews: Warfield, Kuyper, Van Til, and Plantinga on the Clarity of General Revelation and Function of Apologetics.* Lanham, MD: University Press of America, 2008.
Attridge, Harold W. "Wolterstorff, Rights, Wrongs, and the Bible." *Journal of Religious Ethics* 37 (2009) 209–19.
Audi, Robert, and Nicholas Wolterstorff. *Religion in the Public Square: The Place of Religious Convictions in Political Debate.* Lanham, MD: Rowman & Littlefield, 1997.
Ayers, Michael. *Locke: Epistemology and Ontology.* New York: Routledge, 1999.
Baker, Deane-Peter. *Tayloring Reformed Epistemology: Charles Taylor, Alvin Plantinga and the de Jure Challenge to Christian Belief.* London: SCM, 2007.
Baus, Gregory. "Dooyeweerd's Societal Sphere Sovereignty: A Theory of Differentiated Responsibility." *Griffin's View on International and Comparative Law* 7 (2006) 209–17.
Bavinck, Herman. *God and Creation.* Vol. 2 of *Reformed Dogmatics.* Edited by John Bolt. Translated by John Vriend. Grand Rapids: Baker Academic, 2004.
———. *Prolegomena.* Vol. 1 of *Reformed Dogmatics.* Edited by John Bolt. Translated by John Vriend. Grand Rapids: Baker, 2003.
Berkhof, Louis. *Systematic Theology.* Grand Rapids: Eerdmans, 1996.
Bolt, John. "The Imitation of Christ as Illumination for the Two Kingdoms Debate." *Calvin Theological Journal* 48 (2013) 6–34.
Calvin, Jean. *Calvin: Institutes of the Christian Religion.* Edited by John T. McNeill. Translated by Ford Lewis Battles. Library of Christian Classics 20–21. Louisville: Westminster John Knox, 2001.
Chisholm, Roderick M. *The Philosophy of Roderick M. Chisholm.* Edited by Lewis Edwin Hahn. Chicago: Open Court, 1997.

BIBLIOGRAPHY

———. *Theory of Knowledge*. 2nd ed. Englewood Cliffs, NJ: Prentice Hall, 1977.

Clark, Kelly James, ed. *Philosophers Who Believe: The Spiritual Journeys of 11 Leading Thinkers*. Downers Grove, IL: InterVarsity, 1997.

Clifford, William Kingdon. *The Ethics of Belief and Other Essays*. Edited by Tim Madigan. Amherst, NY: Prometheus, 1999.

Coyle, Douglas L. "Nicholas Wolterstorff's Reformed Epistemology and Its Challenge to Lockean and Rawlsian Liberalism." PhD diss., Baylor University Department of Philosophy, 2006.

Crisp, Thomas M., Matthew Davidson, and David Vander Laan, eds. *Knowledge and Reality Essays in Honor of Alvin Plantinga*. Dordrecht, Netherlands: Springer, 2006.

De Bary, Philip. *Thomas Reid and Scepticism: His Reliabilist Response*. New York: Routledge, 2002.

DeBorst, James Henry, and Nicholas Wolterstorff. "Voting God's Cause." *Reformed Journal* 30 (1980) 2–3.

Dennison, William D. "Dutch Neo-Calvinism and the Roots for Transformation: An Introductory Essay." *Journal of the Evangelical Theological Society* 42 (1999) 271–91.

"Does God Suffer? An Interview with Nicholas Wolterstorff." *Modern Reformation* 8 (1999) 45–47.

Dooyeweerd, Herman. *A New Critique of Theoretical Thought: The Structures of Individuality of Temporal Reality*. Lewiston, NY: Mellen, 1997.

Echeverria, Edward J. "Towards a Critique of the Subject." *Philosophia Reformata* 44 (1979) 86–105.

Edgar, William, and K. Scott Oliphint, eds. *Christian Apologetics Past and Present: A Primary Source Reader: From 1500*. Vol. 2. Wheaton, IL: Crossway, 2009.

Fraser, David Allen, ed. *Evangelicalism: Surviving Its Success*. Saint Davids, PA: Eastern College, 1987.

Ganssle, Gregory E., and Paul Helm, eds. *God and Time: Four Views*. Downers Grove, IL: InterVarsity, 2001.

Greco, John. "Reid's Critique of Berkeley and Hume: What's the Big Idea?" *Philosophy and Phenomenological Research* 55 (1995) 279–96.

Greco, John, and Ernest Sosa, eds. *The Blackwell Guide to Epistemology*. Malden, MA: Blackwell, 1999.

Horwitz, Paul. "Churches as First Amendment Institutions: Of Sovereignty and Spheres." *Harvard Civil Rights-Civil Liberties Law Review* 44 (2009) 79–131.

Hume, David. *Enquiries concerning the Human Understanding and concerning the Principles of Morals*. 2nd ed. Oxford: Clarendon, 1902.

Klapwijk, Jacob. "Antithesis and Common Grace." In *Bringing into Captivity Every Thought*, edited by Jacob Klapwijk, Sander Griffioen, and Gerben Groenewoud, 169–90. Lanham, MD: University Press of America, 1991.

Kooi, Cornelis van der, and J. de Bruijn, eds. *Kuyper Reconsidered: Aspects of His Life and Work*. VU Studies on Protestant History 3. Amsterdam: VU Uitgeverij, 1999.

Kuyper, Abraham. *Abraham Kuyper: A Centennial Reader*. Edited by James D. Bratt. Grand Rapids: Eerdmans, 1998.

———. *Encyclopedia of Sacred Theology: Its Principles*. Translated by J. Hendrik De Vries. New York: Scribner, 1898.

———. *Lectures on Calvinism*. Grand Rapids: Eerdmans, 2002.

———. "Pantheism's Destruction of Boundaries." Translated by J. Hendrik De Vries. *Methodist Review* 5, no. 9 (1893) n.p.

———. *Principles of Sacred Theology*. Translated by J. Hendrik De Vries. Grand Rapids: Eerdmans, 1954.

Locke, John. *An Essay concerning Human Understanding*. Edited by P. H. Nidditch. Clarendon Edition of the Works of John Locke. Oxford: Clarendon, 1975.

MacIntyre, Alasdair C. *After Virtue: A Study in Moral Theory*. Notre Dame: University of Notre Dame Press, 2007.

Marshall, Paul A., Sander Griffioen, and Richard J. Mouw, eds. *Stained Glass: Worldviews and Social Science*. Lanham, MD: University Press of America, 1989.

Moltmann, Jürgen, Nicholas Wolterstorff, and Ellen T. Charry. *A Passion for God's Reign: Theology, Christian Learning and the Christian Self*. Edited by Miroslav Volf. Grand Rapids: Eerdmans, 1998.

Moser, Paul K., Dwayne H. Mulder, and J. D. Trout. *The Theory of Knowledge: A Thematic Introduction*. New York: Oxford University Press, 1998.

Mouw, Richard. *The Challenges of Cultural Discipleship: Essays in the Line of Abraham Kuyper*. Grand Rapids: Eerdmans, 2012.

Oliphint, K. Scott. "Bavinck's Realism, the Logos Principle, and Sola Scriptura." *Westminster Theological Journal* 72 (2010) 359–90.

———. *Covenantal Apologetics: Principles and Practice in Defense of Our Faith*. Wheaton, IL: Crossway, 2013.

———. *God with Us: Divine Condescension and the Attributes of God*. Wheaton, IL: Crossway, 2012.

———. "A Primal and Simple Knowledge." In *A Theological Guide to Calvin's Institutes: Essays and Analysis*, edited by David Hall and Peter A. Lillback, 16–43. Philipsburg, NJ: Presbyterian and Reformed, 2008.

———. "Using Reason by Faith." *Westminster Theological Journal* 73 (2011) 97–112.

Plantinga, Alvin, and Nicholas Wolterstorff, eds. *Faith and Rationality: Reason and Belief in God*. Notre Dame: University of Notre Dame Press, 1983.

———. *God and Other Minds: A Study of the Rational Justification of Belief in God*. Cornell Paperbacks. Ithaca: Cornell University Press, 1967.

———. *Warrant and Proper Function*. New York: Oxford University Press, 1993.

———. *Warranted Christian Belief*. New York: Oxford University Press, 2000.

———. *Warrant: The Current Debate*. New York: Oxford University Press, 1993.

———. *Where the Conflict Really Lies: Science, Religion, and Naturalism*. New York: Oxford University Press, 2011.

Reid, Thomas. *Essays on the Intellectual Powers of Man: A Critical Edition*. Edinburgh Edition of Thomas Reid. University Park: Pennsylvania State University Press, 2002.

———. *An Inquiry into the Human Mind: On the Principles of Common Sense: A Critical Edition*. Edited by Derek R. Brookes. Edinburgh Edition of Thomas Reid. University Park: Pennsylvania State University Press, 1997.

Rorty, Richard. "Religion in the Public Square: A Reconsideration." *Journal of Religious Ethics* 31 (2003) 141–49.

Schmemann, Alexander. *For the Life of the World: Sacraments and Orthodoxy*. Crestwood, NY: St. Vladimir's Seminary Press, 1973.

Shannon, Nathan D. "Believe and Confess: Revisiting Christian Doxastic Intentionality." *Heythrop Journal* (2012) doi: 10.1111/j.1468-2265.2012.00795.x.

Skillen, James W. *The Good of Politics: A Biblical, Historical, and Contemporary Introduction*. Grand Rapids: Baker, 2014.
Sloane, Andrew. *On Being a Christian in the Academy: Nicholas Wolterstorff and the Practice of Christian Scholarship*. Paternoster Biblical and Theological Monographs. Waynesboro, GA: Paternoster, 2003.
Sudduth, Michael. *The Reformed Objection to Natural Theology*. Farnham, England: Ashgate, 2009.
Tipton, Lane G., and K. Scott Oliphint, eds. *Revelation and Reason: New Essays in Reformed Apologetics*. Phillipsburg, NJ: Presbyterian and Reformed, 2007.
Van Til, Cornelius. *An Introduction to Systematic Theology: Prolegomena and the Doctrines of Revelation, Scripture, and God*. Edited by William Edgar. 2nd ed. Phillipsburg, NJ: Presbyterian and Reformed, 2007.
―――. "Nature and Scripture." In *The Infallible Word: A Symposium by the Members of the Faculty of Westminster Theological Seminary*, edited by Ned B. Stonehouse and Paul Woolley, 263–301. Nutley, NJ: Presbyterian and Reformed, 1978.
van Woudenberg, Rene. "Abraham Kuyper on Faith and Science." In *Kuyper: Aspects of His Life and Work*, edited by Cornelis van der Kooi and Jan de Bruijn, 147–57. VU Studies on Protestant History. Amsterdam: VU University Press, 2000.
Vos, Geerhardus. *Redemptive History and Biblical Interpretation: The Shorter Writings of Geerhardus Vos*. Edited by Richard B. Gaffin. Phillipsburg, NJ: Presbyterian and Reformed, 1980.
Walsh, Brian J., Hendrick Hart, and Robert E. Vander Vennen, eds. *An Ethos of Compassion and the Integrity of Creation*. Lanham, MD: University Press of America, 1995.
Warfield, Benjamin Breckinridge. *Selected Shorter Writings of Benjamin B. Warfield*. Edited by John E. Meeter. Nutley, NJ: Presbyterian and Reformed, 2001.
Witsius, Herman. *The Economy of the Covenants between God and Man: Comprehending a Complete Body of Divinity*. Grand Rapids: Reformed Heritage, 2010.
Wolters, Albert M. *Creation Regained: Biblical Basics for a Reformational Worldview*. 2nd ed. Grand Rapids: Eerdmans, 2005.
Wolterstorff, Nicholas. "Are Concept-Users World-Makers?" In *Philosophical Perspectives*, edited by James E. Tomberlin, 1:233–67. Atascadero, CA: Ridgeview, 1987.
―――. *Art in Action: Toward a Christian Aesthetic*. Grand Rapids: William B. Eerdmans, 1980.
―――. "Art, Taste, and Society." *Reformed Journal* 26 (1976) 5–7.
―――. "The Assurance of Faith." *Faith and Philosophy* 7 (1990) 396–417.
―――. "Barth on Evil." *Faith and Philosophy* 13 (1996) 584–608.
―――. "Between the Times." *Reformed Journal* 40 (1990) 16–20.
―――. "Beyond Beauty and the Aesthetic in the Engagement of Religion and Art." In *Theological Aesthetics after von Balthasar*, edited by Oleg V. Bychkov and James Fodor, 119–33. Ashgate Studies in Theology, Imagination, and the Arts. Aldershot, UK: Ashgate, 2008.
―――. "Can a Calvinist Be a Progressive?" *Gereformeerd Theologisch Tijdschrift* 88 (1988) 249–58.
―――. "Can Human Rights Survive Secularization? Part I." *Perspectives* 23 (2008) 10–14.

———. "Can Human Rights Survive Secularization? Part II." *Perspectives* 23 (2008) 12–17.
———. "Can Scholarship and Christian Conviction Mix? A New Look at the Integration of Knowledge." *Journal of Education and Christian Belief* 3 (1999) 35–50.
———. "Canon and Criterion." *Reformed Journal* 19 (1969) 10–15.
———. "Christian Political Reflection: Diognetian or Augustinian." *Princeton Seminary Bulletin* 20 (1999) 150–68.
———. "Christianity and Human Rights: An Introduction." In *Religion and Human Rights*, edited by John Witte and M. Christian Green, 42–55. New York: Oxford University Press, 2011.
———. "Christianity and Social Justice." *Christian Scholar's Review* 16 (1987) 211–28.
———. "Crossing the Threshold of Divine Revelation." *Faith and Philosophy* 28 (2011) 102–8.
———. *Curriculum, by What Standard?* Grand Rapids: National Union of Christian Schools, 1969.
———. "Death in Gaza." *Reformed Journal* 38 (1988) 2–5.
———. *Divine Discourse: Philosophical Reflections on the Claim That God Speaks*. New York: Cambridge University Press, 1995.
———. "Divine Simplicity." In *Philosophical Perspectives*, edited by James E. Tomberlin, 5:531–52. Atascadero, CA: Ridgeview, 1991.
———. "Does Truth Still Matter?: Reflections on the Crisis of the Postmodern University." *Crux* 31 (1995) 17–28.
———. "Herman Dooyeweerd: An Appreciation." Paper presented to the Calvin Faculty Forum, mid-1960s. All of Life Redeemed, http://www.alloflieredeemed.co.uk/dooyeweerd.htm (accessed Feb. 23, 2015).
———. "Duties and Rights: Looking for Help in Understanding Justice." *Books and Culture: A Christian Review* 16 (2010) 25–27.
———. *Educating for Life: Reflections on Christian Teaching and Learning*. Edited by Gloria Goris Stronks and Clarence W. Joldersma. Grand Rapids: Baker, 2002.
———. *Educating for Responsible Action*. Grand Rapids: Eerdmans, 1980.
———. *Educating for Shalom: Essays on Christian Higher Education*. Edited by Clarence W. Joldersma and Gloria Goris Stronks. Grand Rapids: Eerdmans, 2004.
———. "An Engagement with Rorty." *Journal of Religious Ethics* 31 (2003) 129–39.
———. "Escaping the Cage of Secular Discourse." *Christian Scholar's Review* 40 (2010) 93–99.
———. "Evangelicalism and the Arts." *Christian Scholar's Review* 17 (1988) 449–73.
———. "Evidence, Entitled Belief, and the Gospels." *Faith and Philosophy* 6 (1989) 429–59.
———. "Faith and Reason: Philosophers Respond to Pope John Paul II's Encyclical Letter *Fides et Ratio*." *Books and Culture: A Christian Review* 5 (1999) 28–29.
———. "Forty Years Later." *Perspectives* 24 (2009) 6–11.
———. "God Everlasting." In *God and the Good: Essays in Honor of Henry Stob*, edited by Lewis B. Smedes and Clifton Orlebeke, 181–203. Grand Rapids: Eerdmans, 1975.
———. "God in Time." *Philosophia Christi* 2 (2000) 5–10.
———. "The Grace That Shaped My Life." *Reformed World* 56 (2006) 251–64.
———. *Hearing the Call: Liturgy, Justice, Church, and World*. Edited by Mark R. Gornik and Gregory Thompson. Grand Rapids: Eerdmans, 2011.

———. "Herman Bavinck—Proto-Reformed Epistemologist." *Calvin Theological Journal* 45 (2010) 133–46.

———. "How God Speaks." *Reformed Journal* 19 (1969) 16–20.

———. "How Much More Blood." *Reformed Journal* 37 (1987) 2–3.

———. "How My Mind Has Changed: The Way to Justice." *The Christian Century* 126 (2009) 26–30.

———. "How Philosophical Theology Became Possible within the Analytic Tradition of Philosophy." In *Analytic Theology*, 155–68. Oxford: Oxford University Press, 2009.

———. "How Social Justice Got to Me and Why It Never Left." *Journal of the American Academy of Religion* 76 (2008) 664–79.

———. "Hume and Reid." *The Monist* 70 (1987) 398–417.

———. "The Idea of a Christian College." *Reformed Journal* 12 (1962) 15–20.

———. "If God Is Good and Sovereign, Why Lament?" *Calvin Theological Journal* 36 (2001) 42–52.

———. "In Reply." *Perspectives* 23 (2008) 17–19.

———. *Inquiring about God: Selected Essays*. Vol. 1. Edited by Terence Cuneo. Cambridge: Cambridge University Press, 2010.

———. "The Integration of Faith and Learning—The Very Idea." *Journal of Psychology and Christianity* 3 (1984) 12–19.

———. "Is It Possible and Desirable for Theologians to Recover from Kant?" *Modern Theology* 14 (1998) 1–18.

———. "Is Reason Enough? A Review Essay." *Reformed Journal* 31 (1981) 20–24.

———. *John Locke and the Ethics of Belief*. Cambridge Studies in Religion and Critical Thought 2. New York: Cambridge University Press, 1996.

———. "John Locke's Epistemological Piety: Reason Is the Candle of the Lord." *Faith and Philosophy* 11 (1994) 572–91.

———. *Journey toward Justice: Personal Encounters in the Global South*. Grand Rapids: Baker Academic, 2013.

———. "Just Demands." *Christian Century* 127 (2010) 30–34.

———. "Justice as a Condition of Authentic Liturgy." *Theology Today* 48 (1991) 6–21.

———. "Justice as Inherent Rights: A Response to My Commentators." *Journal of Religious Ethics* 37 (2009) 261–79.

———. *Justice in Love*. Emory Studies in Law and Religion. Grand Rapids: Eerdmans, 2011.

———. *Justice: Rights and Wrongs*. Princeton: Princeton University Press, 2008.

———. "Letter to a Young Theologian." *Reformed Journal* 26 (1976) 13–18.

———. "Liberating Scholarship." *Reformed Journal* 31 (1981) 4–5.

———. "A Life in Philosophy." *Proceedings and Addresses of the American Philosophical Association* 81 (2007) 93–106.

———. "Liturgy and Lament." *Perspectives* 27 (2012) 24.

———. "Liturgy, Justice, and Holiness." *Reformed Journal* 39 (1989) 12–20.

———. "Liturgy, Justice, and Tears." *Worship* 62 (1988) 386–403.

———. *The Mighty and the Almighty: An Essay in Political Theology*. Cambridge: Cambridge University Press, 2012.

———. "The Mission of the Christian College at the End of the 20th Century." *Reformed Journal* 33 (1983) 14–18.

———. "The Mission of the Christian College at the End of the 20th Century: Thoughts on the Future of the Christian College." Edited by Michael L. Peterson. *Faculty Dialogue* (1988) 37–46.
———. "The Moral Significance of Poverty." *Perspectives* 6 (1991) 8–11.
———. "Not Presence but Action: Calvin on Sacraments." *Perspectives* 9 (1994) 16–22.
———. "On Avoiding Historicism." *Philosophy Reformata* 45 (1980) 178–85.
———. "On God Speaking." *Reformed Journal* 19 (1969) 7–11.
———. *On Universals: An Essay in Ontology*. Chicago: University of Chicago Press, 1970.
———. "Once Again, South Africa." *Reformed Journal* 27 (1977) 10–11.
———. *Practices of Belief: Selected Essays*. Vol. 2. Edited by Terence Cuneo. Cambridge: Cambridge University Press, 2010.
———. *Reason within the Bounds of Religion*. 2nd ed. Grand Rapids: Eerdmans, 1984.
———. "Reid on Common Sense." In *The Cambridge Companion to Thomas Reid*, edited by Terence Cuneo and Rene van Woudenberg, 77–100. Cambridge: Cambridge University Press, 2004.
———. "Reid on Common Sense, with Wittgenstein's Assistance." *American Catholic Philosophical Quarterly* 74 (2000) 491–517.
———. "Reid on Justice." In *Reid on Ethics*, edited by Sabine Roeser, 187–202. Philosophers in Depth. Basingstoke, UK: Palgrave Macmillan, 2009.
———. "Remember to Remember." *Reformed Journal* 39 (1989) 11–14.
———. "Reply to Allen J. Harder Concerning the Possibility of Christian Anarchy." *Christian Scholar's Review* 4 (1975) 339–41.
———. "Response: The Irony of It All." *The Hedgehog Review* 9 (2007) 63–69.
———. "Response to Helm, Quinn, and Westphal." *Religious Studies* 37 (2001) 293–306.
———. "Response to My Commentators." *Studies in Christian Ethics* 23 (2010) 197–204.
———. "Resurrecting the Author." *Midwest Studies in Philosophy* 27 (2003) 4–24.
———. "Scholarship Grounded in Religion." In *Religion, Scholarship, and Higher Education: Perspectives, Models, and Future*, edited by Andrea Sterk, 3–15. Essays from the Lilly Seminar on Religion and Higher Education. Notre Dame: University of Notre Dame Press, 2002.
———. "The Silence of the God Who Speaks." *Philosophia* 30 (2003) 13–32.
———. "Six Days in South Africa." *Reformed Journal* 35 (1985) 15–21.
———. "South African Crucible: Two Prophetic Voices in a Land of Racial Pain." *Sojourners* 9 (1980) 30–33.
———. "Teaching Justly for Justice." *Journal of Education and Christian Belief* 10 (2006) 23–37.
———. "Theory and Praxis." *Christian Scholar's Review* 9 (1980) 317–34.
———. "Thomas Reid on Rationality." In *Rationality in the Calvinian Tradition*, edited by Hendrik Hart, Johan van der Hoeven, and Nicholas Wolterstorff, 43–69. Lanham, MD: University Press of America, 1983.
———. *Thomas Reid and the Story of Epistemology*. Modern European Philosophy. New York: Cambridge University Press, 2001.
———. "Thomas Reid's Account of the Objectivated Character of Perception." *Reid Studies* 4 (2001) 3–15.

———. "Three Functions of Arts in Theological Education." *Theological Education* 31 (1994) 97–100.

———. "To Theologians: From One Who Cares about Theology But Is Not One of You." *Theological Education* 40 (2005) 79–92.

———. "The Travail of Theology in the Modern Academy." In *The Future of Theology: Essays in Honor of Jürgen Moltmann*, edited by Miroslav Volf, 35–46. Grand Rapids: Eerdmans, 1996.

———. "Trumpets, Ashes, and Tears." *Reformed Journal* 36 (1986) 17–22.

———. "Two Approaches to Representation, and Then a Third." *Midwest Studies in Philosophy* 16 (1991) 167–79.

———. *Understanding Liberal Democracy: Essays in Political Philosophy*. Edited by Terence Cuneo. Oxford: Oxford University Press, 2012.

———. *Until Justice and Peace Embrace*. Kuyper Lectures for 1981, delivered at the Free University of Amsterdam. Grand Rapids: Eerdmans, 1983.

———. "The Way to Justice." *Christian Century* 126 (2009) 26–30.

———. "What Is Cartesian Doubt?" *American Catholic Philosophical Quarterly* 67 (1993) 467–95.

———. *What New Haven and Grand Rapids Have to Say to Each Other*. Stob Lectures of Calvin College and Calvin Theological Seminary, 1992–1993. Grand Rapids: Calvin College and Calvin Theological Seminary, 1993.

———. "What Reformed Epistemology Is Not." *Perspectives* 7 (1992) 14–16.

———. "What Sort of Epistemological Realist Was Thomas Reid?" *Journal of Scottish Philosophy* 4 (2006) 111–24.

———. "Why Animals Don't Speak." *Faith and Philosophy* 4 (1987) 463–85.

———. "Why Care about Justice." *Reformed Journal* 36 (1986) 9–14.

———. "Why Care about Justice?" In *Evangelicalism: Surviving Its Success*, edited by David Allen Fraser, 156–67. Saint Davids, PA: Eastern College, 1987.

———. "Wolterstorff Responds." *Reformed Journal* 37 (1987) 8–9.

———. *Works and Worlds of Art*. Oxford: Oxford University Press, 1980.

———. "Worship and Justice." In *Major Themes in the Reformed Tradition*, edited by Donald McKim, 311–18. Grand Rapids: Eerdmans, 1992.

———. "The Wounds of God: Calvin's Theology of Social Injustice." *Reformed Journal* 37 (1987) 14–22.

Wolterstorff, Nicholas, and Joseph Houston. "God and Darkness in Reid." In *Thomas Reid: Context, Influence and Significance*, 77–101. Edinburgh: Dunedin Academic, 2004.

Woolsey, Andrew A. *Unity and Continuity in Covenantal Thought: A Study in the Reformed Tradition to the Westminster Assembly*. Grand Rapids: Reformed Heritage, 2012.

Yolton, John W. *John Locke and the Way of Ideas*. London: Oxford University Press, 1956.

———. *John Locke: Problems and Perspectives: A Collection of New Essays*. London: Cambridge University Press, 1969.

Index

Alston, William P., 57n2, 59n5, 60
antithesis, 6–7, 8n21, 120n104, 188
apologetics, 12n31, 141n53, 171
Aquinas, Thomas, 12n31, 98n43
atonement, 166n25
Augustine, 61, 96n36, 98n43

Bavinck, Herman, 5n13, 10n28, 11n30, 12n31, 13, 14n34, 19n40, 107, 107n65, 160n9
belief-forming dispositions, 18–19, 24, 34–49, 54–56, 60, 62–63, 66, 73, 78, 81, 161–63

Calvin College, 5–6, 118, 160, 169
Calvin, John, 95n32, 98n43, 107n65, 176n50
Cartesian, 1, 3, 24
Chisholm, Roderick, 32, 75–76, 164
Clifford, W. K., 32
common grace, 6n15, 160n9
common sense, 10, 13, 24, 34n41, 42n69, 47–49, 162n15, 174, 182
Covenant(al), 97n39, 100, 109, 117–18, 188, 190–91
creation-order, 84, 87, 100–110, 118, 146n68, 150n80, 166–67, 175–76

Dennison, William, 6n13
deontology/deontological, 20, 23n1, 26, 28–30, 33, 53, 56, 57–60, 66, 69, 73n43, 77, 77n61, 81–84, 86, 120n105, 125, 128–29, 140, 142, 154, 162, 165, 167–68, 172–73, 176, 180–81, 184, 188

Descartes, Rene, 20, 44–46 (*see also* Cartesian)
divine speech, 3, 61
Dooyeweerd, Herman, 6, 8n21, 101, 106, 143, 147, 178n54, 180n56
doxastic anthropology, 10, 11, 18–20, 24, 31n30, 34–35, 37, 39–40, 49–52, 54–56, 59, 78, 122, 129, 134, 153, 154, 161–62, 165, 186
doxastic optimism, 19, 24, 36, 42–50, 55, 81, 162–63

Echeverria, Edward J., 80n72
empiricism, 42n70
entitlement, 1–2, 10n28, 13, 16, 18–20, 22, 23–34, 44, 53, 56–57, 62, 64, 66–67, 69, 71–74, 76–84, 123, 155n96, 162, 165, 168–69, 171, 174, 177, 181, 186
epistemic desiderata, 81, 83n82
eschatology, 7, 20, 58, 90n9, 105–6, 118, 120n4, 139n48, 147, 160n9, 165–66, 179–80, 186, 188
evidence, 12n31, 13n32, 19, 21, 25, 30, 32n33, 35, 37, 48, 50, 53, 104, 130, 146n67, 156, 157n2, 159, 162, 171, 179n55, 182, 184
evidentialism, 31, 155, 171

flourishing, 89–91, 93–94, 99–101, 107–12, 115, 118, 124–26, 137n42, 139, 144, 149, 156, 169n28, 172n42, 179–80, 183
Free University of Amsterdam, , 2, 86n1, 137, 138n44

INDEX

Gaffin, Richard B., 191n78
God, attributes of, 15, 96n39, 98n43, 175, 176n50,
Gutting, Gary, 155

Hart, Carroll Guen, 105, 114n91
human rights, 3, 87, 89–96, 102–4, 11, 117, 119–20, 139, 142, 165, 167, 170–73, 178, 183
Hume, David, 34, 36–39, 42, 46, 49–51

incarnation, 96n39, 98n43, 99, 114n91, 135
induction/inductive beliefs, 34, 36–38, 48, 51, 57, 162, 182–84
intention(ality), doxastic, 14, 33n39, 43, 55, 58–66, 68
intention(ality), ethical, 19, 30, 33, 49, 53, 54–55, 58–66, 108–9, 163
intention(ality), divine creational, 37, 48, 90–91, 104–5, 108–9, 115–16, 141, 180

Jellema, William Harry, 8–9, 160
Jesus Christ, 6, 99, 107, 109, 116–17, 120, 124, 135, 147, 167, 169, 173–74, 176–77, 179, 186–88
justice, 18, 87–92, 94–103, 107, 110–20, 124–27, 135–37, 139, 141–44, 147–49, 151–54, 164–67, 170–73, 178, 181–83, 185n67
justification (epistemic), 1, 18, 23–26, 28–29, 51n2, 57, 73n41, 79n71, 80, 83n82

Kant, Immanuel, 6n15, 8n21, 25, 32n33, 188n74
kingdom of God, 8, 12, 99, 107, 116–17, 141, 160n9, 165–66, 179
Kuyper, Abraham, 6–8, 11, 12n31, 13, 15, 20, 87, 100–104, 106, 109, 114n89, 199–20, 141n53, 143–45, 150n80, 159n5, 160–61, 169, 171, 188
Kuyperian, 6n15, 8, 11, 12n31, 15, 20, 89, 100–101, 141, 143, 145, 159n5, 160n9, 171, 173, 180n56, 182, 186–87

Locke, John, 3, 13, 30–32, 34–37, 39, 41, 42n70, 43–44, 47, 49–51, 53, 59–61, 74, 82, 162–64

MacIntrye, Alisdair, 57n1, 65n19
Mouw, Richard, 6n15, 101n48

Neo-Calvinism, 5, 8n20, 11, 13n32, 20, 87, 92n15, 95n32, 100, 103–5, 106n62, 106n64, 107–10, 112n79, 114n91, 118–19, 121, 123, 143–48, 150, 160, 166, 168, 170

Oliphint, K. Scott, 10n28, 12n31, 96n39, 98n43, 141n53, 176n50, 191n78

perception, 37, 38n56, 44–47, 51, 52n97, 57n2, 61–62
Plantinga, Alvin, 3n4, 6, 8–10, 19, 24, 35, 39n60, 42, 45n79, 46, 47n84, 48–55, 57n2, 157, 161, 163
pluralism, 20, 120, 135n35, 139n48, 185–86
proper function, 10, 44n35, 49, 51–54, 92–93, 163

redemptive history/redemptive historical, 5n13, 21, 146n68, 149, 173, 176n50, 177–82, 185n67, 186, 188, 191
Reformed Epistemology, 9–11, 12n31, 13–15, 17, 28n30, 42, 45n79, 57n2, 107n65, 15/112, 171
Reid, Thomas, 3, 10–11, 13, 18–19, 24, 34, 36–52, 53n98, 54–56, 58n4, 59n5, 60, 71n36, 78, 81, 107n65, 129, 134, 153–54, 161–63, 165, 182, 186, 190
relativism, 75, 78–82, 185n67, 186

Schmemann, Alexander, 113, 115n92
skepticism, 10, 19n40, 40, 44, 47–48, 162n15
Sloane, Andrew, 11n29, 17n38, 18n39, 20n42, 28n21, 30n28, 57n3, 73n41, 81, 82n79, 83n82, 118n98, 188n74

speech act, 61
sphere sovereignty, 101n48, 103, 106, 143, 150

Tipton, Lane G., 176n50

Van Til, Cornelius, 10n28, 12n31, 176n41
Vos, Geerhardus, 5n13, 10n28

warrant, 49, 54n101, 57n2
Wolters, Albert, 8n20, 101n48, 105
Woudenberg, Rene van, 6n15, 145n66,

www.ingramcontent.com/pod-product-compliance
Lightning Source LLC
Chambersburg PA
CBHW070325230426
43663CB00011B/2226